MELVILLE AND THE VISUAL ARTS

Melville's Ionian form, Venetian tint. The Khasneh, or Treasury, Petra.
Courtesy of the Tourism Office, Embassy of the Hashemite Kingdom of
Jordan.

for Grace

Contents

Preface

I F MELVILLE READ Frederic Henry Hedge's *Prose Writers of Germany* (1848), and it seems likely enough that he would have read it, he knew the strictures that Gotthold Ephraim Lessing drew against literary pictorialism. In the preface to "Laocoon, or the Limits of Poetry," as translated by Hedge, Lessing pointed out that "false criticism" misleads authors, and

> has engendered a fondness for sketching in poetry and introducing allegory into painting. Men have attempted to make the former "a speaking picture," without properly understanding what Poetry can or ought to *paint;* and to make the latter "a silent poem," not considering in what degree Painting is capable of expressing universal conceptions, without departing too far from her destination and becoming a kind of arbitrary *writing*.

There is little doubt that Melville clearly understood Lessing's complaint. But, having studied the matter deeply and seen what poets and prose writers had already accomplished, he no doubt felt secure in pursuing, with all his literary tact, the venture of making speaking pictures. And, in any case, Lessing's battle had long since been lost. An article that Melville could have read, "Lessing's Laocoön," probably by J. D. Whelpley, in *American Review* in 1851, discussed Lessing's ideas at some length and concluded that "Were the principles of our critic . . . to pass into literature as critical canons, we conceive a great and serious injury would be inflicted upon the arts" (19). There were already innumerable literary accounts of artworks, including descriptions of painting and statuary, and Melville and others would continue to render, in the narrativity of prose and poetry, the immobility of statue and picture.[1]

Melville's engagement with the art analogy is broad and exemplary in its persistence and is displayed throughout the whole range of his career. Pictorialism appears in some, though not all, of his prose fiction, in much of his poetry, and in a few of the attempts he made in literary and art criticism. His study of the various plastic arts was a crucial element in the development of his imaginative being. A whaleship may have been Ishmael's Yale College and Harvard, but Ishmael's creator did his advanced work in a larger, more productive theater of learning. Melville studiously attended picture galleries, exhibitions, and museums. His journals of 1849–50 and 1856–57 testify to the intensity of his interest. His collection of prints, gathered for years within the limits of a small income, gives a good idea of what he wanted to preserve, possibly to aid his nearly faultless ability to retain pictorial images. With as many as four hundred individual prints, and with illustrated books that he owned bringing the total up to more than a thousand pictures, all this in a personal collection, ready for daily study, he had an unusual resource for his work. He read ancient and modern poetry and the fiction of his contemporaries and understood exactly how literary artists dealt with the visual arts. To a degree probably unusual for his time and situation, he read art criticism, art history, and studies of the works of individual artists and schools of art. He knew the writings of Giorgio Vasari, Roger de Piles, Charles Du Fresnoy, John Dryden, Johann Winckelmann, Joshua Reynolds, Luigi Lanzi, Madame de Staël, John Ruskin, and James Jackson Jarves. He read Frank Cundall's book about the painters of Holland, John William Mollett's studies *(Sir David Wilkie, Rembrandt, Meissonier,* and *The Painters of Barbizon),* Cosmo Monkhouse's *Turner,* and Owen John Dullea's *Claude.* His marginalia in the books he owned, even those primarily about other topics, indicate his alertness to any remarks about the arts. He carefully marked Goethe's account of his Italian journey, with its many references to encounters with art. His copy of Madame de Staël's *Corinne,* purchased in 1849 (and no longer available), must, with its disquisitions upon art, have provided much for him to think about.

In one of his most remarkable descriptions of a work of art, the lost city of Petra, Melville has his speaker, Rolfe, offer a reaction to the sight: "One starts. In Esau's waste are blent / Ionian form, Venetian tint" (*Clarel* 2.30.17–18). The passage marks the two major functions of literary pictorialism. Art allusion is textural, on a small scale; it embellishes and emblazons, in "Venetian tint," a passage of prose or poetry. An example is the "Hawaiian savage," whose carving is "as close packed in its maziness of design, as the Greek savage, Achilles' shield" (*Moby-Dick* 270). On the other hand, "Ionian form" is achieved by means of *ekphrasis,* the literary description of a work of visual art, a passage, usually of some length and complexity, that contributes to the structure of the tale or poem. The ekphrasis of Petra, taking a whole canto of the poem, admirably fills such a function by being central to an interpretation of the whole work. It is my hope that a close look at both structural and textural elements in certain of Melville's writings will give a sense of how his visual imagination expresses itself in ever-more secure and sophisticated literary technique.

In his *George Eliot and the Visual Arts,* Hugh Witemeyer wisely points out that generalizations about the relations of literary works to such things as schools of art are really not very workable. Quoting Bernard Richards on following "the guidelines of what poets and painters actually saw and read," Witemeyer states, as his own guiding principle, the necessity for associating Eliot's writings "primarily with pictures and pictorial traditions which she knew" (6). I agree with Witemeyer's conscientious narrowing of the focus of such study and have attempted to do something similar in this discussion of Melville's debt to art and his contribution to pictorialism.[2]

Studies of Melville's whole-hearted involvement with the plastic arts have laid the groundwork for our increased comprehension of this complex topic. In *Melville's Reading* (1966; 1988) Merton Sealts tabulated the great extent to which Melville depended upon books and magazine articles for his art education. Sealts's reconstruction of the lecture on statuary in Rome (1957) and his careful notes give a good sense of the ways in which Melville studied works of art. Morris Star's dissertation, "Melville's Use of the Visual Arts" (1964), helped to lay out the range of the subject and suggest modes of study. Hennig Cohen's perceptive notes to his edition of Melville's *Selected Poems* (1964) called attention to the frequent use of the visual arts in the poetry. Some individual essays during the 1970s and 1980s noted the persistence of Melville's sense of the plastic arts, and Stuart M. Frank's *Herman Melville's Picture Gallery* (1986) exhibited many of the illustrations that must have served Melville in the writing of *Moby-Dick.*

Two books in particular have contributed much to my study. With *Savage Eye: Melville and the Visual Arts* (1991), a collection of essays by several hands on a wide variety of subjects connected with the art analogy, editor Christopher Sten did much to establish the almost unimaginably wide scope of the subject. Robert K. Wallace's *Melville and Turner* (1992) and his detailed accounts of the various collections of prints once owned by Melville have given a solid footing to the sometimes scattered knowledge that we have of Melville's painterly concerns. There is still much to learn as we uncover further evidence about what Melville saw, when he saw it, and how it affected his literary performance.

This study begins with an introduction to the forms of the art analogy and suggests a line of literary influence that must have shaped Melville's own practice, from Homer through contemporaries such as Wordsworth, Keats, Heine, Irving, Poe, and Hawthorne. A second chapter, necessarily too brief, attempts to give some account of Melville's experience of art through observation, print collecting, and reading. Each of these topics, rich in range and detail, is worth a whole book. Melville painstakingly collected prints and many of the books he owned are illustrated with masterworks of art. *The Works of Eminent Masters,* for instance, contains nearly two hundred engravings thus made available for his constant study. Living in New York from 1863 to the end of his life, he could and did visit art exhibits and bookshops and, no doubt, printshops.[3]

Separate chapters are then devoted to full studies of Melville's use of the visual arts in four of his long works, *Redburn, Moby-Dick, Pierre,* and *Clarel.* This is a selective list that may seem to ignore some of Melville's early work and some of his most important writings. By the time of *Redburn* (1849), he had already published three novels. But in *Typee, Omoo,* and *Mardi,* he makes little use of ekphrasis and art allusion. In his "Overview" to *Savage Eye,* a fine summary of Melville's experiences as writer and viewer, Christopher Sten persuasively suggests that these novels "do not lend themselves particularly well, because of their exotic Polynesian subject matter, to the display of a rich knowledge of Western artistic culture" (4). In *Melville and Turner,* Robert K. Wallace gives excellent examples of Melville's very few uses of art allusions in these books (103–7), but as his account indicates, Melville did not fully engage the subject in these early tales, though there is rather more art allusion to be found in *Mardi* than in the earlier books. This was a period (1845–48) of intense activity for the new author, and he was busy writing and learning. As he later reported to Hawthorne, "until I was twenty-five, I had no development at all." The development was now occurring at a tremendous pace: "Three weeks have scarcely passed, at any time between then and now, that I have not unfolded within myself." During this time he moved from tentative applications of the art analogy to mastery and massive use of the techniques in *Redburn,* which, written in the spring of 1849, would demonstrate how that unfolding manifested itself in a cohesive pattern of literary pictorialism.

White-Jacket, written hastily immediately after *Redburn,* is, in the pictorial sense, a backward step, its narrator being more in the line of the bluff Tommo or Taji rather than the inward, sensitive, art-conscious Wellingborough Redburn. By the time of *Moby-Dick,* nearly two years later, Melville had been to the Continent and to England where, unlike poor Redburn, he had made himself foot-sore trailing around to museums full of the paintings he had never before seen, learning from Samuel Rogers and other English connoisseurs and reading, always reading. Ishmael thus comes before us equipped with visual imaginativeness, impressive knowledge, and "a devout love for all matters of barbaric vertu." Melville's sense of form and tint could be exercised at its highest pitch of accomplishment. In *Pierre*, coming immediately after *Moby-Dick*, Melville creates yet another exemplar of this whelming part of his own nature, which sees the beauty in a Manilla rope, in the "exquisitely defined" flukes of the whale, and in "that sweetest, most touching, but most awful of all feminine heads—The Cenci of Guido."

The lengthy work on *Clarel* produced one more Melvillean persona of the sensitive art-minded youth, eager for experience and enriched by the evidence of eye and mind. Clarel is an Ishmael who never went to sea but led a cloistered life of study and contemplation. His reaction to the landscapes of the Holy Land, the historic sites, and the throngs of visitors, all with their rich personalities and quirks of character, offered Melville grand opportunities for the exercise of some brilliant ekphrastic writing.

In my last chapter, I move backwards to a consideration of the writings published between 1853 and 1876. Arranging sketches and tales in a volume, *The Piazza Tales*, Melville sought to impose upon his collection the discipline of the art analogy. The nominal author of *The Encantadas*, Salvator Tarnmoor, like Salvator Rosa, who is doubtless his master, sees the wildness of landscape in the Galapagos Islands but not as works of visual arts. Architectural and sculptural elements dominate the brooding atmosphere of "Benito Cereno" and "The Bell-Tower." Bartleby scrapes out an existence of sorts in the deserted Wall Street purlieus that so resemble Petra. I have treated these with what I hope is sufficient emphasis to show how Melville thought about artworks during his rather hurried composition of shorter works of fiction. I have left out discussion of *Israel Potter* since Melville, creating his tale upon the skeleton of memoirs, does not make any prolonged use of the art analogy. And, though *The Confidence-Man* obviously offered splendid opportunities for panoramic views of the great Mississippi River, he did not avail himself of its splendors. The detachment from the scenes he depicted in *Battle-Pieces* did allow, in some poems, for the use of the paintings of Elihu Vedder, Sanford Gifford, J. M. W. Turner, and Raphael, as well as photographs and magazine illustrations that highlighted the Civil War; but the prevailing themes of the book lie elsewhere.

The writings that followed the publication of *Clarel* do not always focus upon the advantages of the art analogy. In the poems of *John Marr and Other Sailors*

(1888), the narrative is intensely personal and is bolstered by a wide range of historical reference. The retired sailor's quest into "retrospective musings" is intended to be a struggle with the pain of his day-to-day existence, and it is successful to the point where he can exclaim, at the end of the book, "Healed of my hurt, I laud the inhuman Sea." There are certainly vivid images in the poems—the prairie, like the bed of a dried up sea; a wrecked ship, "Dismasted and adrift"; a raft whose survivors have perished; the Maldive shark, with "saw-pit of mouth" and "charnel of maw"; and the iceberg, a "lumbering lubbard," dangerous to all ships—but Melville seems to draw these from his extensive personal experience rather than from the resources of the plastic arts. *Billy Budd,* too, is enriched by the sense of Melville's long encounters with the sea and sailors. Billy is rendered in the art language that Melville knows well. As Gail Coffler has shown in her excellent study in *Savage Eye* of the iconography that informs the portrait of Billy, he has close ties with the statues of Apollo and Antinous and, it may be added, the Farnese Hercules.

The poems of *Timoleon* and the unpublished poems that engaged Melville's attention in the last years of his life are, many of them, rich in the engagement with works of art. There are poems that describe pictures like Teniers's *Bench of Boors* and a portrait of the Marchioness of Brinvilliers; poems about statuary, like the Hermes, the Hall of Marbles, a medallion at the Villa Albani, and a fragmentary piece of basso-relievo that puzzles the poet; architectural masterpieces, like Milan Cathedral, the Leaning Tower of Pisa, the Parthenon, and Egypt's pyramids. I attempt to deal with these in the last chapter because they seem so important as final notes in the aged poet's contemplation of general aesthetic conclusions and as notations of the role of the plastic arts in the making of literary works.

Melville surely must have derived much pleasure from the enrichment that his own literary art received from the arts of the painter, sculptor, architect, engraver, and other artificers of the visual. He spoke of these matters with the becoming modesty of a man who declared himself "neither critic nor connoisseur," but they impinge constantly upon his thoughts. There is a little poem, scarcely noticed, among those he left unpublished called "Fruit and Flower Painter." Melville would probably have called it a "ditty," to set it apart from verse of more serious intent. He says of the painter,

> She dens in a garret
> As void as a drum;
> In lieu of plum-pudding—
> She paints the plum!

MELVILLE AND THE VISUAL ARTS

Ionian Form, Venetian Tint

Douglas Robillard

The Kent State University Press
Kent, Ohio, and London, England

© 1997 by The Kent State University Press, Kent, Ohio 44242
Library of Congress Catalog and Card Number 97-6780
ISBN 0-87338-575-6
Manufactured in the United States of America

Library of Congress Cataloging-in-Publication Data

Robillard, Douglas, 1928–
    Melville and the visual arts : Ionian form, Venetian tint / Douglas Robillard.
        p.   cm.
    Includes bibliographical references and index.
    ISBN 0-87338-575-6 (alk. paper) ∞
    1. Melville, Herman, 1819–1891—Knowledge—Art.   2. Art and literature—United
States—History—19th century.   3. Visual perception in literature.   I. Title.
PS2388.A75R63   1997   97-6780
813'.3—dc21   CIP

British Library Cataloging-in-Publication data are available.

After two more stanzas in which the poet speaks of the attractive persistence of this artistic lady, he concludes,

> December is howling,
> But feign it a flute:
> Help on the deceiving—
> Paint flower and fruit.

The portrait of the painter is linked to her own art and aesthetic theory. Because any art can feign what is beyond reality, it establishes a crucial inner world of sensual and intellectual values.

Acknowledgments

THE UNIVERSITY OF New Haven has given my work much support. Joseph Chepaitis, as Dean of Arts and Sciences, contributed in many ways. Paul Marx and Donald M. Smith, as chairs of the Department of English, were always helpful. University committees on sabbaticals and grants were generous with assistance. The Marvin K. Peterson Library often obtained hard-to-find books, periodicals, and important articles. The University's journal, *Essays in Arts and Sciences,* published an earlier version of my chapter on *Redburn* and has given me permission to use it here.

The stacks at Yale University's Sterling Library provided an abundance of nineteenth-century periodicals and books and generously gave me stack and borrowing privileges. Summer sessions with Harold Bloom and Robert Caserio gave me additional opportunities to work on my project. Warren Rosenberg, Sanford Marovitz, Robert Milder, and Thomas Heffernan chaired conferences that led me to develop some ideas in papers. Since 1993, the excellent Howard-Tilton Memorial Library at Tulane University has offered me the riches of its nineteenth- and twentieth-century collections, which provided some of the engravings appearing in this book. The Wagner branch of the Jefferson Parish Library, in Metairie, ordered books on interlibrary loan for me when they were not locally available, a service far beyond what anyone could expect.

The illustrations are meant to supply an aspect of Melville's art interests perhaps less available than paintings he knew or than his print collection. The books he owned were often illustrated with engravings and these served, I believe, as a ready source for his study. Of the many illustrations he owned or must have seen, I have selected some that demonstrate his collecting, early and late. His Shakespeare has only frontispieces, but other issues of the set contain engravings. The only book in the list that was probably not in his collection is the Wilson *Picturesque Palestine, Sinai and Egypt*. As Walter Bezanson has shown, Bartlett's *Forty Days in the Desert* had pictures of Petra (*Clarel* 784–85). I wanted to show other views of the city that so fascinated Melville. The Howard Tilton Library and its director, Dr. Philip Leinbach, made it possible for me to use five of these illustrations. The photographic skills of G. Christopher Mathews make clear the details in the engravings.

I am deeply indebted to those at The Kent State University Press who have helped me, to Julia Morton and Joanna Hildebrand for their encouragement and excellent editorial work.

Two friends and colleagues deserve special attention. Robert K. Wallace has read chapters of the book and given them close attention and suggestions for improvement. His own scholarly work in the field, in his articles on Melville's collection of prints and his excellent study *Melville and Turner,* have given aid and acted as a spur to make me do my best to keep up. Christopher Sten read portions of the book and provided some intensive training in stylistics. By asking me to write for *Savage Eye,* his ground-breaking collection of essays on Melville and the arts, he pushed me to think even harder about the subject. I am grateful to him and to The Kent State University Press for giving me permission to use materials from my essays in *Savage Eye.*

ONE

The Sister Arts

"I Shall Ere Long Paint to You as Well as One Can Without Canvas"

I N HIS COPY OF THE *Iliad,* Melville took note of the passage in Book 18 that portrays the shield of Achilles, fashioned to replace the one lost in battle. This elaborate artifact is as much a work of art as an instrument of war. Gathering his tin, silver, gold, and brass, Hephaestus creates "a strong and spacious shield / Adorn'd with twenty several hues." Homer offers a detailed poetic description of the shield's face, with its pictorial representation of constellations, cities, weddings, judgments, armies and battles, vineyards, and dancing. The passage, marked by Melville, reads, in part:

> To these the fiery Artizan did add a new-ear'd field,
> Large and thrice plough'd, the soil being soft, and of a wealthy yield;
> And many men at plough he made, that drave earth here and there,
> And turn'd up stitches orderly, at whose end when they were,
> A fellow ever gave their hands full cups of luscious wine;
> Which emptied, for another stitch, the earth they undermine,
> And long till th' utmost bound be reach'd of all the ample close. (Cowen 2:29)

The copy of the *Iliad* that Melville owned, the Chapman translation, was one that he received from George Duyckinck in 1858, so his markings must have been made then, or even later; but he had long known the poem and its beautiful representation of the Achillean shield and had made use of it in his writings. In *Moby-Dick,* for example, Ishmael, acting as a connoisseur and critic of art forms, discusses the portrayals "Of Whales in Paint; in Teeth; in Wood; in Sheet-Iron; in Stone; in Mountains; in Stars." During his exhaustive catalog of artistic effects, he refers to the efforts of the "white sailor-savage" who will "carve you a bit of bone sculpture, not quite as workmanlike, but as close packed in its maziness of design, as the Greek savage, Achilles's shield; and full of barbaric spirit and suggestiveness, as the prints of that fine old Dutch savage, Albert Durer" (270).

Melville cares much for allusions to the arts and uses them often in his compositions, calling up the names of artists and works of art to vivify his descriptions and remind his reader of similitudes. In the early "Fragments from a Writing Desk," he speaks, rather vaguely, of "several magnificent pictures illustrative of the loves of Jupiter and Semele, Psyche before the tribunal of Venus, and a variety of other scenes" (*Piazza Tales* 202). In *Typee,* Tommo is reminded of "monstrous imps that torment some of Teniers' saints" (211), a reference to one of Melville's favorite painters, who will receive fuller treatment in the late poem, "The Bench of Boors," a rather detailed description of a Teniers painting. In *Mardi,* Taji, an enthusiastic but somewhat unfocused dilettante, describes "the Chondropterygii and other uncouth hordes infesting the South Seas" and invokes the names of painters, "old Wouvermans, who once painted a bull bait," or Gudin or Isabey, "who might have thrown the blue rolling sea into the picture" under "one of Claude's setting summer suns." His vision of "God's creatures fighting fin for fin a thousand miles from land, and with the round horizon for an arena, is no ignoble subject for a masterpiece" (42). Such a masterpiece as Taji envisions would have been a strange collaboration for Wouverman, one of Melville's likeable Dutch painters, and Gudin and Isabey, Melville's contemporaries, with their seas below a Claudean sunset in an odd pastiche of seascape and cannibalism. The reference is still somewhat vague and it is difficult to know what Melville knew of these painters, but he is beginning to make his taste in art better known.

Théodore Gudin (1802–1880) was noted for his early marine paintings, *Coast Scene, Shipwreck on Coast of Genoa, Agitated Sea, Rescue of the Passengers of the Colomb,* and the like. Eugène Isabey (1804–1886) painted such subjects as *Storm, Ships at Anchor, View of Dieppe,* and *View of Boulogne Harbour.* In Carlo, an immigrant boy aboard ship, Wellingborough Redburn sees "such a boy as Murillo often painted" (247), and, moved by the sight of Jackson, the sailor, he says that "this man was still a picture, worthy to be painted by the dark, moody hand of Salvator" (275). Bartleby is observed as "a sort of innocent and transformed Marius brooding among the ruins of Carthage," an allusion to a popular subject for painters; and, in the same story, Wall Street on a Sunday morning "is deserted as Petra," the ancient city that Melville, without ever seeing it, admired for its magnificent architecture (*Piazza Tales* 27–28). In *Clarel*, Melville has the prodigal speak of "Earth's loveliest portrait, daintiest," which he identifies as "Titian's Venus, golden-warm" (4.26.236–39). *Billy Budd*, the narrator of that tale tells us, possesses "that humane look of reposeful good nature that the Greek sculptor in some instances gave to his heroic strong man, Hercules." Such a system of reference and allusion greatly enriches the texture of Melville's writing, as it does for all authors who make much use of it.

As we see from Homer's striking depiction of the shield, the poetic description of a work of visual arts has a hallowed place in literature. In his study of literary pictorialism, *The Sister Arts* (1958), Jean H. Hagstrum refers to the technique as "iconic" and offers a definition: "In such poetry the poet contemplates a real or imaginary work of art that he describes or responds to in some other way" (18). Hagstrum adds the term "ecphrastic" to mean "that special quality of giving voice and language to the otherwise mute art object" (18n.34). Since Hagstrum's publication, other critics have taken issue with his terminology. Writing of Keats's "Ode on a Grecian Urn," Leo Spitzer prefers to use the term "ekphrasis" to refer to "the poetic description of a pictorial or sculptural work of art . . . the reproduction, through the medium of words, of sensuously perceptible *objets d'art*" (72). Others have chosen Spitzer's ekphrasis over Hagstrum's iconic. In his study of Spenser's pictorialism, John B. Bender uses it to define the "literary description of real or imagined works of visual arts" (51). Murray Krieger has used it in the sense of "the imitation in literature of a work of plastic art" and, in his imaginative and expansive study of the subject, *Ekphrasis* (1992), has discussed the historical background and the limitations of the term.[1]

Ekphrasis has always been, and continues to be, a wonderfully apt literary technique for establishing the direction of a major portion of a work of literature and sometimes the structure of the entirety of a novel or long poem. In *The Sense of Life in the Modern Novel*, Arthur Mizener calls attention to Anthony Powell's use of a careful description of Poussin's painting *A Dance to the Music of Time*. Mizener quotes a substantial portion of this ekphrasis of a fine artwork "in which the Seasons, hand in hand and facing outward, tread in rhythm to the notes of the lyre that the winged and naked greybeard plays." The quotation continues, exhibiting the movements implied in the painting as "partners disappear only to reappear again, once more giving pattern to the spectacle: unable to control the melody, unable, perhaps, to control the steps of the dance." Mizener then remarks that the description of the painting "really tells us all we need to know about the design" of this lengthy work of fiction (92–93). Since the essay in which this analysis appears also deals with the novels of James Gould Cozzens,

Mizener might have added, though he does not, that the American author's description in the opening pages of *By Love Possessed* of an objet d'art, a finely shaped clock illustrating the motto "Love Conquers All," is an ironic ekphrasis dominating the entire novel.

The term, however, is subject to almost infinite expansion. As Krieger points out, early Greek usage included "a verbal description of something, almost anything, in life or art." Krieger adds that "the ekphrasis, as an extended description, was called upon to intrude upon the flow of discourse and, for its duration, to suspend the argument of the rhetor or the action of the poet . . . a device intended to interrupt the temporality of the discourse, to freeze it during its indulgence in spatial exploration" (7). This comment seems a good basis for an understanding of the place of the ekphrastic motive in literature. It is an important descriptive technique whose limits need to be set somewhere between the breadth of "almost anything" and the narrowness of Spitzer's definition. Studying George Eliot's uses of the visual arts, Hugh Witemeyer takes the sensible course of associating her writings "with pictures and pictorial traditions which she knew" (6). An examination of some of Melville's uses of the technique should help to make his limits clear.

Melville's writings display a clear understanding of the possibilities of ekphrasis, and he uses the technique with great skill. He describes paintings, statues, buildings and the carvings which decorate them, and ships as elaborate in their architecture as any land-bound building. He sometimes depicts people as if they themselves were works of art, comparing them to statues or paintings or even architectural masterpieces. He defines them as characters by associating them with the artworks they encounter in the various events of their lives. When he uses some form of ekphrasis in his prose and poetry, he links it, as often as not, with specific works of art. With the Homeric description of the shield of Achilles in mind, he has the young Wellingborough Redburn go to supper at a boarding house called the Baltimore Clipper. At the supper table Redburn observes "a mighty pewter dish, big as Achilles' shield." Melville then moves beyond the relative simplicity of art allusion to create a parody of the Homeric ekphrasis. Redburn sees the supper table as a large work of art, the "shield" of "smoking sausages" at one end, "head-cheese" in the middle, "and at the opposite end, a congregation of beef-steaks, piled tier over tier. Scattered at intervals between, were side dishes of boiled potatoes, eggs by the score, bread and pickles" (*Redburn* 134). This is, of course, a lighthearted and humorous use of the technique, and it does not greatly advance the movement of the novel. But there are more serious and powerful ekphrases in Melville's work that do involve great emphases in the form and development of his fiction and poetry. Redburn lovingly describes the glass ship in his home and gives a highly distinctive account of the travel books that he reads, exhibiting his pleasure in their look and feel. Later in the novel, he carefully reports the appearance of the artworks in the "Palace of Aladdin," when he and Harry Bolton visit that house in London. Ishmael describes paintings in the Spouter-Inn and the Whaleman's Chapel and depicts the *Pequod*, Ahab, and Queequeg in painterly terms. When he undertakes to portray the whale, he speaks of himself as an artist and sets out to "paint to you as well as one can without canvas" the awesome proportions and subtle colorings of his subject (*Moby-Dick* 260). In "The Piazza," the introduction to *The Piazza Tales*, Melville says that the lack of a piazza would be as bad "as if a picture-gallery should have no bench" (2), and thus fortified with a vantage point from which he can, in leisurely fashion, view the artworks available in the stories, he portrays the architectural oddities of Wall Street in "Bartleby, the Scrivener"; the elaborate, decaying naval architecture of the *San Dominick* in "Benito Cereno" and its gruesome figurehead sculpture of skeleton and inscription; the Salvatorean landscapes and seascapes of "The Encantadas"; and the campanile and domino of "The Bell-Tower."

As Melville collected his impressions of Europe in 1857, he seems to have planned for a work of some length to be called "Frescoes of Travel by Three Brothers: Poet, Painter, and Idler" (*Journals* 154). Some of the poems in *Timoleon* appear to have been part of that plan. There is a satisfying ekphrasis of "Milan Cathedral" depicting the building standing upon the "old plain of Lombardy." Everything in the view consists of sharp, narrow points, reaching skyward. The cathedral and "Its tribes of pinnacles / Gleam like to ice-peaks." As do the pinnacles, the "Statues of saints over saints ascend / Like multitudinous forks of fire." The poet meditates upon the "master-builder's" motive and suggests that the saints, "Sublimely ranked in marble sessions clear," signify "the host of heaven."

"Pisa's Leaning Tower" portrays the old campanile as "tiers of architraves" and as a "maker's master-work." In the poet's eye, the building takes on a vivid consciousness as it "debates":

> It thinks to plunge—but hesitates;
> Shrinks back—yet fain would slide;
> Withholds itself—itself would urge;
> Hovering, shivering on the verge

as a "would-be suicide," ready to plunge to its destruction. The poem is an ekphrastic delineation of a powerful personal response. Melville recorded his observations of the tower on March 23, 1857: "Campanile like pine poised just ere snapping. You wait to hear crash. Like Wordsworth's moor cloud, it will move all together if it move at all. Pillars all lean with it. About 150 of 'em. There are houses in wake of fall" (*Journals* 114). The allusion is to lines from Wordsworth's "Resolution and Independence" that carry the burden of suicidal impulses felt by the poem's speaker, held by "fears and fancies," thinking of the suicidal Chatterton and the early death of Burns, and concluding that "We poets in our youth begin in gladness; / But thereof come in the end despondency and madness." These moods adequately match Melville's own feelings at the time of seeing the tower, and, in composing his poem, he displaces the personal, human catastrophe to the more impersonal scenic impending disaster. William Bysshe Stein's elaborate reading of the poem calls attention to the close links between the poem and Melville's "The Bell-Tower." Stein's view, that the ruinous fall of the tower "foreshadows a religious inevitabliity—the catastrophic extinction of Christianity," is, perhaps, too broad in its interpretation, but he perceptively sees the vision that Melville sees, of "intellectual and spiritual suicide" limned in the poem (117).

Other poems in *Timoleon* are, similarly, well-worked-out pieces of ekphrastic description. "The Bench of Boors" depicts the forms and colors of a painting by David Teniers. "The Marchioness of Brinvilliers" carefully describes a seventeenth-century picture of an infamous poisoner, a piece of portraiture possibly by Charles Le Brun. Other poems in the collection both describe and comment. "The Parthenon" is about the impressions that the famous structure makes upon the beholder from various points of observation. "Greek Architecture" counsels "reverence for the Archetype." "The Great Pyramid" expresses the viewer's overwhelming astonishment at the massive, timeless quality of the architectural masterpiece that dares "Time's future infinite" and considers that the builders "Usurped on Nature's self with Art."[2] Ekphrasis, in short, is a powerful literary tool that Melville came to use with increasing confidence and skill to balance against the narrative impulse of his work.

In an important passage in *Clarel,* Melville has Rolfe describe the city of Petra, which the pilgrims will not have an opportunity to visit. He enumerates the colors, the "purple gloom / Of cliffs" and the "rosy stain" of stone before speaking of the shape of the ruins, "Of porch and pediment in crag." Then, in a brief, vivid outburst, he expresses his feelings about the scene: "One starts. In Esau's waste are blent / Ionian form, Venetian tint" (3.30.17–18). The passage fuses brilliantly in a pictorial image Melville's sense of the literary art. He knew well the tints of Venice, having visited that city in 1857 and noted in his journal the "Great gorgeousness of effect" of the colors in the place. The women he saw reminded him that "The rich brown complexions of Titian's women drawn from nature after all . . . . The clear, rich, golden brown. The clear cut features, like a cameo."

Venice pleased him. "Rather be in Venice on rainy day," he wrote, "than in any other capital on fine one" (*Journals* 119–20). His affection for the city appears again in the poem "At the Hostelry" in the words of Paul Veronese to Gerard Dow, contrasting Italian and Dutch art: "Her sunsets—there's hearth-light for you; / And matter for you on the Square. / To Venice, Gerard" (*Collected Poems* 327). A term like "Venetian tint" seems to fit very well his concepts of embellishment, color, and chiaroscuro as part of the sister arts.

"Ionian form" is even more important than "Venetian tint," and Melville's sense of form is intense, his struggle for form obsessive and persistent in the novels, the stories, and the poetic collections. As he wrote, he educated this urge to form by a constant reference to the design in works of visual art. An expression of his concern can be found in his marking a passage from the preface that Matthew Arnold composed for the 1853 edition of his *Poems:* "what distinguishes the artist from the mere amateur, says Goethe, is *Architectonicé* in the highest sense; that power of execution, which creates, forms, and constitutes" (Cowen 1:75). When Melville calls this feeling for structure "Ionian," he is using the word, in a general sense, to mean Greek architectural patterns. In *Timoleon,* the poems that speak of Greek buildings underline the ways in which this matter engrosses his attention. "The Attic Landscape" matches the natural with artifice in which "The clear cut hills carved temples face, / Respond, and share their sculptural grace." Of "The Parthenon" he says, "In subtlety your form's defined" and calls the temple "Art's meridian." Seeing the columns of a ruined temple in "Off Cape Colonna," he reflects that they are "sublimed to fancy's view, / A god-like group." And, in a more general poem on "Greek Architecture," the poet finds its virtue: "Not magnitude, not lavishness, / But Form—the Site." To accomplish both form and tint in his writings, he calls upon all the enticements of the visual arts.

A VARIED SCOPE OF READING

Although Melville came to use the art analogy in individual and sophisticated ways, he assiduously studied his literary models, following, no doubt, the advice of Isaac Disraeli's *The Literary Character,* which he emphatically marked in his copy of the book: "'Our best and surest road to knowledge,' said Lord Kaimes, 'is by profiting from the labours of others, and making their experience our own'" (Cowen 1:511). Melville put the matter well in his description of Pierre Glendenning's ardent study of his precursors: "A varied scope of reading, little suspected by his friends, and randomly acquired by a random but lynx-eyed mind, in the course of the multifarious, incidental, bibliographic encounterings of almost any civilised young inquirer after Truth" (*Pierre* 283).

The literary artist, like the visual artist, learns the trade by careful study of the masters and diligent imitation of their finest strokes.

In addition to his Homeric borrowings, Melville's epigraphs to the sketches in "The Encantadas" were evidence of his enthusiastic reception of landscape description in *The Faerie Queene*. Melville tended to see Spenser's poetry through the eyes of eighteenth- and nineteenth-century enthusiasts who drew rather loose analogies between painting and poetry. As he must have known, Spenser had often been lauded for this pictorial quality of his writings. Alexander Pope claimed that upon reading "a canto of Spenser two or three days ago to an old lady . . . she said that I had been showing her a gallery of pictures." Leigh Hunt devoted a considerable part of his book *Imagination and Fancy* (1844), which features the Pope quotation, to matching selections from Spenser to paintings by Raphael, Correggio, Titian, Guido Reni, and Salvator Rosa. He declared in his preface that the book was "intended for all lovers of poetry and the sister arts," and, in his introductory comments to the section offering "A Gallery of Pictures from Spenser," he spoke of "the old family relationship between poetry and painting." Although we cannot be sure that Melville read Hunt's book, its American edition, under the title of *The Poetry of Imagination and Fancy*, was published by Wiley and Putnam, publisher of his first novel, and advertised in *The Literary World* in 1847. Melville's markings in his copy of Spenser's poems demonstrate his attentiveness to their pictorial values. The set of Spenser that he marked was published in 1855, and inscriptions indicate that he did not have access to it until 1861 (*Sealts* #483). The epigraphs for "The Encantadas," therefore, came from earlier readings of Spenser; those from *The Faerie Queene* are all taken from Cantos 9 and 10 of the first book and from Canto 12 of the second book. The pictures that the epigraphs limn emphasize the "darke, dolefull, dreary," the "ugly shapes and horrible aspects," and the "caitive wretches, ragged, rude, deformed" that Melville, in his pseudonymous guise of "Salvator Tarnmoor" wanted to depict. As Carol Moses shows in her study of Melville and Spenser, the second sketch of "The Encantadas" draws upon Book 2 of *The Faerie Queene*, which details the journey of Guyon to the Bower of Bliss, where "the palmer is able to vanquish the sea monsters they meet with his 'vertuous staffe'" (135). The tortoises of Melville's sketch are portrayed as artworks, with the "calipee or breastplate being sometimes of a faint yellowish or golden tinge." His later markings as he read and reread *The Faerie Queene* show his continued interest. In the first book some twenty-three stanzas are marked from the ninth canto. In the second book the ninth canto, with twenty-four markings, and the twelfth canto, with twenty-two markings, receive the most attention. Hunt remarked that Spenser "took a painter's as well as poet's delight in colour and form, lingering over his work for its corporeal and visible sake . . . in short, writing as if with a brush instead of a pen."

In reading Shakespeare, Melville responded to the imagery of artworks and marked his copy of the volumes as he read. In *Venus and Adonis* he used a side-line to indicate his interest in the complaint of the amorous Venus to a cold Adonis: "Fie, lifeless picture, cold and senseless stone, / Well-painted idol, image dull and dead, / Statue contenting but the eye alone" (ll. 211–13). Many of the sonnets are marked in their entirety, among them the twenty-fourth, in which the poet says

> Mine eye hath play'd the painter, and hath stell'd
> Thy beauty's form in table of my heart.
> My body is the frame wherein 'tis held,
> And perspective it is best painter's art. (Cowen 2:487)

These are conventional images involving the literary transformation of the painter's art by importing the idea of the framed portrait and the painterly device of perspective, but they illustrate the possibility of complexities. The poet has created a fictitious picture, painted, indeed, not upon canvas but within the lover, for the picture is "in my bosom's shop," whose windows are "glazed with thine eyes." Once the metaphor of the artwork has been introduced, it can lead the eye into varied vistas.

It appears that Melville knew something of John Dryden's poetry and prose. Sealts lists a copy of Dryden's *Poetical Works* as a presentation copy from Melville to Mrs. Morewood (*Sealts* #191), and, in his own copy of *The Literary Works of Sir Joshua Reynolds,* he read and marked Dryden's "A Parallel of Poetry and Painting," a piece written as a preface to the translation that Dryden made of Charles Du Fresnoy's *De Arte Graphica.* In a poem like the ode "To the Pious Memory of the Accomplisht Young Lady Mrs. Anne Killigrew," Dryden calls attention to the parallel by adding to his title the complimentary assertion that his subject has been "Excellent in the Two Sister-Arts of Poesie and Painting." His praise of the young woman's poetry disposed of in the first parts of the poem, he turns "To the next Realm" where "she stretched her Sway, / For Peinture neer adjoyning lay." As artist, she "perfectly could represent / The Shape, the Face, with ev'ry Lineament." Her genius is such that "Her Pencil drew, what e're her Soul design'd, / And oft the happy Draught surpass'd the Image in her Mind." The poet praises her landscape art and makes room for her portraiture as well. For King James II, "Her hand call'd out the Image of his Heart / His Warlike Mind, his Soul devoid of Fear" as well as Queen Mary's beauty in the lines, "Her Dress, her Shape, her matchless Grace, / Were all observ'd as well as heavenly Face." Hagstrum, who has written well of Dryden's knowledge of the sister arts and the uses of them in the poetry, calls attention to examples in "Absalom and Achitophel" and "All for Love" (176–202).

A number of eighteenth-century English poets were much involved in the study of the visual arts, were acquainted with artists and read the treatises that appeared, and often collected examples of Italian and French art in engravings. Elizabeth Manwaring's extensive study of the influence of Claude Lorrain and Salvator Rosa upon English writers, artists, and critics, quotes an anonymous poet who distinguishes between Italian and Dutch art: "Why do Salvator's daring strokes delight, / While Mieris' care and labour Tire the sight?" (50). Manwaring cites James Thomson's use of the pictorial landscape in *The Seasons* (101–06), and Hagstrum points out the iconic tendencies in *Liberty* as well as in *The Seasons* (246–61). Sorting among the sayings of minor figures in eighteenth-century England, Manwaring discovers the author of the essay "Of the Sister Arts," asserting that "The nearer the Poet approaches to the Painter, the more perfect he is; and the more perfect the Painter, the more he imitates the Poet" (20).

Pope studied painting with Charles Jervas and sent him a copy of Dryden's translation of Du Fresnoy with a poem that read, in part, "Read these instructive leaves, in which conspire / Fresnoy's close art, and Dryden's native fire." In "An Essay on Criticism," he develops the analogy between the sister arts by pointing out defects of critics, whose

> *Lines,* tho' touched but faintly, are drawn right.
> But as the slightest Sketch, if justly trac'd,
> Is by ill *Colouring* but the more disgrac'd,
> So by *false Learning* is *good Sense* defac'd.

The sources of his pictorialism in "The Rape of the Lock" are masterfully traced by Hagstrum to paintings by Titian and Guido Reni (220–22), and Hagstrum especially calls attention to an index that Pope added to his translation of the *Iliad,* listing under the heading of "Painting, Sculpture &c." the passages of the poem that he believed to be picturesque, with some attention to the shield of Achilles (231–32). Thomas Gray, perhaps the most learned of the poets of the time, took careful notes on his visits to Continental collections of paintings and, in his vast course of study, read Vasari, Du Fresnoy, Bellori (Hagstrum 288) and, as William Jones has shown in *Thomas Gray, Scholar,* studied "Potter's Antiquities of Greece," "Kennet's Antiquities of Rome," "Richardson on Painting," and numerous Italian treatises dealing with "Architecture, Sculpture, Painting, & Antiquities. &c" (Jones 152–57). In its pictorial aspects, Gray's "Elegy Written in a Country Churchyard" is greatly indebted to Nicolas Poussin's *The Shepherd of Arcady* and "The Bard" to Raphael and Parmegiano, as Gray himself noted (Hagstrum 295–96, 310–11).

It seems likely that Melville learned much from his study of contemporary writers who included aspects of the art analogy in their works. He knew Wordsworth's poetry well and must have read those poems that dealt with the sister arts of painting and sculpture. His copy of *The Complete Poetical Works of William Wordsworth* was published in 1839, and we cannot be sure when he acquired it, but the volume contains more than a hundred markings and annotations (Heffernan 339). Melville marked a passage from "Laodamia" and commented that the "line must have been suggested by the 'Antinous,'" a statue he knew well. He likewise marked and commented upon a passage from Wordsworth's "To B. R. Haydon, Esq.," displaying his considerable knowledge of the life and career of the British painter. As Heffernan notes, Melville annotates one of the poems about Haydon with the remark that "Wordsworth should be held partly responsible for Haydon's suicide, for he encouraged him in a career which necessarily ended there" (345–47).[3] Wordsworth's poems include sonnets to painters like Haydon and G. H. Beaumont, the memorial sculpture of Nollekens, a portrait painted by Margaret Gillies, and two poems addressed more generally "To a Painter," whose picture at first leaves the poet dissatisfied and finally allows him, gratefully, to "see its truth."

Wordsworth wrote occasional poems about scenes and events that attracted his attention during his travels, and some of these center around artworks. "Memorials of a Tour in Italy, 1837" features a poem about Raphael, two translations from Michelangelo, and an ekphrastic description of the Pillar of Trajan. The poem, "Lines Suggested by a Portrait from the Pencil of F. Stone" allows the poet to study the picture of the woman and comment, in painterly terms, on

> the tender shade,
> The shade and light, both there and everywhere,
> And through the very atmosphere she breathes,
> Broad, clear, and toned harmoniously.

A poem, "Upon Seeing a Coloured Drawing of the Bird of Paradise in an Album," gives the poet license to reflect upon the inadequacy of art to mirror the splendors of nature. The extensive markings in his copy of Wordsworth suggest what Melville found valuable in his poetry. There are similarities in the way

Wordsworth seizes upon occasions to speak of artists and works of art that he encounters in his tours and the associations of the arts observed by Melville during his tours and then converted into poetry, especially in poems in *Timoleon*.

It is significant that, among the books that Melville owned, we find an illustrated edition of Keats's *The Eve of St. Agnes*. Of all the poets whose work Melville knew, Keats presents the most highly developed response to the visual arts, and the poem is rich in pictorial imagery. The Beadsman, walking along the chapel aisle, passes the "sculptur'd dead" and sees how the "carved angels, ever eager-eyed / Star'd, where upon their heads the cornice rests." The richness of embellished architecture appears in the passage "A casement high and triple-arch'd there was / All garlanded with carven imag'ries / Of fruits, and flowers, and bunches of knot grass."[4] But the finest example in Keats's poetry of the art analogy is the "Ode on a Grecian Urn," an ekphrastic work in which the poet creates, through his literary art, a work of sculptural art, dwelling upon such descriptive details as the lovers, the priest, and townspeople in a procession toward a sacrifice and, in a particularly imaginative passage, the town that is not even portrayed on the urn he is depicting. Meditating upon this work of art, the poet gives voice to it in the admonition that "Beauty is truth, truth beauty." Keats's December 1818 letter to his brother George gives further evidence of his response to the visual arts:

> A year ago I could not understand in the slightest degree Raphael's cartoons—now I begin to read them a little—and how did I learn to do so? By seeing something done in quite an opposite spirit—I mean a picture of Guido's in which all the Saints, instead of that heroic simplicity and unaffected grandeur which they inherit from Raphael, had each of them both in countenance and gesture all the canting, solemn, melodramatic mawkishness . . . . When I was last at Haydon's I looked over a Book of Prints taken from the fresco of the Church of Milan the name of which I forget—in it are comprised Specimens of the first and second age of art in Italy.

Melville certainly knew the "Ode," for he refers specifically to it by writing "The legend round a Grecian urn, / The sylvan legend" in contrasting the landscape of Keats's Greece with the Dead Sea (*Clarel* 2.29.1–2). Keats's rich visual imagination is matched by that of Melville, for both writers were stimulated by the study of artworks and literary compositions that include painting and others of the sister arts.

Melville read Byron's poetry, and, like many others, knew *Childe Harold's Pilgrimage*. The poem's fourth canto, describing its hero's travels in Italy, is, to some extent, a guidebook of the visual arts. The poet describes the *Venus de Medici,* the goddess who "loves in stone and fills / The air around with Beauty" (49), the statue known for a long time as the *Gladiator* (140), and the art treasures of the Vatican, where two of Melville's choice statues repose: the Laocoön, with its "torture dignifying pain, and the *Apollo Belvedere,* "the God of Life, and Poesy, and Light" (160–61). Melville owned *The Poetical Works of Byron* and marked some stanzas of *Childe Harold's Pilgrimage. He* also marked an important passage from *The Prophecy of Dante,* with references to St. Peter's, along with a note from the writings of Sir Joshua Reynolds's *Discourses* on the works of Michelangelo. He underlined Byron's reference to "the marble chaos" and must have looked at the footnote that referred to "the statue of Moses on the monument of Julius II." Further along in the volume were notes on Michelangelo's *The Last Judgment* and anecdotes about the artist's professional life.

We have no volume of Robert Browning's works from Melville's library, but he must have been acquainted with Browning's poetry about the visual arts. In his copy of *The Works of Eminent Masters, in Painting, Sculpture, Architecture, and Decorative Art,* Melville took note of a title, "The Unknown Masterpiece," and annotated it with the remark, "'Pictor Ignotus' of Browning" (Cowen 2:737). The story attached to this is different from the one in Browning's poem. It deals with the discovery by Rubens, in a monastery in Madrid, of a painting "of the most sublime and admirable talent," showing a monk. Though Rubens pressed for the identification of the painter, it was never revealed to him. But it is Browning's poetic tale that Melville seems to find significant in a personal way. The "Unknown Painter" sometimes feels his "heart sink, as monotonous I paint / These endless cloisters and eternal aisles / With the same series, Virgin, Babe, and Saint," but takes comfort in the fact that "no merchant traffics in my heart." If Melville knew "Pictor Ignotus," it seems likely that he also knew others of Browning's art poems. "My Last Duchess" is an ekphrastic description of a portrait. In "The Bishop Orders His Tomb at Saint Praxed's Church" a worldly man of god revels on his deathbed in thoughts of the artistic masterpiece that his tomb will be, with "peach-blossom marble," a slab of "antique-black," the Nero-antico, a beautiful black marble, a lump of lapis lazuli, and a bas-relief that shows "The Savior at his sermon on the mount, / Saint Praxed in a glory, and one Pan / Ready to twitch the Nymph's last garment off." In "Andrea del Sarto," the monologue of "the faultless painter," he confesses his inferiority to Raphael; and "Fra Lippo Lippi" is a poetic testament of a painter whom Melville admired enough to put into his own poem, "At the Hostelry." Browning's account of Lippi was drawn from Vasari, and Melville would have enjoyed the conjunction of the two texts. For Melville,

Browning's poems illustrate the point of view of the artist, justifying himself and his works.[5]

American writers also provided sources of word painting for Melville to ponder. Washington Irving's New York Dutchmen were associated with the paintings of Flemish and Dutch genre painters and portrayed with the kind of earthy realism that Brouwer, Dow, Steen, and Ostade provided for willing American viewers. In "Rip Van Winkle," the strange group of men that the hero encounters in the mountain are carefully depicted and "reminded Rip of the figures in an old Flemish painting, in the parlour of Dominie Van Shaick, the village parson."[6] The adoption of a pseudonym like Geoffrey Crayon, the use of *The Sketch Book* as a title, and the language of the introductory sketch, "The Author's Account of Himself," all emphasize the pictorial presence. In Europe "were to be seen the masterpieces of art"; the author views scenes of life "with the sauntering gaze with which humble lovers of the picturesque stroll from the windows of one print shop to another." Those who travel "bring home their port folios filled with sketches." An "unlucky landscape painter" filled his sketch book "with cottages, and landscapes, and obscure ruins." Irving sets out to paint as well as one can without canvas the varied scenes of England's art heritage, including Westminster Abbey. Melville's first chapter of *Redburn*, with its sketch of a boy's early education in the arts, resembles Irving's introduction to *The Sketch Book*.

Drawing upon art resources different from those employed by Irving, Edgar Allan Poe creates ekphrastically an ideal Helen as artwork, where "in yon brilliant window niche / How statue-like I see thee stand, / The agate lamp within thy hand!" His similarly ideal raven is posed "upon the sculptured bust" of Pallas Athene, goddess of wisdom and the arts. The narrator of "Ligeia" sees her sculpturally, with ivory forehead, hyacinthine hair, a nose like the ones portrayed on Hebraic medallions, and a chin showing "the contour which the God Apollo revealed but in a dream to Cleomenes," the Greek sculptor. After Ligeia's death, the narrator decorates the bridal chamber of his decaying abbey with an architectural masterpiece of phantasmagoric fantasy, as improbable as it is beautiful: a "bridal couch, of Indian model, and low, and sculptured of solid ebony"; a sarcophagus of black granite; and tapestry rich "with Arabesque figures."

Poe's most impressive ekphrastic work appears in "The Fall of the House of Usher" where the author has his narrator attempt to give an account of Roderick Usher's paintings. They imitate the pictures painted by Fuseli, he observes, and adds that one "may be shadowed forth, although feebly, in words," a sensible warning for the writer who invades the visual. The shadowing forth takes this form:

A small picture presented the interior of an immensely long and rectangular vault or tunnel, with low walls, smooth, white, and without interruption or device. Certain accessory points of the design served well to convey the idea that this excavation lay at an exceeding depth below the surface of the earth. No outlet was observed in any portion of its vast extent, and no torch, or other artificial source of light was discernible—yet a flood of intense rays rolled throughout, and bathed the whole in a ghastly and inappropriate splendor.

Despite his caveat, the author demonstrates his capacity for rendering in his prose the subtleties of form, color, light, and shade.

The question of the influence of Hawthorne's pictorialism upon Melville is more problematic. If, as Melville suggests in "Hawthorne and His Mosses," he did not become well acquainted with Hawthorne's writings till the middle of 1850, then he had worked out the procedures of his pictorial writing very well by that time. Several of the stories in *Mosses from an Old Manse* might have appealed to Melville for their use of the art analogy. "Egotism; or, The Bosom Serpent" presents George Herkimer as a sculptor, but little is made of his art. On the other hand, "Drowne's Wooden Image," though Melville does not mention it in his review of *Mosses,* could well have influenced Melville's thinking. The young carver in wood, given mostly to second-rate sculpture, creates a ship's figurehead that displays genius and then lapses once more into mediocre work. As a character and commentator in the story, the painter John Singleton Copley sees the value of the figurehead, objects to its being painted, and gives advice to the carver, probably mistakenly. Drowne's most important activity is finding the image in the wood by carving it until "the work assumed greater precision and settled its irregular and misty outline into distincter grace and beauty." He is an artist who has to seek, by painful steps, the beauty within his materials, a useful likeness, perhaps, to Melville's sailors who carve scrimshaw or to Queequeg, who works at refining the features of Yojo, his little carven god. "The Artist of the Beautiful" presents, in Owen Warland, the figure of the artist who could leave his work unfinished. A prophet dies young, a poet leaves his work unfinished, and "The painter—as Allston did—leaves half his conception on the canvas to sadden us with its imperfect beauty." Ishmael calls his work of classifying the whale an incomplete job, like the uncompleted Cologne Cathedral. The portrait of the whale that he contemplates presenting will, of necessity, never be completed.

The best study of Hawthorne's uses of the visual arts, Gollin and Idol's *Prophetic Pictures,* describes some of the devices that the author uses beyond simple allusion: cataloging artists or artworks, using "art objects to give realistic and (sometimes) symbolic touches to his settings," using art objects for foreshadowing, relating artworks to characters, using artists as characters in stories (39–64). These all achieve a greater or lesser degree of intensity in the texture of a literary work. Hawthorne did a great deal more in *The Marble Faun,* and Witemeyer has indicated that he "taught George Eliot how to use ecphrasis, or the verbal imitation of works of visual art, as a technique of psychological revelation and prophecy." It was, indeed, as Witemeyer has suggested, "a seminal work in the history of literary pictorialism" in its influence on George Eliot's later novels and the writings of Henry James (55). But Melville had already demonstrated such uses in *Moby-Dick* and *Pierre,* and it may be that Hawthorne took some hints from these novels.

Gail Coffler suggests in "Melville, Dana, Allston" that Melville read Washington Allston's *Lectures on Art and Poems* (1850), a volume edited, after Allston's death, by Richard Henry Dana, Jr., and her parallel passages from the lectures and *Billy Budd* are significant (2–5). If Melville read the lectures, it is likely that he also read the poems. Allston's volume is just the sort of book that Melville would have been interested in exploring, and it may well have presented him with ideas and forms for his own work. Allston's poetry, though scarcely significant, would have some things to offer. A fairly long poem, "The Two Painters," is cast as a debate between two deceased artists (Allston 237). The octosyllabic couplets offer, among other goods, a lecture on painters, including Raphael, who

> soon with health his sickly style
> From Leonardo learned to smile;
> And now from Buonarotti caught
> A nobler Form

and may have suggested to Melville the couplets that predominantly fill the form of *Clarel.* Other Allston poems are on art subjects as well, as their titles indicate: "Sonnet on the Statue of an Angel," "On Greenough's Group of the Angel and Child," "On Michel Angelo," "Rubens." Some have more portentous titles: "Sonnet on the Group of the Three Angels Before the Tent of Abraham, by Raffaelle, in the Vatican" and "Sonnet on a Falling Group in the Last Judgment of Michael Angelo, in the Capella Sistina." The depiction of the falling group wrings from the poet the exclamation "How vast, how dread, o'er whelming, is the thought / Of space interminable" (273). It is likely that Melville supplemented a reading of these poems, if he did read them, by seeing the work of Raphael and Michelangelo in his visits to the Vatican. How much Melville could have learned from Allston's poetry is conjectural, but he did have the habit of picking up hints from even unlikely sources. Allston's short poems fall into the pattern of little poems on art topics that frequently appeared in *The Literary World* during the 1840s, when Melville was associated with the magazine. It would have struck quite forcibly the well-developed sense of irony in Melville that the greatest American painter of his time was moved to paint as well as one can without canvas.

Analogies between the sister arts came as naturally to writers of the nineteenth century as they had to those who compared poetry and painting in earlier times. Well after Melville's own venture into the art analogy, Henry James, a constant visitor to museums and exhibitions, demonstrated his skills in his art criticism. In his fiction, James demonstrated his mastery of subtle forms of art allusion and ekphrasis. The opening chapters of *The American* (1877) pose Christopher Newman in the Museum of the Louvre, closely examining first a Murillo painting, then an artist's copy of it, and, finally, "the great canvas on which Paul Veronese has depicted the marriage feast of Cana." Hans Holbein's art affected both "The Beldonald Holbein" (1901) and *The Ambassadors* (1903). In revising earlier works like *Roderick Hudson* (1876), James brought in references to paintings by Pinturicchio and Daumier. In his literary criticism, he was quick to observe and comment upon the art analogy. Writing of Théophile Gautier in the *North American Review* in 1873, he luxuriated in the act of finding appropriate terms to praise Gautier's pictorial imagination, speaking of the author's "faculty of visual discrimination," his capacity for saying "in a hundred places, the most delightfully sympathetic and pictorial things about the romantic or Shakespearean drama," the way in which his newspaper pieces "form a great treasury of literary illustration," and, in stories that "remind us of those small cabinet paintings," the creation of characters "altogether pictorial" (James 357, 359, 363, 366).[7] It is, perhaps, too much to assume that an elderly Melville read James, but he was an eager scanner of magazines and did read fiction in his later years.

These writers, and many others, offered Melville an entry into the varieties of pictorialism, a literary technique that he wished to know thoroughly and practice confidently. He believed in the arts as part of the skilled and professional life and said so. Redburn, for instance, thinks that the "thorough sailor must understand much" and "be a bit of an embroiderer," "something of a weaver," "a sort of jeweler," and, in addition, a carpenter, a sempstress, and a blacksmith, "for you know nothing till you know all"; the mariner who achieves such completeness is "an artist in the rigging" (121). Ishmael, commenting on the virtues of Manilla rope, finds it as handsome as it is useful, "since there is an aesthetics in all things" (278) and beauty often resides in utility. Clarel finds much to admire in Rolfe, an ideal figure, who is "no scholastic partisan" but, rather, "supplemented Plato's theme / With daedal life in boats and tents" (1.31.17–20). Here, daedal is a magical invocation of the creativity and inventiveness of man's labyrinthine artistry.

In 1862 Melville was giving thought to German literature and art. According to his annotation, he acquired the two volumes of *Germany*, by Madame de Staël, on March 4 and sometime in April (Sealts #487). His extensive markings in his copy of *Germany* indicate his interest in the poems and dramas of Klopstock, Goethe, and Schiller, in the works of Lessing and Winckelmann, and in the philosophical writings of Kant and Fichte. At about the same time, on March 17, he acquired the Bohn edition of the poems of Heinrich Heine, in a translation by E. A. Bowring (Sealts #268); the introduction spoke of "Heine's next great work, his 'Reisebilder,' or Pictures of Travel, written partly in poetry and partly in prose" and observed that the book was "descriptive of his travels in different countries, especially in England and Italy," a passage that Melville marked, possibly considering that it had something in common with his own projected "Frescoes of Travel." As if to emphasize this idea, he annotated the "Pictures of Travel" section with the marginal remark "The poetical part of The Reisebilder" and marked a number of passages from the poetic sequence (Cowen 1:654, 656).[8] He may have been considering the possibility of a volume of "Frescoes" that would combine prose and poetry, and some of his later works, published and unpublished, do combine the two. "Naples in the Time of Bomba" is mostly in poetry but has prose headnotes for the various sections. *John Marr and Other Sailors* opens with a prose description of the last years of the sailor-poet. "Rip Van Winkle's Lilac," part of the planned volume *Weeds and Wildings*, combines prose and poetry in its narrative. The poetical part of Heine's pictures of travel prints the complete set of lyrics dealing with "The Return Home," a theme underlined by Melville's final poem in *Timoleon*, a "L'Envoi" about "the return of the Sire de Nesle," who sings "My towers at last! These rovings end." The question of influence would be exceedingly difficult to fix, but Bowring's translations are often persuasive in capturing the shapes of Heine's lyrics and the poetic attitudes expressed in the many poems in the volume.

Among other poems in Heine's volume, Melville marked the seventh of the nine "Fresco-Sonnets to Christian S——," a suggestive title, and, almost in its entirety, a section of the long poem "Germany," in which the poet speaks of Cologne Cathedral as "a form of monstrous sort" and "black as the devil," meant as a "bastile" for the "cunning papists" until

Luther appear'd and soon by his mouth
A thundering "Halt!" was spoken
Since then the Cathedral no progress has made
In building, the charm being broken. (Cowen 1:655, 657–68)

Melville had already presented a "fresco" of the great building, recording in his journal a visit on December 9, 1849, to "the famous cathedral, where the ever-lasting 'crane' stands on the tower" (*Journals* 35). Subsequently, it became the art object to symbolize his unfinished cetological system in *Moby-Dick*, "the crane still standing upon the top of the uncompleted tower," for great architectural undertakings "ever leave the copestone to posterity" (*Moby-Dick* 145). Perhaps Heine's poem only reminded him of what he had seen and described, or perhaps it gave him an impetus toward thinking about another ekphrasis of the impressive cathedral.

TWO

The Arts Observed

"Old Blurred, Bewrinkled Mezzotint"

A DRAMATIC MOMENT IN Melville's encounters with the sister arts came during his Roman tour. On March 3, 1857, he reported in his journal that he "Rode to Palazzo Barberini to see Cenci.—Expression of suffering about the mouth—(appealing look of innocence) not caught in any copy or engraving" (*Journals* 108). The occasion was certainly momentous, for Melville was seeing a painting that, for some time, had been praised as one of the enduring masterpieces of Italian art, the so-called portrait of *Beatrice Cenci,* attributed to Guido Reni. American travelers like Melville made the painting one of the required stops in their art tours, and all seemed equally moved by the attractive picture. Melville knew all about it even before his viewing. A few days before he visited it, he had purchased a print "for $4. Surprising cheap" (*Journals* 106). The print became a prize of his collection and still survives (Wallace, "Reese" 10–11). It is one of the artworks that he would use well in his writings. In *Clarel,* the character of Vine is at least partially portrayed by a comparison of his facial expression to that of the Cenci portrait.[1]

Melville thought long and hard about the pictures that came under his observant eye. He knew well how they could play a vital role in his descriptive writing by giving him subjects and how even the merest allusion might bring them vividly before his readers. With such a reliable motive behind his studious comprehension of the plastic arts, he was able to indulge his refined senses of color, texture, shape, and form. The most concrete evidence of his prolonged attention to his subject is the large collection of engravings that he accumulated.

Essays by Robert K. Wallace have cataloged the various collections that hold these prints. Nearly three hundred are housed in the Berkshire Athenaeum, more than forty are in the Reese collection, and some eight more in the Ambrose group. There is every indication that Melville not only collected these artworks but that he studied them intently and at length and used them in his writings. The markings on the whale's outer layer of skin exhibit lines, according to Ishmael, like those of an engraving. It is clear from his allusion in *Clarel* that he was well aware of the meaning of terms like "mezzotint." When evoking the name of Piranesi in that poem, he speaks of that artist's "rarer prints." Given that he saw paintings only occasionally but had the engravings easily at hand, sometimes for many years, we may assume that he found in them a crucial resource for the visual aspects of his own writing. A mere listing of artists represented in his collection gives some idea of the range of his interests. There were prints after the work of Rubens, Turner, Flaxman, Stanfield, Nicholas Poussin, Veronese, Titian, Cuyp, Mieris, Metzu, Westall, and Landseer. A group of engravings from Boydell's *Shakespeare Gallery* showed scenes from several of Shakespeare's plays. Engravings of antique busts displayed the heads of Homer, Alcibiades, Aristippus, Xenophon, Machiavelli, Pericles, Plutarch, and other famous personages. The Reese collection of prints is rich in architectural art, and the Ambrose group contains works after Claude, Turner, Swanevelt, and Van de Velde. When we add the illustrated books that now survive from Melville's library, the number of engravings available for his examination adds measurably to his available sources.

Like his contemporaries, Melville had no doubt read over and over again the contention that the paintings of the Italian Renaissance represented the pinnacle of art; but his own reactions are often difficult to assess. His Italian notes seem to betray little enthusiasm for the paintings of Raphael. The "stunning effect of a first visit to the Vatican" on March 2, 1857, was not elaborated upon, except for a reference to the "faded bloom" of Raphael's work which he saw in the Loggie (*Journals* 108). On another visit, on March 9, he saw the "Hall of Animals" and took note of the frescoes and a Raphael painting without further comment. In Naples, he did note that the face of Raphael's Madonna was "touchingly maternal" (103). In Florence, at the Uffizi Gallery, he observed that Giotto's paintings were "predecessors of the Peruginos & Raphael" and that a painting had "faces, attitudes, expressions & groupings I had noted in Rome in Raphael" (115). Titian's paintings seemed to receive a more interested response. At the Uffizi, he was "charmed with Titian's Venus" (115); in Venice he saw "Titians Assumption" and "Titians Virgin in the Temple," but neither invited comment (118). But he saw in the complexions of Venetian women a "clear, rich golden brown" that Titian, he believed, must have colored from nature (119). A picture of Lucrezia Borgia, possibly by Veronese, drew his response that there was "no wicked look about her, good looking dame—rather fleshy" (111).

During the Italian journey, he viewed many Italian paintings, including works by Tintoretto, Veronese, Andrea del Sarto, Perugino, Caravaggio, Domenichino, and, of course, Salvator Rosa and Guido Reni, and his praise was often reserved for the works of painters who held lesser places in the pantheon of art. For instance, he found "lovely" a painting of Galatea, probably by Albani. Again and again, his notes simply recorded seeing pictures without offering a reaction: "A Lady by Titian," "Two portraits of Raphael. . . . One of Titian's women" (109–11), and, on April 10, "Some heads of Titian" (122). He recorded a remark by a "wearied lady" at the Pitti Palace in Florence—"It's as bad as too much pain: it gets to be pain at last"—and thought the lady "was talking no doubt about excess of pleasure in these galleries" (114). His excess of pleasure seemed often to come from the work of non-Italian artists. He noted a "Rubens' Magdalen—excellently true to nature, but very ugly" or a "remarkable Teniers effect . . . produced by first dwarfing, then deforming humanity" (122). In Amsterdam, he saw a "Wonderful picture of Paul Potter—The Bear" (127). He could express disapproval of the Italians; looking at two small paintings by Correggio in Naples, he "Could not see anything so wonderful" in them (103). Among the engravings that he collected was a Titian landscape and a Veronese portrait (Wallace, "Berkshire" 80, 83). Italian painters did play a role in the symposium of his poem "At the Hostelry": Fra Lippo Lippi, "with wicked eye," Tintoretto (*Collected Poems* 322), Carlo Dolce, Veronese, Michelangelo, Salvator Rosa, and Leonardo da Vinci all figure in the poem. Speeches are given to "Spagnoletto," the Spanish artist, Jose Ribera, who earned his nickname by settling in Italy.

Melville's occasionally lukewarm response to these Italian works of art is not surprising. It may have something in common with the disappointment travelers felt when first viewing the art works they had often heard praised. The American painter John Singleton Copley, going to Europe to study in 1774, felt the burden of this frustration. "The differences between Raphael, Titiano, Angelo and the common run of moderately good artists," he wrote in a letter, "is not so great as one would imagine from the praises bestowed on those great men" (Alberts 117). When Hawthorne, having completed his assignment in England, traveled with his family to Italy in 1858, his notebook entries betrayed a similar disappointment with what he was viewing. At the Barberini Palace, on February 20, he recorded that, of the paintings, there were "barely half a dozen which I should care to see again, though doubtless all have value in their way." In the same entry, he recorded seeing "pictures by Domenichino, Rubens, and other famous painters, which I do not mean to speak of, because I cared really little or nothing about them." On March 10, he saw at the Sciarra Palace "Raphael's Violin Player, which I am willing to accept as a good picture," and "Titian's Bella Donna,—the only one of Titian's works that I have yet seen which makes an impression on me corresponding with his fame."

Writing *The Marble Faun* shortly after his Italian art impressions, Hawthorne presented his views in a coherent statement. In the chapter entitled "The Emptiness of Galleries," he has Hilda visit "one of the great, old palaces—the Pamfili Doria, the Corsini, the Sciarra, the Borghese, the Colonna" and observes that "she had lost . . . the faculty of appreciating those great works of art." In his copy of the novel, Melville marked and annotated a long passage that follows that criticizes the art of the Roman galleries while praising the work of Dutch painters like Teniers, Dow, and Mieris. The lack of variety is one topic; perhaps a fourth of all collections "consist of Virgins, and infant Christs, repeated over and over again," and "Half of the other pictures are Magdalens, Flights into Egypt, Crucifixions, Depositions from the Cross, Pietas, Noli-me-tangeres, or the sacrifice of Abraham, or martyrdoms of saints." Comments on mythological paintings, "nude Venuses, Ledas, Graces, and, in short, a general apotheosis of nudity," along with remarks about Raphael, make up another portion of the argument. In his copy of the novel, at the head of the chapter, Melville wrote "Most original & admirable, And, doubtless, too true" (Cowen 1:600). Proceeding with his reading of the passage, Melville marked as "excellent" the statement that "a taste for pictorial art is often no more than a polish upon the hard enamel of an artificial character" (601). Hawthorne often protested in his notebook entries that he lacked the ability to judge art works, but there is no such doubt in *The Marble Faun,* and Melville seemed to feel, at least in the 1860s, that such passages articulated his own thoughts about the art of Italy.[2]

Like many nineteenth-century American lovers of art, Melville found much to praise in the paintings of the seventeenth-century Dutch artists. Peter Paul Rubens must have exerted a special influence upon his visual imagination; among the prints that he owned are a dozen executed after paintings by Rubens. Here, narrative in painting dominates; prints show *Mars Going to War* and *Henry 4th Setting Out to War,* and a whole group is devoted to noble birth, education, and marriage, belonging to the series Rubens painted on Mary de Medici (Wallace, "Berkshire" 75). Visiting Cologne on December 9, 1849, Melville had noted in his journal that it was "where Rubens was born & Mary de Medici died." On the same day, at St. Peter's Church, he "saw the celebrated Descent from the Cross by Rubens" (35–36). On his second European journey, on April 10, 1857, he saw "Rubens' Magdalen—excellently true to nature, but very ugly" (122). It may have been this truth to nature, even to the extent of risking ugliness, that drew him to the work of Rubens. In dealing with the picturesque in the poem "At the Hostelry," Melville had some of his painters underline the thesis that the ugly could be portrayed, as in Rembrandt's "Slaughtered Ox." Among the books he later collected, Melville had John William Mollett's *Rembrandt* (1879), a short biographical monograph that gave an account of the artist's life. Several chapters concentrated upon the "Paintings and Etchings" of the last years, and the book offered chronological lists of the paintings and the etchings. Among the sixteen illustrations in the book were *Resurrection of Lazarus,* a *Self-Portrait, Christ Driving out the Money Changers,* and a *Descent from the Cross.*

Along with Rubens and Rembrandt, Melville evinced a great interest in a number of other Dutch painters of the seventeenth century. Among the pictures he saw at Dulwich in November 1849 was an "old man & pipe" (*Journals* 19), possibly, as Horsford conjectures, a work of Ostade (299). During his 1857 journey, he visited "Picture Gallery" in Amsterdam where he viewed "Keel hauling of a Dutch Surgeon.—The Syndics of Rembrandt & The Night Watch (shadows)—Portrait of a painter & his wife . . . Dutch convivial scenes. Teniers and Breughel" (*Journals* 126). Dennis Berthold has provided an excellent survey of Melville's attachment to the Dutch painters, pointing out that in the poem "At the Hostelry" nine of the artists represented in the art symposium are Dutch and demonstrating the influence of *The Illustrated Magazine of Art,* with its articles on Dutch painters ("Dutch Genre" 220, 227ff). In that poem, Melville takes the occasion to define the picturesque in Dutch terms by having Gerard Dow describe a still life painting with "old oak" and "well scoured copper sauce-pans," with "Pigeons and prawns, bunched carrots bright, / Gilled fish, clean radish red and white / And greens and cauliflowers." The picture is completed by a "peasant / Plucking a delicate fat pheasant" (*Collected Poems* 325–26), an attractive genre scene far from the saints and martyrs of Italian Renaissance art. Among the engravings in Melville's collection were pictures by Mieris, Metzu, Ostade, Cuyp, and Van de Velde (Wallace, "Berkshire" 72–83), and many of the articles in his copy of *The Works of Eminent Masters* featured engravings after Dutch artists, including Steen, Ostade, Mieris, Dow, Rembrandt, Rubens, Cuyp, and Potter. In his writings he would refer to Dutch painting. In *White-Jacket* the sailors aboard the *Neversink* are compared to "a Flemish kitchen full of good fellows from Teniers" (387), and a poem in *Timoleon,* "The Bench of Boors," describes a Teniers painting. Melville evoked the name of Phillips Wouverman in *Mardi* to indicate the kind of struggle scene he envisioned. Ishmael, recoiling from the sublime ambition of Ahab, learns that "man must eventually lower, or at least shift, his conceit of attainable felicity" and finds that lowered, humane conceit in "the wife, the heart, the bed, the table, the saddle, the fire-side, the country," all the elements of a good Dutch painting (*Moby-Dick* 416).

This attraction to Dutch artists was one that other American writers shared. Washington Irving referred to paintings of Teniers in *Tales of a Traveller* and drew a literary equivalent of such art in his description of the Van Tassel farm in "The Legend of Sleepy Hollow." Though he relates the description of the odd company that Rip Van Winkle meets to Flemish art, the people have much in common with the personages depicted in Ostade and Brouwer (Zlogar 49). Hawthorne wrote in his notebooks of "looking principally at the old Dutch Masters, who seem to me the most wonderful set of men that ever handled a brush." He found their true genius in the portraying of the "minutely true" and found Gerard Dow "the master among these queer magicians." Barbara Novak has pointed out the influence of Dutch paintings upon Americans. Private collections housed many paintings and the Boston Athenaeum exhibited works by Cuyp, Hobbema, Potter, and Van de Velde, among others.[3]

One of Melville's earliest art acquisitions was a collection of John Flaxman's illustrations for the works of Dante and Aeschylus (Wallace, "Berkshire" 73). The plates for *The Divine Comedy,* alluded to in *Pierre,* demonstrate how Melville could make use, in his writings, of the artworks that he knew and studied (Schless 65–82).The collection of Flaxman pieces that survives in Melville's portfolio at the Berkshire Athenaeum is quite incomplete and hardly gives an idea of what he must have known about the English painter's work. However, it was possible for Melville to have seen, quite early and easily, a good number of the illustrations that Flaxman drew from the classics. Ichabod Charles Wright's translation of Dante contained "34 illustrations on steel, after designs by Flaxman," and included "Charon's Boat," "Ugolino," "Dis, or Lucifer," "The Gluttons," "The Adoration of the Trinity," and "The Ninth Sphere." An edition of the volume, published by Bohn, is dated 1847. The Alexander Pope translations of the *Iliad* and the *Odyssey* were published "with the entire series of Flaxman's designs," thirty-nine for the *Iliad* and thirty-four for the *Odyssey.* Flaxman did a drawing of "Thetis bringing the armour to Achilles" but did not show the famous shield, with its artistic portrayals, in detail.[4]

This interest in Flaxman's illustrations was a part of Melville's general interest in the artists of Great Britain. In *Melville and Turner,* Wallace has demonstrated Melville's love for the paintings of J. M. W. Turner and for the many prints available of these paintings. More than twenty prints executed after Turner's paintings still form part of Melville's collections and include works like *Boats off Calais, The Grand Canal Venice, Venice—The Dogana, The Fighting Temeraire, Peace—The Burial of Wilkie, Snow-Storm,* and *Rain, Steam and Speed* (Wallace,

"Berkshire" 82–83). Toward the end of his 1857 European trip, Melville went to "the Vernon & Turner galleries" where he saw Turner's paintings of the burial of Wilkie, a *Shipwreck,* and the *Temeraire* "taken to her last birth [*sic*]" (*Journals* 128). The Vernon collection, which Melville leaves undiscussed, was a large accumulation of English paintings that included works by Hogarth, Landseer, Gainsborough, and Constable, among others. Wallace's elaborate study of the influence of Turner upon Melville's writings argues that Turner's "powerful aesthetic of the indistinct," a technique of concealing the directness of form and design, played an important role in formulating the ways in which Melville conceived and used pictorialism in *Moby-Dick.* Wallace demonstrates as well that other aspects of Turner's art—the use of swirling vortices of color, the relative sizes of the human against the inhuman in nature, for instance—also had a great influence upon Melville's work.

In addition to Flaxman and Turner, Melville showed a considerable interest in British painters and in those foreigners who adopted Britain as their workplace. He liked Van Dyck's portraits. Sir Joshua Reynolds's portrayals of *Mrs. Siddons* and of *The Death of Cardinal Beaufort* caught his interest during his visit to Dulwich Gallery on November 17, 1849 (*Journals* 20). In later years, he would acquire *The Literary Works of Reynolds* and read the "Discourses on Art" and the notes that Reynolds provided for William Mason's translation of Dufresnoy's *De Arte Graphica.* It is likely that he saw paintings by Sir David Wilkie during his tours of England, although he does not mention them in his journals. One of the books he acquired late in life was John William Mollett's study *Sir David Wilkie* (1881). Mollett gave an account of Wilkie's life and career and offered illustrations of a number of Wilkie's paintings, including *The Pedlar, The Village Politicians, The Cut Finger,* and *The Jews' Harp,* all of them British versions of the Dutch genre pictures that Melville admired.

Melville displayed a considerable interest in American art and artists. Living in New York in 1847, he registered at the New-York Gallery of Fine Arts. Evert Duyckinck took him to a showing of the new rooms at the Art-Union and there he met and conversed with William Sidney Mount. Mount's paintings would surely have interested him, portraying as they did scenes of ordinary American life in something of the manner of the Dutch genre painters. Pieces like *The Rustic Dance* (1830), *Eel-Spearing at Setauket* (1845), and *The Power of Music* 1847), all "realistic views of American scenery" (Flexner 30), brought a great deal of praise to Mount's work and made it available to many viewers. In England on November 21, 1849, Melville recorded visiting Greenwich Hospital, where he saw "Fine painting by West of St. Paul" (*Journals* 23). Benjamin West had entered a competition in 1786 to paint an altarpiece for the chapel at Greenwich Hospital, *St. Paul's Shipwreck at Malta* (Alberts 185–86, 366).

Melville made a point of visiting, or attempting to visit, American artists who were living and working in Italy. These visits were part of the itinerary for tourists and were carefully advertised in the guidebooks. On March 27, 1857, he recorded a visit to the studio of Hiram Powers and saw "His America. Il Penseroso, Fisher Boy." As for Powers himself, he was a "plain man. Fine specimen of an American" (*Journals* 116). Powers, the best-known American sculptor of his time, had the habit of fashioning female nudes and giving the statues symbolic or suggestive names. *Greek Slave,* a sensational success with American audiences of the mid–nineteenth century, portrayed the chaste nude in chains. *America* was another nude, and *Il Penseroso* played upon the current popular device of finding equivalents in the visual arts for literary subjects, this one from Milton. A few days earlier, on March 10, Melville noted that he had visited no less than three of the advertised studios. One of these belonged to William Page, who apparently offered his fellow American a "Long lecture," perhaps, as Melville recorded, on "Titian—kneading of flesh—Middle tint" (*Journals* 111). Page apparently liked to lecture; he "expounded theories of art with an eloquence that would have made the Sirens abandon their reef and swim for him" (Flexner 180). He was able to go to Italy because he received commissions to paint copies after Titian, and his own pictures "needed only the cracks of age to be mistaken for Titians" (Flexner 187). At the studio of Edward Bartholomew,who died the year after the visit, Melville saw "His Eve. Bust of young Augustus" and apparently did not receive a lecture. In *Melville as Lecturer,* Merton Sealts has indicated that in 1858 Melville visited "the studio of an Albany sculptor, Erastus Dow Palmer—perhaps in connection with the subject matter of his lecture" (27). If he knew Palmer well enough to discuss the lecture on Roman statuary, it is likely that he had a good knowledge of Palmer's work.

When Melville and his wife visited the Shaw family in Boston during the 1840s, it would seem likely that he might take these occasions to visit the art exhibits at the Boston Athenaeum. Sealts points out, however, that there is no record of Judge Shaw taking Melville there as a guest (Sealts 46, 56n.1). But even if he did not have opportunities to visit the museum, he may have known quite a few details about the art collection through the exhibition catalogs regularly issued by the Athenaeum; Perkins and Gavin give a full accounting of these publications in their *Art Exhibition Index.* During this period, the Athenaeum had a collection of copies of sculptural art and painting. Jonathan Harding lists a copy of the *Apollo Belvedere* and a bust of Homer as well as copies of a painting of Allori's *Judith and Holofernes, The Martyrdom of Saint Sebastian* after the painting by Guido Reni, and *The Piping Shepherd* after Albert Cuyp (69–72); he also cites John Gadsby Chapman's copies of David Teniers's *The Musician,* Gabriel Metsu's *Woman Tuning a Mandolin* (19), and Giordano's *The Flaying of Marsyas* (81–82), among others. When Josiah Quincy's *History of the Boston Athenaeum* was published in 1851, Melville may have been stirred to read it.

As a registrant at the New-York Gallery of Fine Arts, Melville had the un-usual opportunity of studying some of the best American art.[5] Luman Reed (1787–1836) had assembled an impressive collection, and after his death his heirs established the gallery and bought the paintings for it. There were paintings by Thomas Cole, including the series *The Course of Empire,* and several works by Asher B. Durand and some by William Sidney Mount. It is curious that only one print after the work of an American artist survives in the collections that Melville owned, for, doubtless, he did have others. The engraving by W. G. Jackman was made for the *New York Illustrated Magazine* in 1846, after *The Death Struggle,* a painting by Charles Deas (Wallace, "Reese" 14–15). Deas (1818–1867) was known as a painter of frontier scenes. *The Death Struggle* was shown in New York at the Art-Union in 1844, as John McDermott reports in his article on Deas. Other frontier topics included a trapper, voyageurs, and a prairie fire (McDermott 308). In *The Literary World* of May 29 and June 12, 1849, reports were given of show-ings of paintings by Deas at the National Academy of Design (309).[6] One might well have expected Melville to own at least a few more of the many engravings that portrayed the frontier, scenes of American rustic life in the manner of Mount and others, or the sort of scene that Clarel, marooned and lonely in Jerusalem, imagined set among the Kaatskills, with "Farmhouse and stack, last lichened barn / And log bridge rotting in remove" (1.1.168–69). His allusion, in chapter 42 of *Moby-Dick,* to the "White Steed of the Prairies"(191) is seemingly cast as a frontier picture, and Ishmael's remark that Death, "the king of terrors, when personified by the evangelist, rides on his pallid horse" (192), argues a knowl-edge of Benjamin West's famous portrayal of *Death on the Pale Horse,* or per-haps, as Wallace suggests, Turner's picture of the same subject (*Melville and Turner* 40–44). Much of the painterly argument in *Pierre,* the "rural bowl of milk" that Melville promised Sophia Hawthorne (*Correspondence* 219), centers about Ameri-can art and artists, rustic genre scenes, local portrait painters, and fake pictures offered as originals of the masters. When reading and marking James Jackson Jarves's *The Art-Idea,* Melville took especial note of what Jarves had to say of Washington Allston.

Melville knew something about the work of at least two American artists and wrote ekphrastic descriptions of their pictures. Attendance at the 1865 exhibition of the National Academy of Design in April 1865 led to his writing the poem "'The Coming Storm,'" based upon a painting by Sanford R. Gifford (1823–1880). Gifford lived in New York and had his work on display year after year at the Academy—among others, *An October Afternoon* in 1866, *Cape Ann* in 1867, *San Giorgio, Venice* in 1870, *San Maria delle Salute, Venice* in 1872, *The Golden Horn, Constantinople* in 1873, *Venetian Sails* in 1874. But Melville had earlier opportunities to know Gifford's work. The "Distribution of the American Art-Union for 1849" featured, among the two hundred pictures that it advertised, four by Gifford—*Schroon Lake, Solitude,* a *Sketch from Nature,* and *Creek Scenery, Ulster County, N.Y.* (*Literary World* 135 [September 1, 1849]: 187). Another poem in *Battle-Pieces* was "Formerly a Slave," based, as Melville noted, upon a picture by Elihu Vedder (1836–1923). After 1865 Melville continued to cultivate his interest in Vedder. He acquired a copy of *The Rubaiyat of Omar Khayyam,* in the Edward Fitzgerald translation, with illustrations by Vedder. There were many other opportunities for him to see examples of Vedder's pictures and illustrations. An illustrated edition of Tennyson's *Enoch Arden* was published in 1865; and Vedder designed covers for the February and August 1882 issues of *The Century Illustrated Monthly Magazine* and for the Christmas 1882 issue of *Harper's New Monthly Magazine.* And, most importantly, Melville dedicated *Timoleon* to Vedder, a recognition of the painter as "my countryman" and as an important figure in the American art world.[7]

The National Academy's new building was dedicated in April 1865. The ceremony, planned for the middle of the month, had to be postponed until April 29 because of the assassination of President Lincoln, so Melville's attendance at the exhibition must have occurred after that date.[8] It is entirely speculative to consider Melville's further connection with the National Academy of Design, but it is at least suggestive that the Academy's building was located at the corner of Twenty-third Street and Fourth Avenue, not far from Melville's house at 104 East Twenty-sixth Street, and he may well have visited it regularly in later years. Of the two painters whose work attracted him in 1865, Gifford continued to exhibit regularly at the National Academy. He had two pictures shown in 1866 and three in 1867 and again in 1868. From 1870 to 1880, the year of his death, twenty-four of his paintings were shown. Vedder was less consistent than Gifford, probably because of his residence in Italy, but in 1865, the year Melville first saw his work, he had six pictures on display. There were further showings of his paintings in 1866, 1867, 1874, and 1882.[9]

Melville's friendship with Richard Lathers and his visits to Lathers's home opened a large art collection to him. He was able to study a number of statues and other sculptural works of art. Lathers owned a number of paintings, among them at least a few that were significant for Melville's visual thinking—a *Rape of Europa,* a *Sibyl,* and some Dutch genre works. There were copies of a number of famous paintings—Raphael's *Transfiguration* and two Madonnas, two Correggios, a Veronese, and two Murillos, as well as works by Reynolds, Claude, Domenichino, Salvator Rosa, and Canaletto. Lathers also owned engravings, after works by Dürer, Piranesi, Le Brun, Turner, and Landseer (Cohen, "Lathers" 3–25).

Information about Melville's possible association with the Metropolitan Museum of Art is skimpy because he apparently did not register as a member. He must have been well aware of the new museum that was developing after the Civil War. Dr. Henry W. Bellows, the Melvilles' minister of All Souls Church, so concerned with their marital difficulties in the 1860s (Kring 1–9), was a prominent member of the planners of the museum and may well have introduced Melville to its treasures. The museum's purchase of 174 paintings, "principally Dutch and Flemish, but including representative works of the Italian, French, English and Spanish Schools" (Howe 135–36), would have interested him. The museum's second location, the Douglas Mansion at 128 West Fourteenth Street, between Sixth and Seventh Avenues, placed the collection relatively near Melville's home during the years 1873–79, and the acquisition and display of the large Cesnola collection of ancient statues, bas reliefs, pottery, inscribed stelae, and the like would have been worth his intense study (Howe 161, 167–70). The museum's removal in 1880 to its location in Central Park made it easily available to Melville, who liked to walk in the park.

There are no records of attendance by Melville; but the museum's records do indicate the gift of a painting by "Jane L. Melville" and list Mrs. Allan Melville as "a Fellow for Life" from 1884 to 1889. This was apparently the widow of Melville's younger brother, Allan (1823–1872), Jane L. Dempsey, who died in 1890.[10]

Photography developed with astonishing speed during the whole of Melville's maturity and his writing career, and he was clearly affected by its power and potential. In portraiture, its contrasts with the art of painting must have been obvious to him from personal experience. His portrait, painted by Joseph Oriel Eaton, was available for comparison to a portrait photograph made later in his life. He understood how a photographic portrait could delineate truthfully the details of human character, as "On the Photograph of a Corps Commander," from *Battle-Pieces,* demonstrates. He must have had the opportunity, especially in his later years, of seeing many photographs, though they do not seem to have made enough of an impression upon his mind for him to feature them in the late poetry.

When Melville drew upon his impressions of art for a lecture topic, he avoided speaking about paintings and, instead, focused upon the statuary that he had viewed in Rome. "The deeds of the ancients were noble," he was reported to have said at the conclusion of his lecture, "and so are their arts" (*Piazza Tales* 409). Busts of Demosthenes, Socrates, Julius Caesar, Seneca, and Plato, as well as statues of Nero and Tiberius, were his topics. The *Apollo Belvedere,* much admired in nineteenth-century guidebooks and art criticism, drew enthusiastic praise from Melville: "there is a kind of divinity in it that lifts the imagination of the beholder above 'things rank and gross in nature'" (402). The *Laocoön,* "the very semblance of a great and powerful man writhing with the inevitable destiny," made a deep impression upon him, partly because he saw clearly that "half of its significance" came from "the fable that it represents; otherwise it would be no more than Paul Potter's "Bear Hunt" (403). This is a clear-headed assessment of the way in which Melville and his contemporaries viewed art, finding much of its compelling power in the literary narrative attached; this is true of the *Laocoön* and of such paintings as Guido's *Beatrice Cenci,* which, without its pathetic story of murder and execution, is merely a very pretty portrait of a pretty girl. The viewers tended to read into the expressions their own interpretations of the anguished principals in the artworks. It was, of course, not only the ancient statuary that impressed Melville. He spoke of Michelangelo's *Moses* and Benvenuto Cellini's *Perseus* in as glowing terms as he referred to the *Farnese Hercules.*

During his 1849 journey to England and Europe, Melville managed to see much of the sculptural arts. At the British Museum on November 16 he saw "big arm & foot—Rosetta Stone—Nineveh sculptures—& c" (*Journals* 19). His journal for November 30 indicates his seeing at the Louvre "Admirable collection of antique statuary. Beats the British Museum" (31). On December 2 he "saw tomb or rather monument of Cardinal Richelieu. Good sculpture" (32). At the Hotel de Cluny there were "Glorious old cabinets—ebony and ivory carving" (33). In the gardens of Versailles were "Apollo & the horses on the fountain" (35), which, as Horsford notes, would have been the Bassin d'Apollon. At the same time, Melville must have seen, though he did not mention it, the Bassin d'Encelade of Gaspard Marsy (346), which would become a central art motif in the composition of *Pierre.*

During the 1856–57 journey, he saw much sculpture. In Liverpool, shortly after arriving in England, he recorded viewing "Nelson's statue, with peculiar emotion, mindful of 20 years ago" (50). Like Redburn, he was recalling his early trip to England and its effect upon him. The sculptural arts of Palestine were mostly devoted to decorative basso relievos and friezes in tomb and church, and the main impression of Greece was of temples. But in Naples, he visited the "Hall of bronze statuary," where he could see "Plato (hair & beard & imperial) Nero (villianous [sic]) Seneca (caricature) Drunken faun on wine skin" and, among the marble sculptures, "Hercules Farnese—colossal, gravely benevolent face" and "The group of the bull. Glorious" (103). In Rome he saw statues of Antinous, Apollo, Athena, and the "gigantic" statues of the Apostles at St. John Lateran. He visited the Vatican more than once and saw the *Apollo Belvedere,* the *Laocoön,* and some animal sculptures in the "Hall of animals."

He visited the studios of several sculptors. The English artist John Gibson (1790–1866) tinted his statues, and Melville was able to see "his colored Venus." Then, on the same day, he went to the studio of Edward Bartholomew to look at an *Eve* and a bust "of young Augustus" (111). His most rewarding visit was probably the one to the studio of Hiram Powers, who was already notorious for his *Greek Slave,* seen in many copies and reproductions. Melville saw his *America,* a partly nude female figure, an *Il Penseroso,* and a *Fisher Boy.* To Melville's eye, Powers himself was a sculptural work of art, a "plain man. Fine specimen of an American" (116).

In all his journeying, Melville took special note of monumental works of architecture. Hampton Court was "justly renowned for its beauty" (16). He saw St. Paul's, where he sat and listened to the choir, and, with George Adler, visited Westminster Abbey. He found Dulwich a "sequestered, quiet, charming spot" (20). The Bow Church in Cheapside was a "Curious old church indeed" (21). In Paris he visited Notre Dame, "A noble old pile" (31), and the church of St. Roche, with its "noble interior" (32). Versailles was "A most magnificent & incredible affair altogether" (33), and the cathedral at Cologne was "one of the most singular" structures in the world (36). When he visited St. Sophia in Constantinople in December 1856, he described its dome as a "firmament of masonry" and took note of the buttresses and of the "positive appropriation of space" in the interior (67). The pyramids in Egypt drew a lengthy description and meditation, as he found in them "Precipice on precipice, cliff on cliff"; they "loomed" as "something vast, indefinite, incomprehensible, and awful" (75–76). In Greece he found the Parthenon "elevated like cross of Constantine" and commented on the "Strange contrast of rugged rock with polished temple" (99). The cathedral at Milan was "Glorious. More satisfactory to me than St. Peters," and he suggested that he, or perhaps someone else, "Might write book of travel upon top of Milan Cathedral" (121). It is in *Timoleon,* his last volume of poems, that these architectural impressions find voice, for there are pieces on the tower in Pisa, the Milan Cathedral, the Parthenon, and the Egyptian pyramids. Among the prints Melville collected are pictures of the Rouen Cathedral, the monastery of San Saba, Holland House, and Maecenas's villa at Tivoli (Wallace, "Berkshire" 72–86). The Reese collection has prints of *Denton Chapel, Woburn Abbey, Llanthony Abbey* in Monmouthshire, *St. Mary's* in Shrewsbury, and *A View of the Abbey Church at Shrewsbury.* There are views of Westminster, *Tynemouth Castle, Ostenhanger House, Witton Castle,* and other prominent architectural scenes (Wallace, "Reese" 17–42).[11]

Along with his passion for collecting engravings, Melville apparently was determined to learn details about the arts of engraving. From the generalizations about prints in *Redburn,* Melville moved to considering critical analysis of the pictures of whales in J. Ross Browne's *Etchings,* which were "wretchedly engraved," and the "fine engravings" after Garneray and even the skin of the whale with its straight marks, "something like those in the finest Italian engravings," which "but afford the ground for far other delineations" (*Moby-Dick* 165, 267, 306). His desire for such knowledge was probably realized by the acquisition in 1875, and probably as a gift to Mrs. Melville, of Georges Duplessis's *The Wonders of Engraving,* part of an "Illustrated Library of Wonders" that included volumes on sculpture, Italian art, architecture, glassmaking, and Pompeii. Duplessis offered workmanlike chapters on the art of engraving in Italy, Spain, the Low Countries, Germany, England, and France, along with an introductory chapter on the origins of engraving and a closing chapter on processes—wood, copperplate, etching, drypoint, mezzotint, and color. There were illustrations of a Rembrandt landscape, *Two Cows* by Paul Potter, a Ruysdael *Cornfield,* a Hogarth print, and a *Sunrise* after Claude Lorrain.

THE BOOKS NOT ALL HAVE TOLD

Melville's direct experience of art through his visits to museums, galleries, and exhibitions, and his collection of engravings enabled him to study examples of the plastic arts and fix, in his superb visual memory, details that he would be able to call up in his writings. Just as important for his self-education was his reading of what others said about the sister arts. He collected books—perhaps many more than those surviving in various collections—many of which have marked passages that indicate what especially interested him. The history of ancient art and of Italian painting, studies of individual painters or schools of painters, and informed commentary from travelers made up much of this reading, along with collateral studies of gems, the art of engraving, flower arrangements, and, very likely, the art of heraldry. He probably read Winckelmann's history of ancient Greek art and did read Luigi Lanzi's *History of Painting in*

Italy, the volumes borrowed from Evert Duyckinck. He also borrowed Duyckinck's set of Giorgio Vasari's *Lives of the Most Eminent Painters,* though he later acquired his own copy. A didactic poem, Charles Dufresnoy's "The Art of Painting," engaged his interest, though much of it is given to instructions to the would-be painter. When John Dryden translated Dufresnoy's poem, he provided an introduction entitled "A Parallel of Poetry and Painting," and this, too, was part of Melville's reading. Sir Joshua Reynolds's "Discourses" on painting, the annual addresses to the Royal Academy, were read and marked, and it seems likely that Melville might have read the similar addresses by Martin Shee, James Barry, and Henry Fuseli, all readily available. The comments of an American art critics like James Jackson Jarves and, possibly, Horace Binney Wallace, the ever-lengthening *Modern Painters* of John Ruskin, the technical articles of Charles Eastlake, and the essays of William Hazlitt contributed to his knowledge. The periodicals of the 1840s and 1850s—*The Literary World, American Whig Review, United States Magazine and Democratic Review, Putnam's Magazine*—all ran articles about art and artists and reviews of exhibitions. Later on there were many pieces of art criticism in the *Atlantic Monthly, Harper's Monthly, The Galaxy, Appleton's Journal, Scribner's Monthly, The Nation,* and other popular magazines, and it is likely that Melville scanned at least some of this material.[12]

In his copy of Goethe's notes from Italy, Melville underlined a passage written from Verona. Goethe had been looking at paintings by Tintoretto and Veronese and now observed that "It lies in my nature to admire, willingly and joyfully, all that is great and beautiful, and the cultivation of this talent, day after day, hour after hour, by the inspection of such beautiful objects, produces the happiest feelings" (Cowen 1:568). Apparently, Melville took the passage to apply as well to his own studies, for, when he acquired the volumes of Goethe, in December 1849, he had already been busy inspecting the art available in England and, to a lesser extent, what he could see in a quick trip to the Continent. The more than eighty markings in the travel letters indicate Melville's great interest in Goethe's little book about his Italian journey. These were not a jumble of random notes but a carefully edited version that Goethe drew in 1814 from material composed in 1786. The last portion, dealing with Rome, was not prepared till 1829 and so represents the work of the elderly author. Melville's underlinings, sidelines, and check marks illustrate well what he found valuable in this highly sophisticated commentary upon ancient and Italian arts. He marked Goethe's praise of Raphael's painting of St. Cecilia and his placing the artist at the highest point of art (569). A page or so later he sidelined Goethe's estimate of Guido Reni as the painter of "anatomy—a flaying scene—always some suffering, never an action of the hero" and did not mark but surely must have noted the summary statement that "to admire or to be charmed with them one must be a madman" (570). In Rome, Goethe saw Raphael's *Transfiguration*, of which he already owned a colored print, and meditated poignantly upon the way in which the original and the copy are "quite different," for "every true relation and false relation becomes immediately evident" (572). For Melville as a collector of prints who, only occasionally, had the opportunity to see original paintings and statues, this is a revealing situation for the art lover. And, indeed, he would be able to compare his purchased print of *Beatrice Cenci* with the original or speak, in *Clarel*, of "some print, / Old blurred bewrinkled mezzotint" (1.36.30–31). A similar reservation appears in a passage he marked from Goethe's observations about the *Apollo Belvedere*, "infinitely ravishing" in its marble original, "for that sublime air of youthful freedom and vigour, of never-changing juvenescence, which breathes around the marble, at once vanishes in the best even of plaster casts." But he likewise marked the succeeding description of "a Medusa-mask, above the size of life, in which the attempt to portray a lofty and beautiful countenance in the numbing agony of death has been indescribably successful" (Cowen 1:573). A number of Goethean references to the writings of Winckelmann were marked, showing an interest that seems confirmed by Melville's reading of Winckelmann's *History of Ancient Art* in 1852 (Sealts #559). Goethe's visit to Naples and to the grotto of Posilippo was marked (Cowen 1:576), and the entire passage seems to throw some light upon Melville's poem "Pausilippo." Part of Goethe's note says that "I can pardon all who lose their senses in Naples. . . . Just as it is said, that people who have once seen a ghost, are never afterwards seen to smile, so in the opposite sense it may be said of him, that he never could become perfectly miserable, as long as he remembered Naples." In Melville's poem, the name

> imports that none
> Who take the prospect thence can pine,
> For such the charm of beauty shown
> Even sorrow's self they cheerful weened
> Surcease might find and thank good Pan. (*Collected Poems* 242)

At Girgenti, Goethe was struck by the appearance of a Temple of Jupiter, whose ruins, "Like the bones of a gigantic skeleton . . . are scattered over a large space" (Cowen 1:582). Melville marked the passage in which Goethe describes his measuring of a huge column and, perhaps, made use of it later when comparing the skeleton of the whale to large architectural blocks like Pompey's Pillar or Gothic spires (*Moby-Dick* 453–54).

Though we do not possess the first volume of this set of Goethe's writings, it is not difficult to guess what Melville might have found useful in the author's tale of his early encounters with the arts. The father, Johann Casper, was an enthusiastic collector of artworks, and the young Goethe, as a student in Leipzig, took lessons in drawing and speaks of the ways in which his drawing master, Oeser, a collector of drawings and engravings, inspired in him a reverence for Winckelmann. At this point, Goethe's reading of Lessing's *Laocoön* moved him, as he said, "out of the region of scanty perceptions into the open fields of thought" (Cowen 1:268, 270, 280). Goethe was particularly drawn to the paintings of the seventeenth-century Dutch painters and studied the work of Rembrandt and Rubens, as well as Ostade, Schalken, and others, looking "to see nature in art." In Mannheim, he was able to see casts of antique sculpture, including *Laocoön,* the *Apollo Belvedere,* and the *Dying Gladiator* (Cowen 1:434–35). These statues were among the ones that Melville made a special effort to see during his Italian visit of 1857 and that he discussed in his lecture on Roman statuary. Goethe's comments on the *Laocoön* must have been of special interest, since this statue figures prominently in Melville's writings.[13]

Another book that Melville purchased in 1849 was *Corinne,* a novel by Madame de Staël, after hearing it discussed aboard ship on October 27 (*Journals* 9). We no longer have Melville's copy of this book, but, beneath a fairly thin fictional fable, it reads like a guidebook to the arts in Italy. The beautiful Corinne, "Attired like Domenichino's Sibyl," looks, to Lord Nevil, like a "Grecian statue" or "a priestess of Apollo" (*Corinne* 18). Furthermore, she is a gifted and brilliant artist and displays a fine sense of the great treasures of Italy as she takes him on a tour, lecturing about everything she believes he should know. They visit the St. Angelo Castle and St. Peter's and pay particular attention to statues of Castor and Pollux, Marius, and Marcus Aurelius. Seeing the large public baths, they reflect on how these buildings once contained art treasures: "In the baths of Caracalla were the Farnese Hercules, the Flora, and the group of Circe. Near Ostia, in the baths of Nero, was found the Apollo Belvidere" (64). At the Vatican, "that palace of sculpture," they note that "the ancients dignified grief by heroic composure" and study the *Laocoön* and *Niobe,* the statue of Tiberius, and the *Apollo.* A chapter on painting gives Corinne the opportunity to display her learning, as she and Nevil argue whether "the nature of the subjects selected by the Italy's great masters admit the varied originality of passion which painting can express" (127). They mention Raphael, Michelangelo, Mantegna, Perugino, and Leonardo da Vinci in the course of their debate. Corinne's own collection, "composed of historical, poetic, religious subjects, and landscapes," gives rise to more ideas as she speaks of portraits of Brutus, Marius, and Belisarius. She displays

"Albano's infant Christ asleep on the cross" and "Titian's Jesus bending under the weight of the cross." She owns paintings drawn from scenes in literary works, Dido and Aeneas, "the dying Clorinda" from Tasso, Macbeth in combat with Macduff, and Racine's Phedra. Her landscapes reflect her liking for "Salvator Rosa's style . . . rocks, torrents and trees." In Salvator, "The absence of man in the midst of nature excites profound reflections" (133–36), an idea that gives Melville's "Salvator Tarnmoor" a pictorial anchor in his description of the deserted Encantadas. Lord Nevil visits the Sistine Chapel alone, where he sees "the pictures of Michelangelo—the Day of Judgment treated by a genius worthy so terrible a subject" (154).

Perceptive authors like Goethe and Mme. de Staël would do much to broaden Melville's experience of works of art, much more, probably, than the guidebooks of France and Germany that he received in London in 1849. The direct experience of how other literary artists wrote of the sister arts must have helped to determine how Melville himself would approach this task. But he also read widely in art history, theory, and criticism. The popular Bohn Library editions offered readers a considerable range of reading matter. Evert Duyckinck owned the Bohn edition of Luigi Lanzi's *History of Painting in Italy* (1847), which Lanzi (1732–1810) revised several times, the final revision appearing in 1809. Melville borrowed Lanzi in 1859, along with an edition of Giorgio Vasari's *Lives of the Most Eminent Painters, Sculptors, and Architects,* also in a Bohn edition. Lanzi's work is itself rather dry, but it is full of quotations from Vasari, Winckelmann, and other art historians. Lanzi's descriptions of artworks follow a conventional and much-approved literary pattern of depicting in dramatic fashion with narrative movement the essentially static presentation of a painting. In his account of the *Transfiguration* of Raphael, for example, he offers an ekphrasis: "A youth possessed is presented to them, that they may expel the evil spirit that torments him, and in the possessed, struggling with the presence of the demon, the confiding faith of the father, the affliction of a beautiful and interesting female, and the compassion visible in the countenances of the surrounding apostles, we are presented with perhaps the most pathetic incident ever conceived" (Lanzi 1:378–79).

But, in addition to reinforcing the literary portrayal of artworks, Melville's reading in art history, criticism, and scholarship offered much of profit as he learned to appreciate art first through the help of prints and copies and later through visits to museums, galleries, and various exhibitions. William Hazlitt's *Encyclopaedia Britannica* article on "Fine Arts," reprinted with Haydon's piece on "Painting" (Sealts #263), was put together from some of Hazlitt's earlier art criticisms and offered the author's "most complete statement on the history and function of painting" (Barrell 315). A highly influential volume, Hazlitt's *Criticisms on Art* (1843) was acquired by Melville in 1870 and annotated. It contained the encyclopedia article and reprinted Hazlitt's "Criticisms on the Picture Galleries of England," an account of the artworks at the Dulwich Gallery, Windsor Castle, and Hampton Court, among others. But it seems likely that he had read Hazlitt's contributions to art criticism much earlier than 1870. As Robert K. Wallace has noted, these essays could have served as a guidebook for Melville during his 1849 stay in England, for he gave an account of his visits to these three institutions in his journal (*Melville and Turner* 252, 265–69).

Hazlitt's art writings, coming from an excellent essayist who was a more than adequate painter, were valuable influences upon Melville, as Wallace's excellent summaries demonstrate. The essay, "On Gusto," with its introductory dictum, "Gusto in art is power or passion defining any object," proposes that there is gusto in Titian's coloring, his representation of flesh, "like nothing else," where "The blood circulates here and there, the blue veins just appear." Likewise, "Michelangelo's forms are full of gusto" and "convey an idea of great muscular strength, of moral grandeur, and even of intellectual dignity; they are firm, commanding, broad, and massy, capable of executing with ease the determined purposes of the will." Melville comes close to this sentiment in *Moby-Dick* when, finding human analogues for the powerful flukes of the whale, he says, "When Angelo paints even God the Father in human form, mark what robustness is there" (376). With gusto as his criterion, Hazlitt is able to find great merit in some of the paintings of Rubens, all of Rembrandt, Titian's landscapes, and especially a painting of Actaeon hunting. He can criticize, as lacking in gusto, Correggio's paintings and Claude's landscapes. He also finds gusto in the ancient Greek statues, in Shakespeare's dramatic invention, "in Pope's compliments, in Dryden's satires, and Prior's tales; and among prose-writers, Boccaccio and Rabelais." His quick conspectus of literature and the sister arts is an invitation to Melville's reading and art observing.

We have little solid evidence of what Melville was reading during the 1840s. Many of the books that would have been of use to him then were acquired in later years, including Vasari, Hazlitt's *Criticisms on Art,* Ruskin's *Modern Painters,* Sir Joshua Reynolds's "Discourses," and other prose works. My guess would be that, while he may not have read some of the books available during these early years, he could often fill in his knowledge from the large amount of art criticism, gossip, and the like appearing in the magazines of the 1840s and early 1850s. Certainly *The Literary World,* during the period 1847–55, when he occasionally wrote for it and almost surely read it regularly, was filled with articles and reviews on the arts. The issue for February 10, 1849, for instance, contained a review of Lanzi's *The History of Painting in Italy,* a "Letter from Washington" dealing with the "Sale of the Works of the Old Masters," and part of a long review of Layard's *Nineveh and Its Remains.* Many of the issues were taken up with the activities of the Art-Union, describing and reviewing the contents of exhibitions or running advertisements of the distributions of Art-Union art. There were poems about artists and artworks: a sonnet on Murillo's *The Flight into Egypt,* a sonnet on Powers's sculpture *The Greek Slave,* sonnets on paintings by Rubens and Ludovico Caracci, and a poem on Titian's *The Assumption of the Blessed Virgin.* Most issues carried advertisements of art books. Wiley and Putnam, acting as agents for the Bohn Library, offered Lanzi's *History* in the issue of August 21, 1847, "with fine portraits of Raphael, Titian, and Correggio," along with "Lectures on Painting, by the Royal Academicians" and *Lives of the Italian Painters,* Michelangelo and Raffaello, in one volume. The issue of November 4, 1848, carried a full-page advertisement of "The Distribution of Prizes by the American Art-Union," with Thomas Cole's series *Voyage of Life* in four pictures, to be distributed as one prize; the pictures purchased for distribution included, among others, W. S. Mount's *Loss and Gain,* Bingham's *Stump Orator,* Deas's *Wounded Pawnee* and *Western Scenery,* and Durand's *The Village Church—Moonlight* and *Dover Plain, New York.*

Another prominent journal, *The United States Magazine and Democratic Review,* offered articles, reviews, and poems on art subjects. Since the magazine carried a review of *Mardi* and a comment on *Omoo* in an article devoted to de Tocqueville, it is easy to imagine Melville reading it regularly. Commenting on "American Works of Painting and Sculpture" in the January 1847 issue (vol. 20), the anonymous critic casually affixes, as epigraph, the opening Latin lines of Charles Du Fresnoy's *De Arte Graphica* without identifying them, assuming, no doubt, that they would be well known. His remarks support and extend both art knowledge and art prejudices. Since art "is a faithful imitation of nature," it follows that "whatever is good in its distinctive class of art, however low the subject, is worthy of respect . . . . Thus, Teniers and Gerard Dow will live probably for an equal time with Raphael" (47). His assertion validates a love of realistic Dutch art, somewhat at the expense of the work of the Italian Renaissance. In specific remarks on the Art-Union exhibition, he gives attention to John Vanderlyn's *Landing of Columbus,* Asher Durand's *Old Man's Lesson,* and a painting by Charles Deas, disappointing after the great success of *The Death Struggle.* In the May 1847 issue a brief review of the exhibition of the National Academy of Design calls attention to the paintings of Leutze, Huntington, Gray, and Mount. A particularly stimulating essay in July 1850 (vol. 27) is "Recollections of the Vatican," which traces the route Melville would take in 1857 and speaks of the same statues that the Melvillean lecture on Roman statuary would cover. The author remarks that "Of the Laocoon none should speak, unless they have some new word of value to say." Canova's *Perseus* and the *Antinous,* as well as the *Apollo,* an *Ariadne,* "a noble Jupiter, and one whose beauty and majesty cannot be appreciated in the day, and a Hadrian," are among his subjects (69–71). But the journal also has its share of inferior poems celebrating such subjects as "The Incognita of Raphael" and "Coreggio: The Fate of Genius."

Analogies between the sister arts came as naturally to writers of the nineteenth century as they had to those who compared painting and poetry in earlier times. Henry James was a constant visitor to museums and wrote excellent criticisms of painting, some of which Melville may have encountered in the magazines. As a writer of fiction, James was a master of subtle forms of art allusion and ekphrasis. In *The Ambassadors,* for instance, Lambert Strether's trip to the French countryside allows him to appreciate the vista as if it were a painting by Lambinet. Holbein's art affected both *The Ambassadors* and "The Beldonald Holbein." In revising some of his earlier works, he drew in references to painters and paintings—Pinturicchio and Daumier in *Roderick Hudson*—and in literary criticism he was quick to observe and comment upon the art analogy. Composing a review of Théophile Gautier, which appeared in the *North American Review* in 1873, James luxuriates in appropriate terms to praise Gautier's pictorial imagination and speaks of the author's "faculty of visual discrimination," his capacity of saying "in a hundred places the most delightfully sympathetic and pictorial things about the romantic or Shakespearean drama," the way in which his newspaper pieces "form a great treasury of literary illustration," and, in stories that "remind us of those small cabinet paintings," the creation of characters "altogether pictorial" (*Literary Criticism* 357, 359, 363, 366).[14]

Like his fictional counterpart, Wellingborough Redburn, Melville enjoyed reading travel books. Redburn confesses that, as a boy, he "went through many courses of studying them, and never tired of gazing at the numerous quaint embellishments and plates, and staring at the strange title pages" (141), and, of course, Redburn takes great pleasure in enumerating the various beauties of the books, their complicated titles, and the general effect that they have upon a reader. One sees that Melville likes lingering over the words and phrases that describe bindings, book sizes, and title pages and finds the usual travel book—with its capacious appetite for descriptions of landscapes, buildings, artworks, and strange peoples—a rich, rare source for his own imaginative descriptive writing. The travel books that Redburn studies are intended as fictional accounts, but, as Willard Thorp has demonstrated, they are carefully based upon existent travel books published between 1798 and 1845 that were readily available to Melville. Two of the volumes offer details about the old and new Paris and the ancient and modern Rome with its architecture, paintings, and sculpture. Redburn is impressed by the *Picture of London* with its pictorial reproductions of St. Paul's and other architectural pleasures. Similarly, the book about Blenheim gives a picturesque tour of the premises with descriptions of paintings, tapestry, and furniture (Thorpe 1147–48). From Redburn's selective description of varied travel guides, we get some sense of what attracted Melville to these sources.

The travel book is likely to work heavily in the ekphrastic realm. As a seasoned traveler in our century, Somerset Maugham discusses in *The Gentleman in the Parlour* the problem of finding a literary equivalent for visual images. He has visited Angkor Wat and wants to speak of the temples: "It would be enchanting to find the apt word and by putting it in its right place to give the same rhythm to the sentence as he had seen in the massed gray stones; and it would be a triumph to hit upon the unusual, the revealing epithet that translated into another beauty the colour, the form, and the strangeness of what he alone had the gift to see" (226). The ekphrasis of place offers the subtle temptations of luxurious prose to the traveler, who generally wants to take full advantage of them.

Melville's journals of 1849–50 and 1856–57 read often like notes for travel books. He conceived of writing some such book under the title "Frescoes of Travel" and, perhaps, was putting his resolve into practice in some of the poems that finally appeared in *Timoleon*. The emphasis upon ekphrasis in *Redburn, Moby-Dick,* and *Clarel* is well placed, for, essentially, they are travel books undertaken by people who obviously love the arts. In some sense, *Pierre* becomes a travel book when the flight to New York and the settling in to such a foreign place begin to occupy the book's plot; and Pierre makes most of his personal and ethical distinctions about life by using the art analogy.

From his markings in Goethe's record of his Italian journey, we see the extent to which Melville was moved by the adventures of the German author. Among the books from Melville's library, Arthur Penrhyn Stanley's *Sinai and Palestine* was certainly one, to judge from his markings, that engaged his full and fascinated attention. As Bezanson has indicated in his notes to *Clarel,* Melville made close use of Stanley to aid him in descriptions of places that he had not seen, notably the city of Petra. But other markings in the volume demonstrate what particularly caught his eye in Stanley's account. For example, he checkmarked a description of the Nile, its "slow, vast volume of water, mild and beneficent as the statue in the Vatican, steadily flowing on between its two almost uniform banks" (Cowen 2:605). Stanley complained that earlier descriptions of the gigantic statues at Thebes had not "given me an adequate impression" and attempted his own impression in a passage that Melville marked: "What spires are to a modern city,—what the towers of a cathedral are to its nave and choir,— that the statues of the Pharaohs were to the streets and temples of Thebes" (606). Similarly, Melville marked passages in which Stanley described the pyramids as well as medallions depicting Justinian and Theodora, "those two great and wicked sovereigns," a phrase that earned a double underlining from its reader. In describing the sea from Jaffa and the "reefs famous in ancient Gentile legends as the rocks of Andromeda" (616), Stanley touched the springs of Melville's visual imagination, the enticement of the great myth of Perseus, Andromeda, and the monster and Guido Reni's painting of the subject. The red earth "from which the first man—the red 'Adam'—was formed" gets Melville's attention as much as Stanley's (618), and the lengthy account of the Church of the Holy Sepulchre (618–20) draws several extended markings.

Although Stanley's description of Petra is clearly Melville's source for the canto "Of Petra" in *Clarel*, he knew of Petra before reading Stanley's book in 1870, as allusions in earlier writings show. There were, of course, many choices. Melville may have read the record that John Burckhardt left of his discovery of the magnificent city in 1812, centuries after it seemed "lost." Also, John G. Kinnear, accompanied by the painter David Roberts, visited in 1839 and published his impressions, as did Harriet Martineau in *Eastern Life: Past and Present* (1848), a spirited account of her journey to the red city, and Austen Henry Layard and John Lloyd Stephens. There were also many magazine references to Petra, often in reviews of these books.

We see, from Bezanson's excellent notes to *Clarel*, how Melville supported his own views of sites in Palestine with the careful descriptions and engravings in William Henry Bartlett's books. As he traveled in Europe, he followed the lead of the handbooks for travelers issued by John Murray. George Duyckinck lent him handbooks for Italy in preparation for his journey in 1849. John Murray himself "Offered to give me some of his 'Hand Books' as I was going on the Continant [*sic*]. So he sent me to the house his Book of the Continant & for France" (*Journals* 19). The handbooks were of considerable value for the tourist in a hurry, and Melville, limited in funds and time, generally was hasty in his movements. Murray's *Handbook for Travellers in Central Italy: Part II. Rome and Its Environs* had reached a fourth edition by 1856 and could well have provided the itinerary for Melville when he finally went to Italy in February 1857. The handbook offered an extensive description of the basilica of St. John Lateran, including the origin of its name, its architecture, and the art treasures it contained. The account of the Vatican was even longer and more elaborate.

The Sistine Chapel, with its ceiling by Michelangelo was of such a nature that "No language can exaggerate the grandeur and majesty of the figures" (150). The Laocoön sculpture received even more special and lengthy treatment with quotations from Pliny and Byron's *Childe Harold* and paraphrases from Winckelmann, Vasari, and Canova (162–63). The *Apollo Belvedere* description also bore the weight of casual learning that cited Pausanias, Winckelmann, and Canova's view that the marble statue was a copy of a bronze original; two complete verses from *Childe Harold* completed the description (163–64). The Hall of Animals was presented in the handbook with an enumeration of its many statues. Other places for the tourist to visit received attention as well in Murray's well-organized volume: the Palazzo Barberini and its special treasure, Guido Reni's *Beatrice Cenci,* "one of the most celebrated portraits in Rome," with the various stories of its being painted just before or just after Beatrice's execution; the Borghese and Farnese palaces; the Villa Albani. One section of the book calls attention to the studios of artists—not making the acquaintance of a single artist would be "inexcusable, as some of our countrymen are amongst the greatest artists in the Eternal City" (247)—and Melville obediently visited the studios of Edward Bartholomew, John Gibson, William Page, and Hiram Powers (*Journals* 111, 116).

Handbooks like Murray's were valuable enough for Melville to study them, and in their urge to be encyclopedic, they provided bits of information that could be used when transformed into his closely knit paragraphs. But just as valuable were such books as Joseph Forsyth's *Remarks on Antiquities, Arts, and Letters During an Excursion in Italy, in the Years 1802 and 1803* (Sealts #219). Melville acquired the third edition (1824) at some unknown date and annotated it very lightly, taking note of a passage about Schiller and underlining what must have seemed to him a delicious phrase about "the short-lived fopperies of literature." A description of "the chapel of the stigmata" was checked and underlined. A remark of Forsyth's—"English poets cannot plead for the sonnet one successful precedent. Even the greatest of them all, Shakespeare, Milton, Spenser, split on this rock and sank into common versifiers"—drew the fire of a Melvillean annotation: "What pedantry is this! Yet its elegance all but redeems it. Forsyth is the most graceful of pedants" (Cowen 1:148–53). However, Forsyth's book probably held more interest for Melville than the marginalia would indicate. There was, for instance, an introductory "Memoir of the Author," a brief account of Forsyth's life (1763–1815), including his travels in an Italy made poorer in art treasures through the depredations of Napoleon; the piece spoke, too, of Forsyth's internment for several years in France. His style in the text is sometimes fetching: "I saw nothing in the class of comic painting except Albert Durer's Misers and a few Teniers, to which perhaps might be added a repose in Egypt, where the Virgin and Child are lulled to sleep by an Angel, who plays the fiddle and leaves poor Joseph to hold the music-book" (239). The *Apollo Belvedere* had been spirited off to France, its place taken by a cast facing the statue of Perseus. Forsyth particularly derided the work of restorers, who boldly "make up dismembered trunks and affix attributes" so that "we lose the freedom of judging on the original trunk, and the pleasurable torment of conjecture" (241–42).

Since Melville saw so little of Greece, having spent only three days there in February 1857, he depended upon such books as Christopher Wordsworth's *Greece: Pictorial, Descriptive, and Historical,* in the second edition of 1844. His copy, acquired in 1871, contains only a few marginal markings, but the book probably contained much of interest and entertainment for Melville. Wordsworth (1807–1885), a British bishop and one-time headmaster at Harrow, had traveled in Greece in the early 1830s. His book was popular, a sixth edition appearing by 1858. Wordsworth's descriptions of landscape and architecture were accomplished, and each edition of the big volume had many engravings depicting the sites he visited. At least one allusion in *Clarel,* to the temple at Sunium then identified with Minerva, seems to have its source in Wordsworth's description. A passage that Melville did mark in the book dealt with Pylos, where "Telemachus, attended by Minerva in Mentor's shape," landed. The passage continues, "Here Minerva rejoiced, as the Poet says, in the piety of the young Pisistratus, Nestor's son, who had requested her to pray" (Cowen 2:734).

At some point, possibly in Florence in 1857, Melville acquired Valery's *Historical Literary and Artistical Travels in Italy* (1852), a fat little volume of more than seven hundred pages of crabbed, double-columned print with no illustrations save for an engraving of Milan Cathedral on the title page. He may have used it, to some extent, during his Italian travels, but his markings seem to indicate later uses. In a passage on Venice, Melville marked a description of Titian's *St. John Giving Alms,* along with Valery's complaint that the picture is lost in the darkness of the church (Cowen 2:708). In Bologna, Valery comments upon "the immortal St. Cecelia," with "the ardour, the triumphant joy of the seraphim singing the sacred hymn in heaven, the purity and simplicity of the saint's features," a passage that Melville marked with additional underlining of "ardour" and "triumphant joy" (Cowen 2:712). One passage in Valery, describing "the celebrated chamber of Correggio" (282) in Parma, is carefully annotated at the back of the book with Melville's note,"Correggio—chamber figures in trellis work," and in Valery's description Melville has marked the description of the ceiling "covered with graceful genii wantoning amid ovals pierced through a vast treillage" (Cowen 2:714, 721). Since Melville did not visit Parma during his Italian journey, he may have regarded the passage as a useful piece of literary pictorialism to be employed later. Receiving from Sarah Morewood an illustrated copy of Bulwer-Lytton's *The Pilgrims of the Rhine* in 1854, Melville commented that "The engravings are beautiful, & I have enjoyed them much." Then, relating visual arts to literary arts, he added that "No doubt too, pictures equally fine will be found in the text when I come to read it" (*Correspondence* 257). The volume contained twenty-seven engravings illustrating Rhine scenes that Melville had visited in 1849 (*Journals* 35–37).[15]

It is possible that Melville's longest involvement with writings on art is to be found in his study and use of an 1854 collection of art articles, *The Works of Eminent Masters* (Sealts #564). He acquired this two-volume collection in 1871 and thus had its 604 pages and nearly two hundred engravings available for study during the last two decades of his life. But the story of this collection is even more complex. The articles and pictures in *Eminent Masters* are reprints of articles from the *Illustrated Magazine of Art*, a periodocal published during 1853–54. Melville read and annotated the first volume of this publication, possibly as early as 1854, and had its first volume bound for his own use (Sealts #291). The articles, miscellaneous in their approaches to art, offered biographical and critical studies of artists and descriptions of art to be found in such places as the National Gallery, the Vatican, and the Bridgewater collection. Articles frequently discussed the sales prices of paintings as of 1854, so much of the material was out of date by the 1870s and 1880s. However, there were valuable hints about the personal appearances, life-styles, and attitudes of painters that Melville could and did make use of in his poem "At the Hostelry" and in other late writings. Dennis Berthold's essay "Dürer 'At the Hostelry'" demonstrates how Melville was able to use these and other available materials to exhibit "the melancholy estate of Albert Durer" (6; *Collected Poems* 331). The engravings in *The Works of Eminent Masters,* many of them clear and detailed, often supported by careful ekphrases by the authors of articles, provided extensive resources for Melville's studies of the sister arts. The two volumes contained essays of considerable length and substance as well as many illustrations. Melville marked essays on Francis Mieris, copperplate engraving, Adrian Brouwer, Adrian van Ostade, Jacques Louis David, and Gabriel Metzu. It is possible that the piece on the craft of copperplate engraving stimulated him to a further study of engraving processes, since he went on to acquire Georges Duplessis's *The Wonders of Engraving* (1871) as a gift for his wife in 1875 (Sealts #195). A piece in the second volume that he did not mark may have yielded part of a poetic topic. The article on Claude

Joseph Vernet (*Works of Eminent Masters* 2:49–58, 61) included an engraving of that artist's *View of Pausilippo,* which could have entered into Melville's composition of his poem "Pausilippo."[16]

Through his course of observation, collection, and reading, Melville's study of the sister arts was constant and persistent.[17] He came to it early, probably much as Redburn, so often his fictive persona, did, in a home that took a love of art for granted. His travels through the world and through books enhanced his belief in the value of the art of the past in a materialistic modern world. In his lecture on Roman statuary, he observed that "To undervalue art is perhaps somewhat the custom now. The world has taken a practical turn, and we boast much of our progress, of our energy, of our scientific achievements—though science is beneath art, just as instinct is beneath the reason" (*Piazza Tales* 408), "a proposition," observed one reporter of the lecture, "which caused some little discussion in several groups of homeward-bound listeners" (750).

THREE

Redburn

"Mythological Oil-Paintings"

AFTER HIS JUVENILE, unsuccessful efforts at ekphrasis in the "Fragments from a Writing Desk," Melville did not attempt to use this literary technique for the next ten years. For a substantial part of that time, he was working as a school-teacher, a "boy" on a merchant ship, and a sailor aboard whalers and naval vessels. Returning to shore in 1845, he began immediately to convert some of his experiences into imaginative novels that had a firm basis in fact. *Typee* (1846), *Omoo* (1847), and *Mardi* (1849) all used the conventional novelistic device of scenic setting with appropriate landscapes or seascapes, shipboard or jungle, native huts or calabooses. But in none of these did Melville link his scenic description with artworks or describe them as if they were works of art.

There are complex reasons for this neglect of what would become a valuable tool in his building of literary technique. He did not, as an apprentice author, know very much about the art analogy. Even as he wrote his first books, he was busy absorbing pictorialism as part of his language of literary description, mostly by finding examples in the fiction and poetry that he was reading. When he had become familiar with its method and its manipulation of detail, he began using it confidently in *Redburn* during the summer of 1849. But another change could be seen in this new book, a change in his use of a narrator. In the first three novels, the first-person narrator, Tommo or Taji, was a rather breezy sort of person, an extrovert, an adventurer, an action-impelled and action-describing personage. In his fourth novel, he created a new type of personage, perhaps indicative of another side of his nature. Wellingborough Redburn might very well participate in actions, but he is essentially a sensitive, inward, bookish, thoughtful young man who survives to become a sensitive, inward, bookish, thoughtful, reminiscent older man capable of rendering his early experiences with the added advantage of hindsight, experience, and the ability to interpret, or to conceal interpretation of, what he has witnessed. The way of looking at the world changed from what it had been in the earlier books. Artistic, even painterly in his apprehension of shapes and tints, Redburn sees the world as artwork and so interprets it to the reader. Ishmael is this sort of character in *Moby-Dick,* and in *Pierre* and *Clarel,* both of which treat the protagonist from a third-person point of view, the pattern continues. Pierre Glendinning is youthful, sensitive to painting, sculpture, engravings, and architecture, and he is unprepared for the rigors of experience. Unlike Redburn and Ishmael, however, he does not survive to recapitulate and meditate upon all that happens to him. Clarel is another such character who finds the pilgrimage to Palestine his own Yale and Harvard and who is abandoned by his creator before he can reflect very much upon his recently gained experience of life and art and deliver himself of carefully considered opinions.

That Melville has not, in his first three novels, quite absorbed the dimensions and possibilities of the art analogy can be seen in his management of scenic description. A passage from *Typee* may make the distinction clear: "The long, measured, dirge-like swell of the Pacific came rolling along, with its surface broken by little tiny waves, sparkling in the sunshine. Every now and then a shoal of flying fish, scared from the water under the bows, would leap into the air, and fall the next moment like a shower of silver into the sea" (10). Something similar can be seen in the scenic writing in *Mardi* some three years later: "How changed the scene! Overhead a sweet blue haze distilling sunlight in drops. And flung abroad over the visible creation was the sun-spangled, azure, rustling robe of the ocean, ermined with wave crests; all else infinitely blue" (66). These are interesting, even excellent, examples of novelistic scenic description, a necessary part of a writer's arsenal of literary devices. But they are not examples of ekphrasis, except incidentally as they qualify as "a description of anything." There is no link to the world of art objects, and there is no attempt to make such a link. At best, Melville depends upon some lightly handled art allusions in his writing. In *Typee,* for instance, the reader encounters "monstrous imps that torment some of Teniers' saints" (211), without a reference to a specific Teniers painting. In *Omoo,* "a folio volume of Hogarth" (310) is alluded to, again the barest of hints. In *Mardi,* Taji speaks of a picture into which "Gudin or Isabey might have thrown the blue rolling sea" and invokes the names of Wouverman and Claude to offer a clearer view, perhaps, of his picturable scene (42). But these scrappy beginnings leave the reader unprepared for the extensive and distinguished application of pictorialism in *Redburn*.

PORTFOLIOS OF COLORED PRINTS

In some of its aspects, *Redburn* is another "sketch book," its artist providing, as Washington Irving's Geoffrey Crayon had done thirty years before, a "port folio filled with sketches." Like Geoffrey, Redburn provides an introductory account of himself. Geoffrey is "fond of visiting new scenes, and observing strange characters and manners." Redburn "frequently fell into long reveries about distant voyages and travels, and thought how fine it would be, to be able to talk about remote and barbarous countries" (5). In his discussion of the novel, Hershel Parker has noted a number of details from Irving's book that Melville may have borrowed and remarks that Evert Duyckinck believed that Melville was influenced by the older writer (*Redburn* 327–28). Irving's careful depiction of such an architectural masterpiece as Westminster Abbey, with its carved arches, columns, sepulchers, and monuments and, in particular, the tomb of Mrs. Nightingale, the work of Roubillac, forms an ideal model for ekphrasis—that is, pictorial writing linked carefully to a work of art. However, "Geoffrey Crayon, Gent." is a young man of leisure while Redburn, the son of an impoverished gentleman, has to earn his way across the sea.

In the first chapter of *Redburn*, Melville takes great care to establish a reasonable basis for his protagonist's fascination with the arts. Redburn, like Melville himself, grew up in a home well furnished with art objects, including oil paintings, engravings, portfolios of prints, and a considerable library that included many illustrated books (Gilman 177), but the Melville of 1849 knew more about the arts than Redburn. Living in New York since 1847, Melville had many opportunities to encounter the bustling art business of the city and to profit from all he saw, perhaps with limitations. As a result, the art young Redburn knows seems to be mostly French. The "oil paintings and rare old engravings" at his home come from the Paris that his father visited; two of the paintings, given the benefit of brief ekphrases, are sea scenes. Melville had developed considerably from his earlier generalized references to artists and paintings to a specificity in his description of a picture's contents, layout, and color. A fishing boat "with three whiskerandoes in red caps," "high French-like land in one corner," and a sea in which the "waves were toasted brown" could be the work of Théodore Gudin, who painted such pieces as *Return of the Fishermen* (1827) and was one of the painters especially noticed in *Mardi*. The second painting in Redburn's home is also subjected to a close scrutiny. It shows "three old-fashioned French men-of-war with high castles like pagodas, on the bow and stern, such as you see in Froissart." A number of the paintings of Eugéne Isabey, another favorite Melville mentions in *Mardi*, would serve well as examples of the art he has young Redburn admiring. In contrast to the brown of the sea in the first picture, this one features "a bright-blue sea, blue as Sicily skies," and the seaman's point of view, still strong in Melville, emphasizes such details.[1]

There were ample opportunities for Melville to study French art in New York. In 1848 the French firm of Goupil, Vibert & Co. had established a gallery at 280 Broadway. The advertisements that Goupil ran in *The Literary World* demonstrated the company's enterprise. Their "splendid gallery of paintings" included "works by Delaroche, Ary Scheffer, Muller, Landelle, Court, Mozin, Guet, Girarded [sic], Waldmuller, Groenland, Brochart, &c, &c, &c." Goupil nevertheless had competition from other firms. At 353 Broadway, Williams & Stevens, "Importers and Dealers in English, French and German line and mezzotint engravings, lithographs, studies, views &c.," also offered prints of works by Delaroche, Vernet, and other artists. William Colman, at 304 Broadway, had "many hundred fine paintings" of ancient and modern artists as well as "beautiful engravings of every variety of subject, many of which are equal if not superior to paintings."[2]

After the details of the paintings, Redburn is excited by the portfolios of colored French prints in his home and enumerates hastily their partial contents. Sea pictures, rural scenes, and views of Versailles; natural history illustrations of rhinoceroses, elephants, and tigers; and "a great whale, as big as a ship, stuck full of harpoons, and three boats sailing after it as fast as they could fly" (6–7) are prominent stimuli for his visual imagination. But the central exhibit of the first chapter is a glass ship, "of French manufacture," kept in a square glass case upon a special table in the sitting room of his home. This piece of naval sculpture, "the admiration of my father's visitors in the capital" and "the wonder and delight of all the people of the village where we now resided," receives a detailed ekphrasis that encompasses almost half of the first chapter and signals some of Redburn's developing talents, his exactitude in matters of observation and memory, and his obvious appreciation of aesthetic values and visual symbolism in the details displayed in an art work. Dolphins and sea horses disport themselves about the glass ship as it plows through a heavy sea. Crew members are rendered imaginatively, and we are made to visualize the sailor in the foretop with "a coil of glass rigging" on his shoulder, the steward with a plate of glass pudding, a glass dog with a red mouth, and the captain with his glass cigar. The dust and down that have collected upon the piece for many years appear, to the young observer, to add a generally artistic effect to the little sculpture, in much the way that a general dirtying and darkening of a painting will change it and inspire an interpretation different from the one that the work in its original state might have excited. The ship does for Redburn what a work of art should do: it pleases his sense of order and beauty and arouses his curiosity beyond the limitations of its surface appearance. It offers a complete and satisfying aesthetic experience. Like any genuinely artistic work, the ship offers the imagination the opportunity to furnish force and action to the still and glassy object. It is capable of inspiring fear. The older man tells us that the boy, alarmed about the ship's predicament, "used to be giving her up for lost and foundered every moment, till I grew older, and perceived that she was not in the slightest danger in the world" (9).

Redburn's glass ship is usually treated as a symbol of the narrator's troublesome condition. William Dillingham sees it as a controlling image for the motif that he traces throughout the book, the boy's hunger (*An Artist* 35–36). Rogin links the ship with Redburn's voyage, "a sign not of the power Redburn will inherit from his father, but of the doom" (64). The glass ship is all of these things, but, far more than a symbol, it is an objet d'art, a sculptural masterwork available to eye and memory. It is the subject of Melville's first fully realized ekphrasis, and he treats the pictorial events skillfully. Commentators upon the sister arts insist that detail is an element of crucial importance in painting and sculpture; Ruskin points out that "the limit of detail is—visibility."[3] The little ship's glass construction mimics reality, as "masts, yards, and ropes were made to resemble exactly the corresponding parts of a real vessel that could go to sea." Its portholes and black guns and even its crew members "were all made of glass, as beautiful little glass sailors as any body ever saw, with hats and shoes on, just like living men, and curious blue jackets with a sort of ruffle round the bottom" (*Redburn* 8). The sculptor detailed the mariners' activities in the rigging or their chopping wood or preparing dinner. As Gilman has observed, there was a glass ship at the Melvill home that the boy Herman visited (38–39), and in his writing he calls upon his marvelous visual memory to recreate it as Redburn is led from description of the artwork to his meditation upon its significance. He has looked at the ship as a boy, but he speaks of it as a man, unsettled by his later life and experience: "We have her yet in the house but many of her glass spars and ropes are now sadly shattered and broken,—but I will not have her mended; and her figure-head a gallant warrior in a cocked-hat, lies pitching head-foremost down into the trough of a calamitous sea under the bows—but I will not have him put on his legs again, till I get on my own, for between him and me there is a secret sympathy" (9). The glass figurehead is both artwork and mirror image. Its calamity is a foreview of the calamitous life that Redburn is destined to live. The fact is, that even with the passage of time he has not quite regained his sea legs and cannot quite manage in the pitching, heavy sea of life. Having lost his youthful innocence, he has not yet gained the calm of experience and wisdom he has been seeking. The little work of art, the ship in the sitting room of his youth, epitomizes for him the lengthy and essentially fruitless struggle of his life up to the point when he relates his story. Changed, debilitated by the blows of time, the ship is an objective correlative for his own perilous and uncompleted journey, not only to Liverpool and London but also through years of life when "I found myself a sailor in the Pacific" (312). The episode of the glass ship offers an unusually clear idea of how Redburn's aesthetic imagination reacts to and plays upon a specific art object.

Aboard ship, Redburn is sensitive to whatever is offered by way of art, and, like others of Melville's sailors, he is impressed by figureheads and takes care to describe the one on the bow of the *Highlander*. It is a handsome piece, "a Highlander, 'in *full fig*,' with bright tartans, bare knees, barred leggings, and blue bonnet and the most vermilion of cheeks." Redburn immediately personifies the figure, "game to his wooden marrow," "standing at his post like a hero," and "a veteran of many wounds of many sea-fights." The piece has been repaired by a figurehead builder who mends it as he would an ancient sculpture, replacing a left leg and a nose and giving it a new paint job (116).

This cheerful ekphrasis of one of the important examples of marine art is prelusive to a much more difficult pictorial event in the novel, the depiction of the dying sailor Jackson as if he were the figurehead of a ship in some imagined painting:

> Brooding there, in his infernal gloom, though nothing but a castaway sailor in canvas trowsers, this man was still a picture, worthy to be painted by the dark, moody hand of Salvator. In any of that master's lowering sea-pictures, representing the desolate crags of Calabria, with a midnight shipwreck in the distance, this Jackson's would have been the face to paint for the doomed vessel's figure-head, seamed and blasted by lightning. (275)

Looking at a man, Redburn sees a painting, a sort of reaction typical of his thought processes. But on his first encounter with Jackson, in the twelfth chapter of the novel, Melville's description of the sailor's appearance and manners resides entirely within the realm of conventional novelistic character portrayal. Redburn's comment on Jackson's "subtle, infernal looking eye" is a good example of this fictive convention. The eye "must have belonged to a wolf, or starved tiger," it outdoes any glass eye for deadliness, and, as Redburn concludes, with Melville's less-than-original novelistic emphasis, "it haunts me to this day" (57). This view of Jackson is certainly pictorial, but it is does not seem inspired by any picture by Salvator Rosa or indeed by any other painter. At this point in the narrative, the infernal Jackson has not struck Redburn so forcefully as to serve as the subject of an artistic conception.

However, in chapter 55, Jackson is "still a picture" and is now to be seen as a possible subject for Salvator Rosa. In this ekphrasis, which may contain elements from several Salvatorean paintings, Redburn's sense of scale is allowed to veer from the panoramic to the close detail work of facial expression. An imaginary painting is put before the reader, and a human figure is placed in it and described as if he were a work of art. By this device, Melville introduces a sensitive allusion to the paintings of Salvator and awakens in the reader a whole repertory of responses to the kind of art that might be aroused by Salvator's wild images of landscape and seascape, rocks, dead trees, banditti, and stressful scenes.

Melville could be sure that an allusion to Salvator would bring forth the expected reaction in a reader of the 1840s. The Neapolitan master (1615–1672) was extravagantly admired for a long time, from shortly after his death to about the middle of the nineteenth century. Ruskin led an attack upon Salvator in his first volume of *Modern Painters* (1843), but his lesson sank in slowly and at midcentury Salvator was still regarded as one of the greatest of painters, his work recognized and frequently mentioned.[4] Art patrons in America frequently ordered copies of his paintings. Thomas Cole, among others, was urged to imitate his work. Engravings of his paintings were available for display and purchase. Melville could have seen some prints of Salvator's works by the time he wrote *Redburn*, including *Jacob Wrestling with the Angel, Banditti in a Desert,* and *Hagar and Ishmael* as well as copies of paintings then in England, either at galleries like the Dulwich or in private collections. He would have had opportunities to see some originals when in 1849, after completing *Redburn,* he voyaged to England and the Continent. His journal of the voyage contains references to his seeing such "gems" as Titians, Claudes, Salvators, Murillos" (*Journals* 20, 298–99).

Salvator's paintings were admired for their "dash" and colorful qualities in portraying wild and savage scenes, replete with rocks, gnarled trees, cataracts, lakes, castles, and a few well-placed and picturesque brigands. James Thomson, an eighteenth-century admirer, had such works in mind when writing "Whate'er Lorrain light touch'd with softening Hue, / Or savage Rosa dash'd, or learned Poussin drew." It was that savagery, picturesquely roughening the ordinary sights of neat house and formal garden, that was most appreciated by those who loved

Salvator's art, and it was surely this aspect of his work that Melville had in mind when he gave himself the pseudonym of "Salvator Tarnmoor" for the magazine serialization of "The Encantadas" in *Putnam's Magazine*. Tarns and moors were almost the private preserves of Salvator's art, and, though the Galapagos featured neither, the volcanic savagery of landscape thrust against the violence of the sea must have been reminiscent of what the Italian painter projected.

Figurehead sculpture, by its very nature, is a far from delicate art, but for Melville it carried the force of prophecy. In the tiny glass ship *La Reine*, the figurehead, "a gallant warrior in a cocked-hat," tragically falls from its optimistic place ahead of all other figures aboard, signaling the stormy accumulation of life's blows. The Jackson figurehead is seamed and blasted by lightning, again the victim of storms. In "Benito Cereno" the San Dominick carries a draped figurehead, as a work of art might be draped to conceal it before an exhibition; when finally exposed, it reveals "death for the figure-head, in a human skeleton; chalky comment on the chalked words below, *'Follow your leader.'*"

QUAINT EMBELLISHMENTS AND PLATES

An important element in Redburn's art education is the study of "some outlandish old guide-books," European and English, from his father's library, and in chapters 30–31 he takes great care to describe them as art objects. These chapters extend our respect for Redburn's visual imagination, for, working with what might well be inferior products, he is able to salvage impressions of unusual beauty and significance. The mind customarily takes in impressions from the whole range of visual objects, whether they be of greater or lesser aesthetic value. The uncritical mind cannot distinguish the good from the bad, but the critical mind can make the distinction. The encompassing mind makes the distinction and goes further, appreciating the good and appropriating what is useful from the mediocre. Redburn's mind works in just this way, sometimes turning obvious defects into actual enhancements. A lengthy ekphrasis of the books offers carefully selected, exact details:

> Among others was a Parisian-looking, faded, pink-covered pamphlet, the rouge here and there effaced upon its now thin and attenuated cheeks, entitled, *"Voyage Descriptif et Philosophique de L'Ancien et du Nouveau Paris: Miroir Fidèle;"* also a time-darkened mossy old book, in marbleized binding, much resembling verdantique, entitled, *"Itinéraire Instructif de Rome, ou Description Générale des Monumens Antiques et Modernes et des Ouvrages les plus Remarquables de Peinture, de Sculpture, et de Architecture de cette Célébre Ville;"* on the russet title-page is a

vignette representing a barren rock, partly shaded by a scrub-oak (a forlorn bit of landscape), and under the lee of the rock and the shade of the tree, maternally reclines the houseless foster-mother of Romulus and Remus, giving suck to the illustrious twins; a pair of naked little cherubs sprawling on the ground, with locked arms, eagerly engaged at their absorbing occupation; a large cactus-leaf or diaper hangs from a bough, and the wolf looks a good deal like one of the no-horn breed of barn-yard cows; the work is published *"Avec privilege du Souverain Pontife."* There was also a velvet-bound old volume, in brass clasps, entitled, *"The Conductor through Holland,"* with a plate of the Stadt House; also a venerable *"Picture of London,"* abounding in representations of St. Paul's, the Monument, Temple-Bar, Hyde-Park-Corner, the Horse Guards, the Admiralty, Charing-Cross, and Vauxhall Bridge. (*Redburn* 141–42)

The passage, about half of a long paragraph giving such details of books presumably influential in young Redburn's life, is rich in humor, some of it jovial, some quite sharply satirical. It is clear that Redburn likes illustrated books redolent of the sister arts and featuring examples of paintings, sculpture, and architecture with interesting artistic bindings and elaborately decorative title pages. With his apparent mastery of the language of bibliographical description, he is fully aware that he is not talking about masterpieces of book production, but his eye is that of an art lover, transforming what is almost beneath notice into suggestive pictures. He takes great pleasure in transcribing the lengthy titles of books, with all their quirks and prolixity. The pamphlet comically metamorphoses into a faded madam. The cactus-leaf diaper, the wolf that, with poor artistry, resembles a cow, and the vignette of barren rock all please his eye and tickle his funny bone. To his imaginative vision, Romulus and Remus will not be served by strong wolfish milk but by the pale imitation variety from a cowlike creature.

Bookbinding is an old and honorable art, and fine bindings are to be prized as much as pictures, statues, and furniture. Melville, with the bibliophile's fascinated attention to the details of binding, would soon write a review of James Fenimore Cooper's *The Red Rover* entitled "A Thought on Book-Binding," which was published in *The Literary World* on March 16, 1850. Using some of the same language as he had in *Redburn,* he expressed the wish that the book had been given "a flaming suit of flame-covered morocco, as evanescently thin and gauze-like as possible," or, perhaps, "bound in jet black, with a red streak round the borders (pirate fashion)." Still, the actual binding was to be praised, for "In the mysterious cyphers in bookbinders' relievo stamped upon the covers we joyfully recognize a poetical signification and pictorial shadowing forth of the horse-shoe, which in all honest and God-fearing piratical vessels is invariably found nailed to the mast" (*Piazza Tales* 237–38). The "pictorial shadowing-forth" is a particularly telling phrase, for Redburn displays the same rather professional approach as Melville to the binder's art, noticing the marbelized look of a binding and understanding that "verd-antique" is the proper designation for the green mottled effect of some covers. And sometimes Redburn simply dismisses an uninteresting binding. In a later portion of his discourse upon travel books, he passes quickly over "a bulky book, in a dusty-looking yellow cover," spending his best efforts upon its elaborate but tedious title page. He notes a green pamphlet "with a motto from Virgil, and an intricate coat of arms on the cover, looking like a diagram of the Labyrinth of Crete." A book in "a classic vellum binding" and a pamphlet "with a japaned sort of cover, stamped with a disorderly higgledy-piggledy group of pagoda-looking structures," complete his roll call of guidebooks. Of the eight volumes mentioned in the paragraph, Redburn has taken care to specify and describe the bindings of seven, leaving out only the binding of the venerable "Pictures of London."

Beyond the simple fact of Redburn's sophisticated knowledge is the careful artistic disposition of his materials, both visually and verbally. Though there is an apparently casual arrangement in his discourse about the eight guidebooks, a seizing of what first comes to hand, this initial impression gives way to a conviction that the passage has been carefully thought out and arranged for maximum aesthetic effect. Redburn is not growing "intolerably flat and stupid," as Melville ironically puts it in the chapter title, when he can so cunningly create, dispose, edit, and exhibit his materials. He is sensitive to colors, moving the reader through a lavish rainbow effect produced by a pink-covered book, a mottled verd-antique, a russet title page, the textures and tints of velvet and brass, a dusty yellow, another green, and the blackness of a japaned effect. The shapes and sizes of the volumes, including pamphlets, a fat bulky tome, and "a small scholastic-looking volume" and the decorations that encompass such things as brass fixtures, a coat of arms, a Latin motto, and a vaguely Oriental illustration offer a pleasing array of bookshelf pleasures to the eye. Willard Thorp, examining volumes of the kind that Melville was describing, indicates that there are changes from the originals that Melville must have seen. The first volume, for instance, called by Redburn a pamphlet, is actually a fat duodecimo. The second volume's title-page illustration of Romulus and Remus suckled by the odd wolf is one of Melville's clever inventions. The pictures in "Pictures of London" do not correspond to what is actually in the volume. The Cambridge guide, with its Virgilian motto and a design like the labyrinth of Crete, appears to be mostly another Melvillean fabrication. "What Melville has done in almost every instance," says Thorp, "is either to exaggerate humorously some pretentious phrase in the title-page or to invent some feature for the book" (1147). Invention is crucial in ekphrasis, for it permits avoidance of literal transcription of what the artist has seen and depicted. But even beyond such uses, an inventive and fanciful process applied to apparently meticulous scholarly description and reference is a feature, from the first, of Melville's writing. He delights in creating a seamless web of verifiable erudition mingled with the most charming deceptions that his fertile imagination can conceive.

We should probably not take too seriously Redburn's assertion that "In my childhood, I went through many courses of studying" the guidebooks from his father's library (141). If we accept the dates of publication of the seven books that Thorp has identified as the originals of those that Redburn studied, they range from 1798 *(The Great Roads . . .)* to 1845 *(The Cambridge Guide).* Thorp concedes that the guide to Cambridge that he cites does not exactly fit Melville's title, and there may indeed be another guide of a date early enough to coincide with Redburn's childhood (1147). But the volubility and exactitude of Redburn's bibliographic description argue for an 1846–49 range of dates when Melville, returning from his sea travels, could learn about the visual and aesthetic qualities of the books that he seemed to be devouring with such intensity.

By way of increasing the reader's aesthetic pleasure, Melville presents expansive, appealing titles for his guidebooks from French and English. Again, Thorp has demonstrated that the author tinkers with real titles rather than simply recording the existent, sometimes intolerably verbose appearance of the originals. The result is visually delightful on Melville's pages as he moves the reader's eye, with careful casualness, through a "Voyage Descriptif," an "Itinéraire Instructif," a fancy description of "The Great Roads, both direct and cross," and a "Description of Blenheim, the seat of His Grace." Visual and tonal qualities merge here and, with the painstakingly orchestrated descriptions of the appearance of the books and their decorations and illustrations, offer a richness of visual effect too complex for ready assimilation. The passage must be studied as one studies a painting, analyzing its parts and its balances and shadings in order to come, finally, to a full comprehension of its individual excellences and the ways in which they bind themselves together.

This chapter seems, at first look, to be a good example of Melville's quickly developing literary pictorialism used simply for decorative effect; and, indeed, it fills such a function in a pleasing way. But Melville's carrying out such a venture would offer only a filler chapter that would not advance the narrative in any important way. However, he has something more immediate in mind. Guidebooks, as Edgar Dryden points out, "profess to be faithful mirrors of reality and hence reliable guides to experience" (63–64). Redburn's most painful discovery is that the usual guides to experience that he so cherishes are anything but reliable, and this is especially true of the "outlandish" travel books that have given him pleasure. The chapter is prelusive to important matters, and Melville here institutes a procedure that he will often follow, that of using art descriptions as introductions to his central themes. In *Moby-Dick,* for instance, Ishmael will require three chapters of prelude on artistic portrayals of whales before he can undertake his own singular ekphrasis of leviathan. In order to present Mortmain's impassioned explication of the Pauline text of sinful mankind's iniquitous mystery, Melville will devote a whole canto of *Clarel,* fittingly entitled "Prelusive," to a careful description of Piranesi's most elaborate etchings of mazelike dungeons and prisons that mirror, visually, "man's heart, with labyrinths replete." In *Redburn,* the long ekphrasis of guidebooks ends with the sentence "And lastly, and to the purpose, there was a volume called 'The Picture of Liverpool.'" The purpose, it becomes clear, is to introduce the travel guide that Redburn's father had used during one of his visits to England. Using the language of booksellers, Redburn describes the tiny volume: its size is octodecimo; it is bound in green morocco; its corners have triangular red patches; there is no title on the binding. The book was once adorned with some of the childish Redburn's drawings of "wild animals and falling air-castles," the juvenilia of the art-trained youth. The father's marginalia of places visited, dinners eaten, and books bought are a further kind of artwork, added to the book's street map, elaborate title page, poetry by John Aiken, and excerpts from the *Aeneid* and Falconer's poem *The Shipwreck.* Redburn lingers over the book; for although it is not anything special in the way of the bookmaker's art, it carried personal associations for him that help "to dim and mellow down the pages into a soft sunset yellow" (143–49).

But still, is this obsession with a preludium only a throat-clearing exercise, a pause before plunging into important matters? It would be superficial of Melville to employ all his technical astuteness upon unimportant things, for his sense of needed elements in structure is always a crucial matter. Redburn tries to give voice to what haunts him in his researches into the oddities of guidebooks. Reading his father's Liverpool guide, he is "filled with a comical sadness at the vanity of all human exaltation" at the thought that the vividly significant present is shortly to be the ruinous past. St. Peter's is built of the ruins of ancient Rome; New York will be a Nineveh; and "explorers" will "exhume the present Doric Custom-House, and quote it as proof that their high and mighty metropolis enjoyed a Hellenic antiquity" (149). The arts in their ruinous condition are a storehouse of error in the past, and the outlandish guidebooks that do not quite lead one to a view of past glories portray, instead, a foreign and bizarre world that is certainly an "out-land."

This careful preparation leads into the next chapter, in which Redburn takes the old guidebook as his tour guide through the city. The chapter abounds in passages of pictorialism, for the observant Redburn encounters sculptural and architectural objects of virtu at every turn of his journey. A large piece of statuary catches his eye, a work

> in bronze, elevated upon a marble pedestal and basement, representing Lord Nelson expiring in the arms of Victory. One foot rests on a rolling foe, and the other on a cannon. Victory is dropping a wreath on the dying admiral's brow, while Death, under the similitude of a hideous skeleton, is insinuating his bony hand under the hero's robe, and groping after his heart. A very striking design and true to the imagination; I never could look at Death without a shudder. (155)

The passage offers the author the opportunity to embellish his narrator's character and let us understand Redburn's attitudes and convictions. As the description of the statue continues, the figures at the base of the pedestal assume importance. They are captives, emblematic of Nelson's victories, and Redburn is "involuntarily reminded of four African slaves in the market-place." This involuntary reminder permits him to contrast his views of the inhumanity of slavery with his father's rather more practical view "of the unhappiness that the discussion of the abolition of this trade had occasioned in Liverpool" (156). Redburn's almost offhand remark is the first in a series of reflections upon his relationship with his father. For a good portion of the book, while we were learning that the boy was apparently unhappy, his attitude toward his father seemed ambivalent, since nothing pointed directly to the father. In chapter 30, for instance, he read the old guidebook and "what a soft, pleasing sadness steals over me, and how I melt into the past and forgotten" (143). The contradictory words imply a deep repression of important memories. And when, a few pages further on, he invokes "my father's sacred memory and all sacred privacies of fond family reminiscences," the invocation has no more serious use than preventing quotation at length from the old tour guide.

James Duban perceptively associates Redburn's walk through Liverpool with "Christ's agonizing procession along the Via Dolorosa" (*Melville's Major Fiction* 39), noting the use of images from Palestine here and elsewhere in the novel—"Sodom-like," "the brink of the Dead Sea," and "the Pool of Bethesda" (40). He conjectures that Melville may have read William H. Bartlett's *Walks*

About the City and Environs of Jerusalem much earlier than 1870, when he acquired a copy of the volume, a likely proposal that underlines Melville's tendency toward a kind of thematic echolalia enriched with each new repetition. Redburn's pilgrimage is entirely bookish, as far as Melville's actual knowledge in 1849 of the Holy Land is concerned, and it concentrates its detailed pictorial effects upon a clear knowledge of Liverpool. The 1857 tour of Palestine, noted carefully in Melville's journal, adds the necessary burden of direct experience, and so the pilgrimage recounted in *Clarel* is resonant with the accumulation of the visual imagination, the reading, and the years of meditation. It is true, however, that Redburn's pilgrimage through the English city, following the elusive father, is as agonizing as any dolorous way in the Holy Land.

Trusting the outdated guidebook, Redburn pursues his father's path only to find that his confidence in it is a "dear delusion." That, of course, is not the father's fault. But the son uses the occasion to point out the differences between his father's financial and social position and his own. While the elder Redburn, as the son imagines, had dressed well for his tour of the city, "little did he think, that a son would ever visit Liverpool as a poor friendless sailor-boy," a thought that leads to the further "reflection that, he then knew you not, nor cared for you one whit" (154). A dismal reflection, indeed, to come from thoughts of the battered guidebook, cherished as an artwork. But Redburn goes further. The Nelson memorial, with its pedestaled captives reminding him of slaves, gives rise to memories of the discussions at home and the unhappy thought "that the struggle between sordid interest and humanity had made sad havoc of the firesides of the merchants, estranged sons from sires, and even separated husband from wife" (156). Pictorialism moves from the decorative and biographical to the ideological in Marianna Torgovnick's continuum of pictorial significance, for Melville's strategy here is to use the family memories of Redburn to reflect upon the historical effects of the slavery depicted on the monument.

"A sadder and a wiser boy" who at last holds a useless guidebook, Redburn still insists that he "did not treat with contumely or disdain, those sacred pages which had once been a beacon to my sire" (157). The artistically arranged tour guide has called up unwonted, perhaps unwanted, memories of a past that he has resolutely buried in a haze of conventional filial reminiscence. He insists upon finding aesthetic values in the volumes he has turned over in his father's library and in the cheap little guidebook that he values beyond its worth because he does not quite trust his own impressions, repressed feelings, and angers. Arguing with himself, he at first declares that he must "follow your nose throughout Liverpool." But, on second thought, he believes that he "can not expect to be a great tourist, and visit the antiquities, in that preposterous shooting-jacket." He concludes, "I am not the traveler my father was. I am only a common-carrier across the Atlantic" (159–60). If these are the words of an older Redburn, assessing his youthful past, he has not yet been able to find much room for self-esteem or even forgiveness for a father who clearly does not deserve acquittal.

OPULENT ENTERTAINMENT

Redburn observes most things as if they were art objects. He is quick to note decoration in unlikely places and to describe it in his usual painterly fashion. When he visits another ship, the *Irriwaddy*, in Liverpool's harbor, he makes the most of its romantic strangeness. On the deck, "I thought I was in Pegu, so strangely woody was the smell of the dark-colored timbers." The name of Pegu, a river and city in Burma, coupled with the obvious alien charms of the ship's name and the darkness of timbers, conjoin to offer as rich a fulfillment as ever the boyish Redburn had hoped for in dreaming about his travels. A moment later he is musing on the oddity of a ship divided between Christianity and paganism: "As if to symbolize this state of things, the 'fancy piece' astern comprised, among numerous other carved decorations, a cross and a miter; while forward, on the bows, was a sort of devil for a figure-head—a dragon-shaped creature, with a fiery red mouth, and a switchy-looking tail" (171). Shipboard art always impresses the sailor Redburn. Aboard a brig from the coast of Guinea, he notices an ancient cannon "covered with half-effaced inscriptions, crowns, anchors, eagles. . . . The knob on the breach was fashioned into a dolphin's head, and by a comical conceit, the touch-hole formed the orifice of a human ear" (175). Melville would always be captivated by the fantastic embellishments of antique cannons. In a note to the poem "The Temeraire," he speaks of old cannons "that were cast in shapes which Cellini might have designed."

Many of the scenes that Redburn witnesses in Liverpool remind him of like scenes in New York and cause him to consider that "all this talk about travel was a humbug; and that he who lived in a nutshell, lives in an epitome of the universe, and has but little to see beyond him" (203). Guidebooks are not trustworthy, for all their vivid words and engravings. Travel is not trustworthy if it offers the traveler hardly more than a repetition of the sights he can readily see at home. The questing intelligence is thrown upon its own devices, unaided by antiquity, history, or even the early experiences of others. That the questing intelligence, in this instance, is the property of a boy, hardly fitted by his own skimpy experience to come to a just assessment of what he observes, is an irony that the mature Redburn, recounting his early adventures, can wryly savor, considering that he will spend much of his life at sea and pass "through far more perilous scenes."

The more mature Redburn has the opportunity to use his hard-earned irony to its fullest degree in chapter 46, "A Mysterious Night in London." The youthful Redburn has struck up a friendship with Harry Bolton, a boy far more worldly and sophisticated. A major theme of the novel is Redburn's passage from the new world to the old, from ignorance to knowledge, from naivete to a measure of worldliness, with its accompanying disillusion. To the extent that it is a study of a boy's education by experience, the novel offers Harry Bolton as a crucial part of that education, although the young Redburn seems reluctant to communicate what he learns from Harry, or perhaps he does not fully understand the knowledge he has acquired. Youth learns quickly but cannot always absorb what it learns and make that a vital element in its actions. Redburn's friendship with Harry is unforced but ambivalent; Harry is attractive but not quite trustworthy; and, to accept him, Redburn has to "drown ugly thoughts" (225) and must "hold back my whole soul from him; when in its loneliness, it was yearning to throw itself into the unbounded bosom of some immaculate friend" (223). Harry is far from immaculate, as the trip to London proves, and, for Redburn, the journey is a disaster, both for what it provides and for what it falls short of offering him in aesthetic experience.

From Liverpool, with its soured offerings, Redburn is eager to visit London, feeling that it will offer the best that travel can give, and he is "half delirious with excitement" as they enter the great city. But Harry's constricted view of such a pilgrimage permits only a visit to a "semi-public place of opulent entertainment," as Redburn designates it, giving it the name of "the Palace of Aladdin" (228). Here, more than anywhere else in the novel, the young Redburn receives only half-formed impressions of an air of corruption and venality, and he cannot quite articulate even these impressions. The older Redburn, as narrator of the adventure, is aware of what the boy does not fully understand, but he too will not articulate his knowledge.[5] Melville, knowing all, is careful not to be too explicit. Instead, presenting the "Palace" as a place for the entertainment of "gentlemen," offering food, drink, gambling, and homosexual entertainment, Melville resorts to a careful interweaving of art allusion and ekphrasis to make his case. The first room the young men enter is depicted in detail:

> The walls were painted so as to deceive the eye with interminable colonnades; and groups of columns of the finest Scagliola work of variegated marbles—emerald-green and gold, St. Pons veined with silver, Sienna with porphyry—supported a resplendent fresco ceiling, arched like a bower, and thickly clustering with mimic

grapes. Through all the East of this foliage, you spied a crimson dawn, Guido's ever youthful Apollo, driving forth the horses of the sun. From sculptured stalactites of vine-boughs, here and there pendent hung galaxies of gas lights, whose vivid glare was softened by pale, cream-colored, porcelain spheres, shedding over the place a serene silver flood; as if every porcelain sphere were a moon; and this superb apartment was the moon-lit garden of Portia at Belmont; and the gentle lovers, Lorenzo and Jessica, lurked somewhere among the vines. (228)

Deception is the motif of this entire section of the novel, and deceiving the eye with painted colonnades and false marble is its pictorial correlative. Redburn finds the scene overwhelming and, as a result, is willing to follow Harry's lead in all matters. He can scarcely be expected to understand all the complexities involved in the setting. It is the elder Redburn, writing years later, who deftly weaves into the description a knowledge of scagliola, the clever imitation marble; one of Guido Reni's mythological paintings; household furnishings that combine utility with the aesthetic; and a reference to *The Merchant of Venice*. Since Venice is a corrupt city, the image of the young, innocent lovers offers an oblique perspective upon Redburn's situation in this contaminated den.

As the scene progresses, however, Redburn becomes increasingly uncomfortable, made so by the behavior of the people he observes. He sees a waiter "eying me a little impertinently, as I thought, and as if he saw something queer about me." Looking at the patrons of the establishment, he notices "that every now and then little parties were made up among the gentlemen, and they retired into the rear of the house, as if going to a private apartment" (229). Since they use terms like "Rouge" and "Loo," they are gamblers. But then Harry conducts Redburn not to the rear of the house but to an upstairs room, and the young man is struck by the extraordinary, changed appearance of its decoration:

> As we entered the room, me thought I was slowly sinking in some reluctant sedgy sea; so thick and elastic the Persian carpeting, mimicking parterres of tulips, and roses, and jonquils, like a bower in Babylon.
>
> Long lounges lay carelessly disposed, whose fine damask was interwoven, like the Gobelin tapestry, with pictorial tales of tilt and tourney. And oriental ottomans, whose cunning warp and woof were wrought into plaited serpents, undulating beneath beds of leaves, from which, here and there, they flashed out sudden splendors of green scales and gold.
>
> In the broad bay windows, as the hollows of King Charles' oaks, were Laocoon-like chairs, in the antique taste, draped with heavy fringes of bullion and silk.

The walls, covered with a sort of tartan-French paper, variegated with bars of velvet, were hung round with mythological oil-paintings, suspended by tasseled cords of twisted silver and blue.

They were such pictures as the high-priests, for a bribe, showed to Alexander in the innermost shrine of the white temple in the Libyan oasis: such pictures as the pontiff of the sun strove to hide from Cortez, when, sword in hand, he burst open the sanctorum of the pyramid-fane at Cholula: such pictures as you may still see, perhaps, in the central alcove of the excavated mansion of Pansa, in Pompeii—in that part of it called by Varro *the hollow of the house:* such pictures as Martial and Suetonius mention as being found in the private cabinet of the Emperor Tiberius: such pictures as are delineated on the bronze medals, to this day dug up on the ancient island of Capreae: such pictures as you might have beheld in an arched recess, leading from the left hand of the secret side-gallery of the temple of Aphrodite in Corinth. (230–31)

Here the young Redburn is overwhelmed by the sensuality of his impressions and the older, cooler narrator of a later date must attempt to give credence to his younger avatar's feelings by citing a bewildering variety and range of references from art, history, myth, and literature. Redburn neglects none of the implications of such description. The apartment pleases, as it is meant to, by its disposition and harmony of arrangement. Carpeting, furniture, wallpaper, and paintings conjoin in Melville's practically seamless mingling of pictorialism and allusion.

The senses of feeling, sight, and smell are invited to participate in Redburn's fully imagined depiction of place. Patterns of material in the ottomans evoke a linked series of images. The plaited serpents, in "sudden splendors of green scales and gold," are a fixture of the iconography of temptation. A passage in *Paradise Lost* that Melville surely must have known describes the ancestor of all tempting serpents displaying himself to Eve:

> his head
> Crested aloft, and carbuncle his eyes,
> With burnished neck of verdant gold, erect,
> Amid his circling spires. (9.499–502)

Further sources can be found in the romantic iconography of Coleridge and Keats. The water snakes in *The Rime of the Ancient Mariner* have something of the look of Melville's plaited serpents, with their "rich attire: / Blue, glossy green, and velvet black." From Keats's "Lamia," the snakelike demon is "a gordian shape of dazzling hue, / Vermilion-spotted, golden, green, and blue; / Striped like a zebra, freckled like a pard."[6] The case for Coleridge is, perhaps, not entirely clear, but for Keats there are useful hints. Lamia has seen Lycius in Corinth, "where 'gainst a column he leant thoughtfully / At Venus' temple porch" (1.316–17). This is the Corinthian temple of Aphrodite, one of the sites of the unmentionable pictures that Redburn recalls. Keats offers the additional hint of "That purple-lined palace of sweet sin" (2.31), the lair of the seductive serpent, Lamia, and could thus give Melville a source for his learned allusion. The serpentine iconography of the Melvillean passage continues in the solidly visual sculptural effect of the "Laocoon-like chairs." Laocoön is a favored Melvillean theme and will appear in *Pierre* and *Clarel*. After observing this great sculptural work during his 1856–57 European art pilgrimage, Melville made it part of his lecture on the statues of Rome, noting the effect of its depiction of "a great and powerful man writhing with the inevitable destiny which he cannot throw off." The statue "represents the tragic side of humanity and is the symbol of human misfortune" (*Piazza Tales* 403–4). The chairs in *Redburn,* immovable pieces, evoke the dynamic impression of serpentining and coiling about a victim.

Melville's central intention in constructing this chapter of his novel is to leave an overpowering impression of luxurious beauty, coupled with temptation and corruption. The room is certainly not intended as a site for gambling. Instead, it is likened first to "a bower in Babylon," a place that is an epitome of sensuous immorality. Since corruption proceeds by attraction, the elements of Melville's picture are rich and appealing, intricate and even contradictory in the cues he furnishes for the observer. In the manner of tapestries, the upholstery offers images of knightly tournaments, all cheerful and innocent enough. But the ottomans, supporting the comfort of the lounges, offer contrary depictions of serpentining splendors and mix the embrace of pleasure and pain. With good reason, too, since the mythological oil-paintings, upon which Redburn lavishes a long, dense, allusive and elaborate paragraph, form the centerpiece of his presentation and make it clear that, whether the young Redburn understands fully all that he sees, there are overwhelming hints of erotic, shameful, and perverse activities. William H. Gilman's study of *Redburn* offers a judgment that Melville's knowledge at this point in his career was "not deep but eclectic," and this is surely correct. Gilman's analysis is supported by Thorp's careful assessment of just how much Melville could extract from the title pages and a few pages of admittedly dreary guidebooks and then convert his remarks into casually learned, allusive, and entertaining prose. Gilman remarks that Melville "uses allusions literally when they help to broaden or intensify the immediate meaning or supply color in an incident that requires it" and cites Redburn's "meditation" on the Liverpool guidebook as a typical example (223–24).

Redburn's long, almost breathless account of pictures that he will persistently not describe in detail serves an important structural purpose in the novel. Something wrong about the scene is emerging, allusive and deceptive, before Redburn's eyes. Alexander bribes high priests to show him pictures similar to the ones the boy is seeing, and, thus, blasphemy mixes with religiosity. When the "pontiff of the sun" tries to hide such pictures from the conquering Cortez, religion and eroticism are conjoined. Looking at other pictures that reflect a secular, rather than religious, view of sexuality, Redburn is reminded of Pompeii and art objects owned by Tiberius. Gilman rightly remarks that "the inclusion of a blatantly pornographic picture is one measure of Melville's sophistication" (224). He is referring to the Emperor's picture of "Atalanta performing a most unnatural service for Meleager" and concludes from this example that Melville is inventing allusions (355n.31). Gilman's judgment is partially true but does violence to Melville's allusive technique, which would be characterized as mosaic, a painstaking placing of varicolored pieces of tile or stone in a mortar base to achieve an orderly pattern or picture. This carefully worked out technique uses allusion inventively and fancifully, but it depends, finally, upon some bedrock of factual source material.

There seem to be clear lines between the allusion to Cortez at the temple of Cholula and its possible source in William Hickling Prescott's *The Conquest of Mexico*.[7] The apparently simple reference to Pompeii has a complicated background. Since the middle of the eighteenth century, Pompeii had been yielding up its treasures and tragedies to the shovels of the archeologists. Reports emerged and lengthy articles appeared in magazines that Melville could easily have read. Edward Bulwer-Lytton, searching for new novelistic material, met William Gall, one of the chief excavators of Pompeii, and visited the site in 1832 and, from all he had learned, created one of his most popular novels, *The Last Days of Pompeii* (1834). Bulwer-Lytton's novel may be Melville's most likely source for the Pompeiian allusion, for, although it is not listed among the books that Melville owned at one time or another, there are clear signs that Melville knew the book. Leon Howard suggests that Captain Ahab was based upon the character of Arbaces, Bulwer-Lytton's villainous high priest. Melville jotted down, in one volume of his set of Shakespeare, a series of notes on magic, "not the (black art) Goetic but Theurgic magic," and his source seems to be a long note that Bulwer-Lytton appended to the novel dealing with the practice of Goetic magic.[8]

Redburn's comment that "such pictures as you may still see, perhaps, in the central alcove of the excavated mansion of Pansa, in Pompeii" is an instance of Melville concocting a convincing allusion from a work of fiction rather than from any factual report or article. Gilman points out that "The house of Pansa in Pompeii is not known to have contained any pictures" (355n.31) and assumes that Melville has fabricated his reference. But we must unravel Melville's thought processes carefully. In Pompeii, there is a "House of Pansa," and Bulwer-Lytton used Pansa as a character in his novel, which, like many other historical fictions, is an amalgam of the real and invented. From Bulwer-Lytton and others, Melville no doubt learned the device of combining the real and the invented and employed it effectively in "Benito Cereno" and *Israel Potter*. Having brought Pansa into his novel, Bulwer-Lytton has him take some friends to the home of Glaucus, where they can admire the art on display. Pansa's commentary on the artworks is revelatory: "How beautifully painted is that parting of Achilles and Briseis!— what a style!—what heads!—what a hem!" (Lytton 28). Pansa is referring to pornographic art displayed, finally, in the nineteenth century, upon the walls of the houses in Pompeii. Melville takes up the hint from Pansa and Bulwer-Lytton and reconstructs it into his own tempting allusion.

Such a richness of inventive reference can hardly be the work of the young Redburn, timorously embarked upon his first, disappointed investigation of London. No boy could know so much. One even becomes suspicious of the older Redburn, the consciousness through which the story is being displayed, seemingly a resident scholar as well as tale teller. The passage offers a clear challenge to look beyond the narrator to the concealed, manipulating novelist. The older Redburn certainly understands what sort of den his younger self has been coerced into visiting by the importunate Harry Bolton. He suspects, if he does not entirely believe, that Harry's virtual abduction of his younger avatar carries confirmation of attempted homosexual seduction, if not violent assault. Harry's plans, whatever they might be, are not carried out, and Redburn, the boy, is left alone with his emotions, as he admits being "mysteriously alive to a dreadful feeling." He compares the feeling to what he had felt on observing the "most squalid haunts of sailor iniquity" and epitomizes all the complexities into a powerful pictorial image in which "All the mirrors and marbles around me seemed crawling over with lizards" (234). His feelings are not quite susceptible to articulation, but he can come close by resorting to painterly terms, finding their correlative in the decorative elements in the room, the fascinations of gilt and gold, and the serpentine iconography of evil. Without Redburn's insistence upon pictorialism and art allusion, important scenes in the novel would remain vague for the reader, who would take the narrator's word for it that Aladdin's Palace is only a gambling house and would miss Melville's carefully wrought point that the boy, reporting accurately what he sees and can comprehend, does not comprehend nearly enough. The contemporary reviewer of *Redburn* who claimed that such a gambling house "existed nowhere (at least in London) but in our sailor-author's imagination" came close to the truth (Gilman 192). Subsequent readers seem to have been misled. Raymond Weaver found the passage false, a "brave and unwilling concession to romance" (107). In his study of the book, William Dillingham states that the place is a gambler's den and fits the episode into an elaborate pattern of "hunger" in the novel. The "description of Aladdin's Palace," says Dillingham, "constitutes a highly imaginative and elaborate metaphor for Harry Bolton," but Dillingham does not say what the metaphor stands for (*An Artist* 43).[9] That Melville used his prose narrative to say that Redburn was in a gambling den merely underlines what he deliberately repressed in his description. Given the restraints of censorship, he could not be literal, and so the only possible technique of presentation would be a system of metaphor that would contradict the narrative assertions. The use of the art analogy made it possible for him to accomplish his aim, concealing it at the level of narrative but revealing it at the level of language.

The working out of such a literary device is important for the development of Melville's art, and, as he continued to write, he made it even more sophisticated and capable of bearing an extraordinary load of ambivalent, even puzzling, and certainly ironic contradiction. The reader finds himself sometimes confused by the almost infinite contrarieties of "Bartleby, the Scrivener" and "Benito Cereno" or the discrepant, bland-sounding innuendoes of the late poems. But Melville himself made clear what he was about in his discussion of Hawthorne's *Mosses from an Old Manse,* asserting that "in this world of lies, Truth is forced to fly . . . and only by cunning glimpses will she reveal herself." The glimpses, well concealed, are offered, as often as not, by Melville's consistent creation of some persona, obsessed by painterly, sculptural, or architectural images that act upon his imagination.

Melville's skill in rendering scenic description is enriched by his careful disposition of the elements of a scene in painterly fashion. Hence, a narrator such as Redburn can fulfill the requirement Hagstrum demands for a pictorial passage, that, although it may not be the description of a work of art, it should be "capable of translation into painting or some other visual art." The Floating Chapel in the harbor at Liverpool, with its house, steeple, and balcony planted upon the hull "of an old sloop-of-war," is carefully depicted (175). The passage offers close-up views next to views of the middle distance and distant suggestiveness. Instead of being a scene drawn from a picture the writer has seen, it is the kind of seascape that an illustrator like Cruikshank, Millais, or Darley might use for a magazine illustration. Chapters 31–41 present an extraordinary sequence, rich in pictorialism, that depicts the youthful Redburn making a descent through the Avernus of Liverpool streets into a hell of human misery, "rendered merchantable" by the work of "undertakers, sextons, tomb-makers, and hearse-drivers" who thrive off the dead. The prisonlike miseries of Launcelott's-Hey and of the booble-alleys, the dock-wall beggars, and "poverty, poverty, poverty, in almost endless vistas" haunt him in his movements through the town. He finally links the world he sees with the quotidian world of illustration, finding the railroad station familiar, although he knows he has never seen it before. Back in America after his voyage, he locates a magazine illustration of the station, where "I saw a picture of the place to the life; and remembered having seen the same print years previous" (206). Art is as much an experience as other sorts of encounters with life, capable of arousing feelings as strong as the primary facts of existence. Here, life, in a turnabout, copies the felicities of illustration, which has come first and made its powerful effect on the viewer. Redburn is presenting a parody of the conventional Liverpool guidebook, based upon his truer experience of the Liverpool that is passing before his eyes.

The Historical Note for the Northwestern-Newberry edition of *Redburn* argues that Melville did not write the chapters of the book seriatim but made insertions to fill out parts of what was otherwise a strictly chronological record of young Redburn's voyage. Such additions could well include the guidebook chapters and some of the Liverpool sequence, as well as Harry Bolton and, thus, the London journey. The assertion that "Melville may have had at one point, in fact, a manuscript without many of the more highly colored scenes of the final book" tells us much about the author's methods of composition (330–32). The novel grew by accretion, and what is added has, almost always, to do with Redburn's dependence upon the art analogy for the expression of his experiences. Newton Arvin discusses these art analogies as, in part, the "symbolic" elements of the novel "imagined and projected with an intensity that constantly pushes them beyond mere representation." In his view, "it is a question of endowing ordinary objects, ordinary incidents, with a penumbra of feeling and suggestion" (107–08). To this analysis, one must add that the scenes in which art is at the forefront are part of a deliberately constructed plan of literary pictorialism. Melville's delight in the beauties of the visual arts causes him to address seriously the techniques of the art analogy as decorative and structural elements in his fiction. *Redburn* is his first extended attempt in this direction, but hereafter in his writings it will be an ever more important consideration.

FOUR

Moby-Dick

"Less Erroneous Pictures"

THE CONTEMPORARY REVIEWER OF *Moby-Dick* in *Harper's New Monthly Magazine* for December 1851—perhaps George Ripley—showed his consciousness of the illustrative and descriptive powers of the novel by commenting on its many characters as "a succession of portraitures" and claiming that they "all stand before us in the strongest individual relief, presenting a unique picture gallery, which every artist must despair of rivaling." And, indeed, the novel is a picture gallery, not only for its portraiture of human characters but for its brave attempts to portray the whale, for its splendid seascapes, for its narrational pictures delineating scenes that marine painters like Gudin and Isabey, otherwise very praiseworthy, had neglected, and for its sense, often elicited from Ishmael, of the powerful force of Nature as artist.

Like Redburn, Ishmael loves art and sees objects and scenes as art objects. Because Melville learned a great deal about art after completing *Redburn,* read much, and visited English and European museums, galleries, and exhibitions during his 1849–50 voyage, it is inevitable that Ishmael will be more knowledgeable than his predecessor.[1] At the very beginning of *Moby-Dick,* Ishmael tries to account for his deep feelings about the sea, and one of his examples evokes, by means of an ekphrastic description, a typical landscape. "But here is an artist," he says. "He desires to paint you the dreamiest, shadiest, quietest, most enchanting bit of romantic landscape in all the valley of the Saco." There follows a careful delineation of the elements that would go into such a painting—trees, hermit, cottage, meadow, and cattle. This is simply the foreground of a rather complicated picture; in the distant background are woodlands and mountains. But the central feature of the painting is water, and "all were vain, unless the shepherd's eyes were fixed upon the magic stream before him" (4–5).

Ishmael, the connoisseur, gives precise details of his imagined painting, using the language of nineteenth-century art criticism to enumerate its beauties. The essence of this "romantic landscape" is its air of timelessness and repose; variants of the word "sleep" appear three times within one sentence, and the picture itself is said to lie "thus tranced," as if in a dazed state between sleep and waking. The pine tree, in a favored form of the pathetic fallacy, "shakes down its sighs like leaves." The diction has a Tennysonian ring, and the landscape is somewhat like that of "The Lotos-Eaters," where "the languid air did swoon, / Breathing like one that hath a weary dream." The stream in Ishmael's picture does not move, but the artist must give it the sense of movement, for that is its magic in an otherwise tranced effect. Melville, fond of langorous landscapes, uses such a one in a late poem, "Pontoosuc," where a lake substitutes for a stream and "further fainter mountains keep / Hazed in romance impenetrably deep" (*Collected Poems* 248). Such a Melvillean landscape aims for the picturesquely beautiful rather than the sublime, a view not only of the Saco Valley but also one he will observe in the Berkshires, at Lake Pontoosuc and at Arrowhead.[2]

This early sortie into the critiquing of landscape art establishes Ishmael's credentials as an experienced observer, able to find the exact words to describe the effects of a painting upon the viewer. Behind his confident language is an impressive amount of writing about the picturesque and the beautiful in the works of William Gilpin, Uvedale Price, and Richard Payne Knight, among others, and in the British poetry of the eighteenth and early nineteenth centuries.[3] Much of what had then been said earned the scorn heaped on it by Ruskin, the "graduate of Oxford," whose *Modern Painters* Melville must have read by 1849. The book would have had a powerful effect upon his thinking about art, for he is caught between the older views of the lovers of the picturesque and the modernism of Ruskinian thought. In the landscape he writes of in *Moby-Dick*, he is describing a typical scene, possibly a Claude, a Cuyp, or a Constable painting. Or he could have in mind the work of an American contemporary, an Asher Durand, a John Frederick Kensett, or almost any of the more or less anonymous painters exhibited by the Art-Union and praised or scoffed at by the art critic of *The Literary World*.

Ishmael's pictorial imagination, exercised by the connection of landscape to water, finds itself challenged by the painting in the Spouter-Inn, "a very large oil-painting" that at first baffles his eye and his cognitive faculties. He offers the acute suggestion that "at first you almost thought some ambitious young artist, in the time of the New England hags, had endeavored to delineate chaos be-witched."[4] The picture, he finds, demands careful study, repeated viewings, and questions posed to others who have seen it. It is, indeed, a paradoxical work of art, a "boggy, soggy, squitchy picture truly" that nevertheless possesses "a sort of indefinite, half-attained, unimaginable sublimity" that makes it, finally, into a "marvelous painting." Since the picture is both soggy and squitchy (or perhaps squishy), its chiaroscuro mostly the result of dirty smoke, defacement, and bad lighting in the entryway, Ishmael's excuse for its sublimity is even more marvel-ous than the canvas itself.

In *Melville and Turner,* Robert Wallace presents a complex interpretation of the Spouter-Inn painting as "arguably the most significant of Ishmael's many attempts to 'paint' the whale in words" (324). Since rendering a portrait of the elusive whale is one of Ishmael's chief concerns, this picture and his comments on it are crucial to the development of the novel. Wallace's study is an intricate demonstration of Melville's understanding of and practice of J. M. W. Turner's "powerful aesthetic of the indistinct" (3). Because the picture itself is a demonstrable exhibit of the indistinct and the indefinite, Wallace's argument that Ishmael's description "es-tablishes the aesthetic of the entire novel" is forceful (325). He convincingly dis-plays Melville's debt, not to any specific Turner painting, but to a review that Thackeray contributed in 1845 to *Fraser's Magazine* (325–27). Manfred Putz rightly discusses the passage as showing Ishmael in "the role of reviewer and outspoken critic of non-verbal presentations of art" who spends time describing his reac-tions to the picture rather than offering a description of the art object itself (160–62). What might be added, though Putz does not do so, is that the picture is almost certainly a poor one; we could hardly expect the entryway of the cheapest inn in New Bedford, "a queer sort of place—a gable-ended old house, one side palsied as it were," to be graced by a marine masterpiece.

However, there are other dimensions to this unique painting. The elements of Ishmael's description offer a humorously inclined observer, puzzled but ear-nest. Since the whole narrative is presented as that of a worldly and wise older speaker, he might well have gotten, and revealed, the point immediately, but instead he leaves his younger self poised on the dilemmas of the unresolved negatives, whose wild conclusions about the picture "might not be altogether unwarranted." Recognizing that his first, rather lewd, impression of the central figure as a "long, limber, portentous, black mass of something" might discredit the painting, he looks at it with an eye to its "half-attained, unimaginable sub-limity" and begins to see new possibilities—"the Black Sea in a midnight gale," which would surely be a dark picture, or the elements in "unnatural combat," exaggerated and grotesque, or, better still, "a blasted heath," a Salvatorean landscape, or, best of all, "a Hyperborean winter scene" or an allegorical "breaking up of the ice-bound stream of Time"—all excellent possibilities for the portrayal of the sublime. But the sublimity is in question, and the terminology is self-defeating. Either the sublime is attained or it is not; and the sublime, however remote, must be, at the very least, imaginable. The reader, who cannot see the picture and can hardly visualize it by using Ishmael's determinedly false disclosures, is at the mercy of this imaginative art critic and is thus at the disadvantage of having to accept Ishmael's conclusion that "In fact, the artist's design seemed this: a final theory partly based upon the aggregated opinions of many aged persons with whom I conversed upon the subject. The picture represents a Cape-Horner in a great hurricane; the half-foundered ship weltering there with its three dismantled masts alone visible; and an exasperated whale, purposing to spring clean over the craft, is in the enormous act of impaling himself upon the three mast-heads" (13). With all its potential for sensationalism, this portrait of an exasperated leviathan is nearer to one of Ishmael's "monstrous pictures of whales" than the wonderfully "bright, but, alas, deceptive" themes that Ishmael has already conceived for it.

Melville's pointed satire in his ekphrasis of the whale painting is so gratifying that it takes attention from Ishmael's study of other art objects in the inn, of which there are many, including examples of primitive art like "monstrous clubs and spears" and the more modern "whaling lances and harpoons," all utilitarian instruments of destruction. Nevertheless, unlike modern tools, primitive ones are aesthetically improved with the embellishment of teeth and hair. In the public room of the inn, itself an architectural maze of ponderous beams and wrinkled planks, are glass cases of "dusty rarities," never enumerated. The bar itself is a masterpiece of folkish art, "a rude attempt at a right whale's head," containing "the vast arched bone of the whale's jaw." The sailors in the bar compare pieces of scrimshaw and "a ruminating tar" is busy carving the likeness of "a ship under full sail" upon the old wooden settle. The sublimity of the whaling painting has been "unimaginable" because Ishmael's description has undercut the sublime with his reductive humor. In the account of the other art objects in the inn, the sublime is domesticated and given a humanizing dimension by being reduced to the rough picturesque. The whale's jaws, which could be fearful, become decorative. The weapons are simply colorful. The menacing teeth of the whale have to give way to the attractions of scrimshaw. Nevertheless, the passage is important to the novel's major themes. By entering the public room, one gains access to "some old craft's cockpits." The bar, however, entered through the whale's mouth, is the comic representation of the belly of Jonah's whale, where the bartender "sells the sailors deliriums and death."[5]

Queequeg, Ishmael's roommate for the night at the inn, is himself a work of art. Adorned with tattoos, his face presents an aspect that, to Ishmael's first astonished view, is repellent. Even upon later and more reasoned observation, he seems "hideously marred about the face," as Ishmael puts it, being careful to add—in the best tradition of the dilettante art observer—"at least to my taste" (49). Ishmael's taste, formed in the raw and rural America of the 1830s, is unprepared for the combination of primitivism and sophistication in the art of an island like Kokovoko, the "true place" that is not on any map. Some of the young Ishmael's art education consists of dropping his provincialism and coming to some understanding of what he sees in a larger world, and he begins well by recognizing that "through his unearthly tattooings," Queequeg "reminded me of General Washington's head, as seen in the popular busts of him" (49–50), possibly one of the many busts of the general executed by Jean-Antoine Houdon. The whiteness of the marble bust and its insistence upon structure and contour make it "an object of virtu." The sculptural refinement of the savage's head, "phrenologically an excellent one," is a triumph of form over mere surface colors and shadings.

In addition to being a highly embellished objet d'art, Queequeg is also an artist. His ebony idol, the object of his devotions, is not, to his way of thinking, complete and self-sustaining. At intervals, he whittles away at its nose to improve the appearance of its little face. This revelation is momentous, although Ishmael does not at first comprehend it. The ebony image is like the vast cathedral at Cologne, an unfinished and never-to-be-finished work of reverential art and an answer to Ishmael's prayer, "God keep me from ever completing anything" (145). Like the cathedral builders, Queequeg locates his artistic ambition close to the facts of his physical and religious life, shaping and reshaping the source of his reverence. He does something quite similar after recovering from his terrible illness, embellishing his coffin lid "with all manner of grotesque figures and drawings; and it seemed that hereby he was striving, in his rude way, to copy parts of the twisted tattooing on his body. And this tattooing, had been the work of a departed prophet and seer of his island, who, by those hieroglyphic marks, had written out on his body a complete theory of the heavens and the earth, and a mystical treatise on the art of attaining truth" (480). "Such artist-savages," says Paul Brodtkorb, "make material worthless in itself into things of value as, patiently, they literally fill their time with meaning" (133). Because Queequeg, "in his own proper person," is a riddle "whose mysteries not even himself could read," the hieroglyphs upon his body are incomprehensible except as art, "a set of empty signs," as Peter J. Bellis suggests, "inscribed on a hollow, lifeless text" (63). After the meanings that once connected the artwork with faith have been lost, the art remains, ineluctably. Queequeg's hieroglyphic and artistic tattoo matches the hieroglyphs carved by Nature upon the visible surface of the whale, and both adumbrate a cosmology and a belief inexplicable because they have become lost mysteries. Ahab realizes with keen distress that these markings are like the water and fruits of King Tantalus, receding when reached for, and thus he exclaims, "when one morning turning away from surveying poor Queequeg—'Oh, devilish tantalization of the gods'" (481).[6]

In what seems to be a less exalted position as artist, Queequeg collaborates with Ishmael to create an object that, by its most superficial description, barely qualifies as an objet d'art. This is the mat in chapter 47, "The Mat-Maker." The sword-mat is work for a lazy day, and the two men are only "mildly employed" in their work. Queequeg, while using the sword and "idly looking off upon the water," now and then "carelessly and unthinkingly drove home every yarn" (214). Nevertheless, this rather crude object evokes, in Melville's ekphrasis, the most carefully calculated and measured of philosophical reflections upon fate and necessity. In John Wenke's perceptive analysis of the passage, "Melville's narrator is alert to the mind's ability to forge symbolic correspondences" (103), and Wenke links this passage with the figural language of weaving that appears in the description of the bower in the Arsacides (109). The careful and elaborate ekphrasis of the temple fashioned from the whale's skeleton is the motive for the introduction of the "weaver-god," who, deafened by his weaving, cannot hear his mortal dependents (*Moby-Dick* 450).

ORIGINAL GROTESQUENESS

Ishmael, self-styled painter in words and our cicerone in the joined worlds of whaling and art, has read and seen all that Melville has read and seen and seems determined that we shall learn all that he has learned. It is easy to tell that he has become fascinated by all the dimensions of the whaling industry, and if he must give us an enormous volume of information, speculation, and myth, well and good. But if he can also pack in the memoirs of travelers, explorers, and whalers, Kantian, Lockean, and Cartesian philosophy, nineteenth-century science, a personal view of free will and necessity, the glories of Shakespearean and Hawthornesque literary art, the exotic thought of Pierre Bayle and Thomas Browne, so much the better. And if, like Melville, he has been studying art and seeing paintings, statues, palaces, and cathedrals, he will certainly want to get in everything he has learned, thought about, and guessed. A great autodidact, Ishmael is also an incorrigible pedagogue.

In Nantucket, there is a choice of whaling ships, but after Ishmael has "peered and pryed about the Devil-Dam" and "hopped over to the Tit-Bit," appropriate activities for a curious young man, given the sexual attractions of ships' names, he observes the *Pequod*, and, "having looked around her for a moment," decides quickly. Given his penchant for art, and even the odd and exotic in art, his quick decision seems inevitable, for the ship is a work of nautical art, designed as much for her odd beauty as for her function. Ishmael's language blooms into metaphor as he tries to describe her. She has "an old fashioned claw-footed look about her. Long seasoned and weather-stained in the typhoons and calms of all four oceans, her old hull's complexion was darkened like a French grenadier's, who has alike fought in Egypt and Siberia" (69). As an epithet for the ship, "claw-footed" may have something to do with the characteristic form of furniture legs, and cabriole is the description of the shape that curves outward and then narrows into an ornamental foot, resembling "the foreleg of a capering animal." The most distinctive of ornamental feet is the claw and ball, or clawfoot shape, found often in Queen Anne and Chippendale pieces. The origins of the clawfoot are not clear but seem to rise from Oriental sources portraying a dragon claw holding a jewel. The sphere held in the claw may be the great sphere of the world, but, like other meaningful art objects, it has lost meaning and is sometimes reduced to simple embellishment. Still, as Ishmael recognizes, the clawfooted little ship does have its claws into the world of oceanic terrors.

The *Pequod*'s complexion, dark "like a French grenadier's," takes its coloration from paintings of the Napoleonic period and the monarchical restoration. The historical canvases of Horace Vernet and Paul Delaroche were popular in the gallery of Goupil and Vibert in New York during the 1840s, where Melville could have studied them. During his European visit, Melville went to the Luxembourg Palace, where he saw pictures "of modern French school," and at Versailles, on December 6, 1849, he viewed "Splendid paintings of battles" (*Journals* 32–33). In their "Explanatory Notes" for *Moby-Dick*, Mansfield and Vincent add the names of Eugène Delacroix, Francois Gerard, and Ary Scheffer to those of Vernet and Delaroche as artists whose work Melville would have seen at the palace (749–50), and in the novel there is a reference to the paintings at Versailles, "where the beholder fights his way, pell-mell, through the consecutive great battles of France" (230). The military paintings of Théodore Géricault may well have been a part of Melville's experience at this time. Two versions of Géricault's *Portrait of a Carabinier* and one of a *Wounded Cuirassier* present the darkened coloration that Ishmael finds so characteristic of the *Pequod*.

Ishmael's next observation has to do with some architectural effects, for the masts of the ship "stood stiffly up like the spines of the three old kings of Co-

logne." This is an allusion to something that Melville did not see. Reaching Cologne on December 9, 1849, he visited the cathedral, whose "everlasting 'crane'
stands on the tower," and inside "saw the tomb of the Three Kings of Cologne—
their skulls." Horsford indicates that a chapel held "three skulls with the names
of Gaspar, Melchior, and Balthazar spelled out on the reliquary in precious stones"
and speculates that Melville's reference to spines could be "in allusion to their
upright figures in relief on the reliquary" (*Journals* 35–36, 348–49). Whatever the
case, Ishmael is conjoining this view of masts to the Spouter-Inn picture, in
which the "half-foundered ship" does not appear and only its spiny masts are
visible. Skulls and spines are death images that will be part of his iconography of
ships' masts and look ahead to the tremendous image of the *Pequod,* at last,
foundered with only its masts showing. Spines and vertebrae (at least the whale's
vertebrae) are featured later in the book as works of art, intimations of the past,
objects of child's play, and refuge for the noble Ahab, victim of the quotidian.
Another deeply disturbing allusion to death occurs in Ishmael's comparison of
the ship's decks to "the pilgrim-worshipped flagstone in Canterbury Cathedral
where Becket bled." On November 6, 1849, Melville visited the cathedral and
stood in the "Ugly place where they killed him" (*Journals* 13, 260). The complexity of Melville's iconographic thinking appears in his exposition of the kinds of
knowledge that Ishmael, as an older narrator, possesses. He later reminds us of
"one of the most remarkable incidents in all the business of whaling. . . . the
planks stream with freshets of blood and oil" during the slaughter and behead-
ing of the whale, "condemned to the pots" (356). The murder of Becket, as Melville
knew, was a well-known iconographic topic.

So far, the pictorial relationships recalled to Ishmael are the ship's "old antiquities." But the new features that he now addresses are the work of Peleg and
others, "pertaining to the wild business that for more than half a century she
had followed." Peleg's adornment of the vessel recalls the great geographical and
cultural range of Melville's allusive pictorialism, for the "grotesqueness" and
"quaintness, both of material and device," are inlaid as "marvellous features"
and are "unmatched by anything except it be Thorkill-Hake's carved buckler or
bedstead." And, further, he notes the resemblance to the "pendants of polished
ivory" that would deck an Ethopian emperor (69–70). Ishmael is well equipped
to handle the niceties of art description, moving easily from a term like "device"
to the specifics of bucklers, bedsteads, and pendants. The geographical breadth
is justified in the case of Peleg, the biblical figure, "for in his days was the earth
divided" (Gen. 10:25). This division is the dispersal of populations after the del-
uge, and, through their arts, the diverse peoples of the world are more closely
drawn together, a theme omnipresent in the novel.

Horsford conjectures that the *Independence,* the ship on which Melville returned from his 1849–50 journey, served, at least in part, as a model for the *Pequod.* Melville recorded that the ship "looks small—& smells ancient" (*Journals* 42, 362). The factual basis may certainly be there, but the ekphrastic passage reveals Melville's intention to create, in painterly and sculptural terms, a work of art mythic in its dimensions. The ship is "a cannibal of a craft, tricking herself forth in the chased bones of her enemies." Chasing is a form of ornamentation achieved by engraving or embossing. The bulwarks are "garnished," or adorned, with the sperm whale's teeth so that they resemble a whale's jaw. We are meant to remember the bar of the Spouter-Inn, with its adornment of the whale's jaw. As a final decorative note, there is a tiller the ship "sported," "curiously carved from the long narrow lower jaw of her hereditary foe," for she scorns "a turnstile wheel at her reverend helm." The ship has become a personage by *tricking, sporting,* and *scorning,* and with good reason, since she is characterized much as are the cathedrals of Cologne and Canterbury. Her helm is *reverend,* as, indeed, she must be in her resemblance to these massive, revered, and ancient structures dedicated in some way to murder and death. This rich embellishment of the *Pequod,* like the richness of Queequeg's tattoo and the elaborate carving of his coffin lid, as well as the intricacy of scrimshaw, is intended to make the point that, often, the most sophisticated artistry of execution is the province of the artist whose skills are part of his life, work, and spiritual condition and thus worth more than the formal results of the trained artist. The builders of the ship have lavished the best of their craftsmanship upon its construction and thus created a work of nautical architecture. Peleg, unconscious of his artistry, has made her into a jewel that would delight the eye of anyone as intoxicated by art as Ishmael clearly is.

The interest in architectural and sculptural effects extends, as we have seen, to the public room of the Spouter-Inn, but it hardly surfaces in the description of the exterior of the Whaleman's Chapel. Considering Melville's fondness for topographical and architectural prints, this seems strange.[7] Once in the chapel, however, Ishmael sees much to attract his eye. The marble cenotaphs and their inscriptions engage his attention and he is moved to careful notice of the pulpit, whose "panelled front was in the likeness of a ship's fluff bows, and the Holy Bible rested on a projecting piece of scroll work, fashioned after a ship's fiddle-headed beak" (43). The ladder, "by no means in bad taste," is part of the general embellishment, with red-worsted man-ropes and mahogany-colored rungs. Ishmael, always drawn to paintings, pays special attention to the picture on the wall behind the pulpit, lavishing some of his best language upon it. It represents a gallant ship beating against a terrible storm off a lee coast of black rocks and snowy breakers. But high above the flying scud and dark-rolling clouds, there floated a little isle of sunlight, from which beamed forth an angel's face; and this bright face shed a distinct spot of radiance from the ship's tossed deck, something like that silver plate now inserted into the Victory's plank where Nelson fell. "Ah, noble ship," the angel seemed to say, "beat on, beat on, thou noble ship, and bear a hardy helm; for lo! the sun is breaking through; the clouds are rolling off—serenest azure is at hand." (39–40)

Behind this typical piece of American nautical and religious painting is a solid basis in fact. Mansfield and Vincent point out that a painting somewhat like this was to be found in the Boston church of Father Edward Taylor, a picture "representing a ship in a stiff breeze off a lee shore" (615–16).

This ekphrasis is of great interest because of the contradictory elements depicted in its description. The storm-driven ship could be right out of one of Salvator Rosa's paintings, or it could be an iconographic representation of the scene in chapter 23, "The Lee Shore," which also features "the storm-tossed ship, that miserably drives along the leeward land."[8] Melville introduces Jean Hagstrum's version of *ecphrasis,* the procedure of "giving voice and language to the otherwise mute art object" (18), and thus the angel can offer a cheering message to the ship, even in its fearsome danger. But, in a remarkable metaphorical turnabout, the cheering angel has a tiny face that reminds the viewer of the silver plate on Nelson's ship, commemorating the death of the admiral and much more in keeping with the somber memorial tablets that decorate the walls of the chapel with their chilling messages.

The tone of the passage is perfectly deadpan, but the painting, as one might expect from a picture stowed away in a New Bedford chapel, is certainly an insipid piece of chapel art that lapses into a foolish sentimentality. It must be compared, for the best effect, with a painting that Melville could have known, J. M. W. Turner's *Fisherman upon a Lee Shore, in Squally Weather*. The painting depicts the violence of the storm, the beleaguered sailors, and even the sunlight breaking through the dark clouds. There is no angel to cheer anyone on, and the conclusion looks perilous.[9] The chapel's painting reflects a complex of Melvillean tone and substance. Ishmael's interpretation of this artwork, like his commentary on the Spouter-Inn picture, shows the thinking of a young man untested by ocean and danger and reasonably comfortable in his superficial religious belief. His creation of the sugary angelic injunction, as suggested by a mawkish picture, is typical of some of the art and art criticism in midcentury America. Painted angels do not—or should not—speak to the beholder, and to pretend that they do is to import an element foreign to the proper study of an art object. Melville is playing off the poorer passages of art critique from *The Literary World* and other journals and, at the same time, slapping the wrist of the American painter who muddies an original conception, a ship in distress from a powerful onshore storm, with false symbolic values. Ishmael will later criticize the "monstrous pictures of whales" when he has grown in wisdom and experience. The chapel painting is a monstrous distortion of the truth, a pictorial delusion that will have to be corrected to something more closely resembling the true form of a seagoing experience. That will come in "The First Lowering" when, fastened to a whale, Ishmael's boat is swamped in a real squall. It will come, with even greater force, in the finale when the *Pequod* sinks and the whaleboats are splintered and drawn into a destructive maelstrom, and Ishmael is just barely rescued by that harbinger of death, a coffin.

CELLINI'S CAST PERSEUS

Portraiture is a major consideration for Ishmael. He promises to offer a portrait of the whale and labors mightily, in many chapters, to redeem his pledge. Without offering a specific assurance, he does a careful job of depicting his companions on the *Pequod*'s voyage, or, at least, considering such portrayals. Through his allusive vignette of Bulkington, for example, he prepares us for a fuller picture that never emerges but would probably have developed clearly if Melville had found room for that sailor in the novel. Ishmael's several observations of Queequeg give a clear picture of that noble and sturdy man "who has never cringed and never had a creditor." Other characters are embodied in the quick pen strokes of Ishmael's sketchbook. Starbuck's thin aridity, Stubb's attitude and pipe, and Flask's stoutness and irreverence are captured with ease. The tawny color, sable hair, high cheekbones, and "black rounding eyes" of Tashtego and the gigantic coal-blackness of Daggoo belong to this genre of character description, partly pictorial and partly novelistic. Ahab, however, is given the full ekphrasis of a virtually uninterrupted portrait and, as Edgar Dryden rightly notes, "owes his existence to the creative voice of Ishmael" (90). This creative voice delineates as art experience what it sees of the world and people.

Ishmael is aboard the *Pequod* for some time before he sees his captain. He has been learning how to cope with the sailor's life and, from what he has heard and imagined, has constructed a preliminary portrait. But when he sees Ahab, "reality," he admits, "outran apprehension." This reality brings forth a rich outpouring of pictorial elements, some relatively straightforward, some complex and tangled. The captain "looked like a man cut away from the stake when the fire has overruningly wasted all the limbs without consuming them" (123). Here is an imaginative reworking of one of many martyrdom pictures, or perhaps of some art criticism of martyrdom paintings. A typical article that Melville may or may not have seen appeared in the *North American Review* in October 1830 and offered a lengthy discussion of an exhibition of paintings at the Boston Athenaeum. Commenting upon Titian's *The Martyrdom of St. Lawrence,* the writer observed that "In the painting, there is, however, no effect of fire observable, either on the person or drapery of the martyr, and his face is turned upward with a perfectly serene and tranquil expression." The author then remarks upon the martyrdom of St. Polycarp, "when the flames that were kindled at the foot of the stake to which he was attached, retired as they rose from the person of the holy man, and formed a sort of hollow sphere around him, refusing even to singe a hair of his head" (311–12).[10] Ahab as fire-consumed martyr is a fitting subject for a remarkable picture, but it is different from Titian's painting, which shows the saint still upon his torture rack. A major theme in martyrdom paintings is the serenity of the saints during their torture; Ahab, however, is not exactly serene, though he can maintain a posture of repose standing on the quarter deck.

Moving from the haunting images of fire and martyrdom, Ishmael then sees the heroic in Ahab: "His whole high, broad form, seemed made of solid bronze, and shaped in an unalterable mould, like Cellini's cast Perseus." While Melville first saw Cellini's *Perseus* on March 24, 1857, at the Uffizi Palace in Florence, the famous statue was already familiar to him through reproductions in bronze and other materials as well as through prints. Ishmael's view of Ahab as Perseus is filtered through a complex web of mythopoeia. Guido Reni's "picture of Perseus rescuing Andromeda from the sea monster or whale" (261) is a prominent feature of that mythic image. Perseus, "the prince of whalemen" (361), the slayer of Medusa, is fashioned by the cunning art of Cellini into the epitome of the heroic act. For Melville, he is the counterpoise to Laocoön, the hero as sufferer.

As Ishmael traces a visual course from his sculptural consideration of Ahab, his description detailing the "rod-like mark" shifts to painterly language. The tree blasted with lightning is a trademark of "savage" Salvator Rosa's landscapes and the common property of writers who compose in the rough picturesque. Anne Radcliffe, Matthew Gregory Lewis, Charles Robert Maturin, Walter Scott, and Mary Shelley all find room for the Salvatorean landscape in their novels. The tree that grows out of tumbled rocks, its livid mark emphasizing the green life within that persists after disaster, is deeply embedded in Melville's literary consciousness. Mansfield and Vincent call attention to a lightning-scarred elm that Melville saw in Pittsfield, as well as the ship's figurehead in *Redburn,* "seamed and blasted by lightning" (670–71), a landscape effect that Redburn associates with Salvator. In spite of Ruskin's derisive remarks in *Modern Painters* about the "ignorance of tree structure," of which "the most gross examples are in the works of Salvator" (sect. 6, chap. 1), and Melville's ready assimilation of Ruskinian dicta about the truth of Turner's paintings, Ishmael, like his creator, comes partly from a pre-Ruskinian era of art appreciation and has been brought up to love the ghastly landscapes of the Neapolitan master, whatever their faults of falseness to nature.

This great scar that winds its way down the captain's body is quite properly identified with a paradoxical likeness of the portrait of the captain with that of Moby Dick. Clark Davis notes that "Ahab has gradually grown into a reflection of the White Whale" and adds that "the physical precedes, generates the spiritual ailment, at the same time that the recognition of the cosmic body, if repressed, reshapes the warped perceiver" (8). The mutilated figure of Ahab, so prominent in this ekphrasis of his first appearance, and so branded by what may be a birthmark or the mark "of an elemental strife at sea" (124) associates his portrait with other examples of the horrific sublime that Melville is likely to have known, the horrifying family portrait in Charles Robert Maturin's *Melmoth, the Wanderer,* the loathsome form of the created creature in Mary Shelley's *Frankenstein,* the scenes imprinted upon the tapestries in Poe's "Metzengerstein," and the marking of a cursed figure in Hawthorne's "Ethan Brand."

As Ishmael continues to regard Ahab, he is much struck by the "singular posture" of the captain, who stands, bone leg steadied in an auger hole, "one arm elevated, and holding by a shroud." Ishmael interprets this posture as showing "an infinity of firmest fortitude, a determinate unsurrenderable wilfulness, in the fixed and fearless, forward dedication of that glance" (124). This is a created picture, perhaps without an exact source, but it has something in common with Melville's view and conception of the statue of Laocoön. The standard view of that artwork is from the much-quoted passage in Byron's *Childe Harold's Pilgrimage* in Murray's guidebooks, which details the old man's tragic predicament: "vain / The struggle; vain, against the coiling strain / And gripe, and deepening of the dragon's grasp." After seeing the statue itself in 1857, Melville immediately converted his deeply rooted impressions for his "Statues in Rome" lecture, describing the Laocoön as "the very semblance of a great and powerful man writhing with the inevitable destiny which he cannot throw off."[11] There are clearly other elements in this first comprehensive view of Ahab, standing "with a crucifixion in his face," but there is something Laocoön-like in his "nameless regal overbearing dignity of some mighty woe."

Later impressions of Ahab paint him as a Faustian or Promethean figure, even, perhaps, as a Miltonic Satan, surely a monomaniac driven to madness by his external and internal wounds. However, the pictorial complexity of this first representation offers a view somewhat oddly at sorts with later depictions, fastening as it does upon the captain as a martyred saint, a crucified Christ, a mythic hero, and an aged but powerful Laocoön-like figure struggling in the grip of destiny. This earliest impression bears out Ishmael's first feelings—even before he has seen his captain—that "I felt a sympathy and a sorrow for him . . . and it did not disincline me towards him" (79). In his later observations, Ishmael draws upon a fund of architectural and sculptural terminology to attempt a revelation, in some measure, of Ahab's "profundities" by taking us to "those vast Roman halls of Thermes" below the "spiked Hotel de Cluny" (185).

A Melvillean journey into these depths is disappointingly recorded in his 1849 journal as "Descended into the vaults of the old Roman palace of Thermis. Baths &c" (*Journals* 33), but his observations, carefully stored, bloom in this dense pictorial limning of "Ahab's larger, darker, deeper part." The monomania is merely a visible level, whereas the chthonic level, man's "awful essence," is the part unseen by the casual tourist, as it were, of human feelings and ailments. Ahab's "awful essence," in state, is "throned on torsoes," the stone-carved bodies of sculptures sheared of heads and limbs. Ahab himself is another such torso, completed in the ivory of his leg, which supports, "like a Caryatid," another broken figure, the architrave, frieze, and cornice of "the piled entablatures of ages." The passage underlines Melville's deep involvement with the appearance and language of architecture, an art form of which he sometimes had, as Bryan C. Short aptly puts it, a "visionary rather than visual orientation."[12] He is eager to use the descriptive language of the art, which he has picked up from reading about antiquities, those of Pompeii, Greece, Petra, and Nineveh, and there is sometimes a tinge of the spurious in his easy assumption of the mantle of omniscience, but his splendid rhetorical dominance makes all seem right.

Through his persistent recurrence to the art analogy, Melville gives Ishmael the resources to put Ahab before the reader in something like his astonishing intricacy. The captain is not to be another Enceladus, the sky-storming hero whose leaden visage Melville would examine at Versailles, and there is no one figure whom he can be made to resemble. He has been struck by the derisive gods but has not been made impotent, however awkward his wounded movement upon his ivory leg.

Ahab's conceptualization of artworks is sometimes as disfigured as his body. His speech to Starbuck on the quarter-deck offers a strangely reductive sense of the pictorialism of the quotidian: "All visible objects, man, are but as pasteboard masks." To see the magnificent pageant of life, the sea, its creatures, humankind and the creations of humankind shrunken into something essentially as crude as images drawn upon pasteboard is to fail terribly the test of vision, betrayed by what Wenke calls "Ahab's fixed theory of reality" (139). A fixed theory becomes an intolerable fixation that excludes seeing and loving. Coleridge's Ancient Mariner, for instance, cannot, at first, see the beauty of the natural and thus acts criminally. But he is eventually eased in his suffering by wandering about and teaching "by his own example love and reverence to all things," as the prose gloss reminds us near the end of the poem. Ahab fails to comprehend some such attachment to the world and suffers for his failure.

THE TRUE FORM OF THE WHALE

Ishmael, artist without brush or palette, depicts the *Pequod* and Ahab in ekphrastic terms and then turns to the more difficult task he has set for himself, to "paint to you as well as one can without canvas, something like the true form of the whale" (224). His cautionary "as well as one can" and "something like" give indications of his hesitancy and his sense that the task may be overwhelming. Before he makes his own attempt, he finds it necessary to review what other painters have made of Leviathan and, in three successive chapters, displays his knowledge of monstrous pictures, less erroneous pictures, and a wide array of examples of leviathanic iconography in many materials and forms. He again takes the stance of art critic, a part he has already acted out in the first chapter and in the depiction of the Spouter-Inn picture, but the differences in Melville's presentation of him as character and speaker are clear. A competent, thoughtful youth puts the Saco Valley painting before the reader, but the man who shoulders his way into the New Bedford inn stares mystified at the picture of a whale engaged in the perilous and pointless task of impaling itself upon the masts of an invisible ship. The Spouter-Inn painting is the first in Ishmael's collection of monstrous pictures of whales, his earliest invitation to correct the predominant images of the salt sea mastodon.

By the time he fronts his huge task, Ishmael has become a confident pilot capable of leading his reader through the shoals of misrepresentation. As Sten rightly observes, the young man does have a "fixation on the question of what distinguishes a true picture from a false one" (*Weaver-God* 176). His casual display of learning and his capacity for puncturing the pretensions of artists are signs of a growing sophistication in worldly matters. His magisterial tone invites trust as he generalizes about "the natural aptitude of the French for seizing

the picturesqueness of things" (*Moby-Dick* 230), and the reader is hardly sur-
prised at his audacity in ascribing the skills of artists to some concept of national character traits. Suffering, or perhaps profiting, from what Arthur Mizener
calls a "pedantry of the particular" (112), he dates matters like "a Dutch book of
voyages, A.D. 1671" or the outline of a whale "killed on the coast of Mexico, August 1793" or Goldsmith in "the abridged London edition of 1807" with a certainty that overcomes any possible objections. He is the well-traveled envoy who
insouciantly drops place names like London, Saratoga, Baden-Baden, Versailles,
Nantucket, the Solomon Islands, and Wapping. He has an easy familiarity with
important names in art, like "that fine old German savage, Albert Durer," Guido
Reni, and William Hogarth; and he has looked at engravings after paintings by
Ambroise Garneray and "some one who subscribes himself 'H. Durand,'" an
admirably brief notation of the much more impressive name of Jean-Baptiste-
Henri Durand-Brager. Ishmael is a voracious reader of travel narratives and
knows "old Harris's collection of voyages" and Colnett's "Voyage round Cape
Horn." Apparently he has studied Pliny, Hakluyt, Lacépède, Cuvier's brother,
and Beale and knows what has become of Jeremy Bentham's skeleton.

The three chapters criticize artistic and technical representations of whales,
renderings of the whale hunt, and examples of folk art notable for the patience
and perseverance that have gone into their creation. As Stuart Frank's gallery
demonstrates, Melville is a careful observer who can find the appropriate terms
for representing what he observes and allows Ishmael to find images of the whale
in rock groupings and mountains, a discovery that permits the contemplation
of Nature as artist and the whale itself as an artwork.[13] He has already given
some intimations of this art theory in his portrayals of Queequeg and Ahab and
will now apply painterly terms to natural attributes. Robert Zoellner makes the
useful distinction between "the whale as experienced rather than as conceived"
(150). What is experienced or perceived is the material of art, and, seeing pictures, carvings, clouds, and real whales, Ishmael the art critic can get proportions, shapes, light, shadow, and a general sort of framing into proper focus. His
intent is to paint the whale in scientifically correct terms, but he will not be
satisfied with "the mechanical outline of things" and is more interested in "life-
like" presentation and "a truthful idea of the living whale." His high praise for
Garneray's pictures results from his conclusion that the "action of the whole
thing is wonderfully good and true." When that is so, he is not really concerned
about accuracy and is willing to pass over the fact that "Serious fault might be
found with the anatomical details" (216–17). He recognizes that perfect accuracy
is not the usual aim of portraiture, for the spirit must be there, along with a
liveliness of conception. Here, Melville's reading about the visual arts helps him

to be clear about the validity of such ideas. As early as the second chapter of *Modern Painters,* Ruskin, citing Sir Joshua Reynolds as his authority, offers a "Distinction between the painter's intellectual power and technical knowledge" and claims that art is but a language, "invaluable as the vehicle of thought, but by itself nothing." Supporting his view with commentary upon the works of Landseer, the Dutch school, Cimabue, and Giotto, Ruskin arrives at a definition designed to satisfy his own standards: the greatest art has to convey to the spectator "the greatest number of the greatest ideas." Such a definition is an approximation of the program that Ishmael undertakes in presenting the whale.

But before anatomizing his subject, Ishmael draws upon his experience to present in "The First Lowering" a scene from a whale hunt that Garneray might have painted. All the elements are there, whaleboats with oarsmen and harpooneers and "the ivory Pequod bearing down upon her boats with outstretched sails, like a wild hen after her screaming brood" (223). This picture, handled in vivid painterly terms, is "a sight full of wonder and awe," a rich canvas of a seascape full of glens and hollows, color and movement. But we should notice that the stance of the scene painter is quite different from that taken by Garneray, Turner, and other artists of whaling scenes. Removed from the action, they look into a framed depiction of whales, whaleboats, and ships usually at rest. However, since Ishmael is an oarsman, he must face away from the whale and sees only what is behind his whaleboat or to his sides. As a result, we are given a picture depending often upon sounds for its effects—the gasps of oarsmen, the hiss of the harpoon being darted. The whale, absent from the picture, is "something" that "rolled and tumbled like an earthquake beneath us." The whaleboat is pulled into the sort of squall that, in Garneray's picture, only distantly threatens a whaleship and boats.

After depicting what a whale hunt is actually like instead of having to conceive it from other artworks, Ishmael proceeds to offer picture after picture of his subject. The skin, the whale's "visible surface," is marked by lines "as in a veritable engraving" (306). Nature, the violent and abusive artist, has incised upon this ready surface "numerous rude scratches, altogether of an irregular, random aspect." Whatever has created this picture, the scratches of rocks, icebergs, or "hostile contact with other whales," Ishmael is surrendering to the human tendency to regard as hieroglyphic, or indecipherable, anything that lies beyond the human system of symbols. But Melville's metaphor of hieroglyphs represents the engraved symbols on the whale's visible surface as sacred and holy, and hence the reference to "the mystic-marked whale." Nature, as an artist, produces objects like stone cliffs that resemble whales or constellations that stimulate the imagination to fanciful imagery, and these are decipherable by humans.

But it also produces pictures beyond the human capacity of recognition. Ruskin makes this point early in *Modern Painters* when he asserts that "The first great mistake that people make is the supposition that they must see a thing if it is before their eyes." Ishmael can observe but, in a typical human failing, does not always see.[14]

Crucial elements in any portrait are the head and features of the subject, and Ishmael has a difficult task in attempting to depict the inhuman heads of sperm whale and right whale. Phrenology and physiognomy, "two semi-sciences," would not, it appears, work very well, but Ishmael is content to try them and "achieve what I can" (345). The trouble with physiognomy is that it, "like every other human science, is but a passing fable" (347) and is not likely to give helpful results. But he does observe that "the whale's vast plaited forehead forms innumerable strange devices for the emblematical adornment of the wondrous tun" (340). Devices and emblems are part of the language of heraldry, a topic that seems to haunt Melville's thinking, though he does not tell us here what specific devices embellish his whale's giant forehead. To describe properly, one must see, and fortunately he is given a dramatic opportunity to observe two whale heads at one time and can use the contrast to great advantage. The sperm whale offers "mathematical symmetry," "more character," the superiority of "pervading dignity," and an aged and experienced look, the result of his greyish "pepper and salt" coloration (329). Each term is verifiable by observation and offers a few strokes to a picture that could match for its psychological correctness the best portraiture of Italian, Dutch, and English artists. The notable difference between human and leviathanic portraits must be in the placement and appearance of the eyes, and here Ishmael reverts to landscape description to catch the peculiarity that an art lover is unprepared to notice: the whale's eyes are separated by the bulk of the head, which "towers between them like a great mountain separating two lakes in valleys" (330). If this is so, then the scene directly before the great creature "must be profound darkness and nothingness to him." The question of the whale's eyes leads Ishmael to offer a pattern of inconclusive language: the separation of eyes "must wholly separate the impressions" that each organ presents; "a curious and most puzzling question might be started"; and "It may be but an idle whim," this "helpless perplexity of volition" in the whale. His language underlines the essentially alien element in the task he has set for himself. Of all pictures, the portrait is the most easily assimilated, the most familiar, in its laying down of forms and colors, for the viewer. Melville would make this point in his later lecture on statuary, that "the aspect of the human countenance is the same in all ages," and would dwell upon the expressive faces of the subjects.[15] Inexpressive in human terms, even if it can possess "more character" and a "pervading dignity," the whale's head will puzzle even its most sympathetic delineator.

Leaving such speculation, Ishmael moves easily from the arts to the practical crafts. The lower jaw of the sperm whale, "like the long narrow lid of an immense snuff-box," is also like a portcullis, a defense mechanism. The whale's extracted teeth are the stuff of decorative crafts, producing "curious articles, including canes, umbrella stocks, and handles to riding whips." The jaw itself is "sawn into slabs, and piled away like joists for building houses" (332). Consideration of the sperm whale's head, beginning in its dignity and character and proceeding into the mystery of its gigantic receptacle for thought and feeling, now dissolves, rather cheerfully, into the business of the useful. But this is an integral part of Melville's pictorial plan, for the two pictures of the heads of sperm whale and right whale form a contrasting diptych.

The "noble Sperm Whale's head" has distinction and "may be compared to a Roman war-chariot." On the other hand, the poor right whale's head "bears a rather inelegant resemblance to a gigantic galliot-toed shoe," and "an old Dutch voyager likened its shape to that of a shoemaker's last" (333). Melville here evokes an important part of his art knowledge, the works of seventeenth-century Dutch genre painters. The resemblance of the head to a shoe or a last might have been sufficient to make Ishmael's point, but he adds visual confirmation by calling it "galliot-toed." The galliot is a single-masted flat-bottomed Dutch merchant ship or seagoing barge, its flatness and amplitude contrasting with the slimmer lines of other vessels. Redburn had seen a galliot in Liverpool harbor, looking like "an old-fashioned looking gentleman, with hollow waist, high prow and stern," and so, probably, had Melville. The galliot is also a prominent feature in Dutch seascapes that Melville might have seen.

His interest in Dutch art comes to light as early as *Typee* and continues in allusions in *Mardi* and *White-Jacket*. In his excellent summary of this aspect of Melville's art knowledge, Dennis Berthold calls attention to "the genre painting in prose that informs much of Melville's work during the 1850s" ("Dutch Genre Painting" 219) and offers an illustrated catalog of such works that may have influenced Melville's writing, including the somewhat "inelegant" *The Fiddler* and *The Drinkers* by Adrian Brouwer and *The Smoker* by David Teniers (233–34, 242). To these might be added such pictures as the *Country Inn* by Adriaen van Ostade and Jan Steen's *Self Portrait* and *The Poultry Yard*. All of these feature the clumsy Dutch shoe prominently. Seeing Dutch paintings at Dulwich on November 17, 1849, Melville mentioned only a painting by Phillips Wouverman by name but was also struck by "The old man & pipe" (*Journals* 20, 298–99). Horsford conjectures that this painting might have been Ostade's *Man Smoking*. It bears some resemblance to the central figure among Brouwer's drinkers, a man who sits on a bench holding a pipe in his mouth, his leg with the inelegant shoe stretched out on the long seat. How many of these or similar paintings Melville saw, or how many prints he may have owned or seen, is guesswork. But Berthold indicates a source for Brouwer, and we know of Melville's attraction to the paintings of Jan Steen.[16]

As we see, the picture of the sperm whale's head begins with nobility, dignity, and aged wisdom, but this impressive vision is undercut by the practical comedy of trade and commerce. By contrast, the picture of the right whale's head begins with comedy, in Ishmael's wry comparison of it to something as clumsy as a galliot or a Dutch shoe, but, as the depiction continues, the head becomes a thing of marvelous beauty. His careful metaphors exhibit it as a bass viol, its spiracles as apertures in an aesthetically pleasing sounding board. The crown of the head resembles "the trunk of some huge oak." The slats of whalebone within the mouth are like Venetian blinds or, in a more elegant analogy, like "the inside of the great Haarlem organ."[17] The contrasts are enriched, finally, by Ishmael's whimsical contemplation: "This Right Whale I take to have been a Stoic; the Sperm Whale, a Platonian, who might have taken up Spinoza in his later years" (335). As philosophers, the whales have approached the assurance of death in typical manners, the sperm whale viewing it with "speculative indifference," the right whale with "an enormous practical resolution." Melville would later complete this analogy in art terms, seeing the bust of Plato as an "aristocratic transcendentalist" with "long flowing locks" and a beard that "would have graced a Venetian exquisite." By contrast, the bust of the Stoic Seneca offers a face "like that of a disappointed pawnbroker" (*Piazza Tales* 401). These Melvillean conclusions come nearly a decade after *Moby-Dick*, but his seeing the busts in Rome only confirms a long-held art adept's view.

Because the head is the most important feature in the portrait, nearly all of Ishmael's dealings with the leviathanic head are artistic matters. Seeing the whale's head, severed from the body and "hung to the *Pequod*'s waist like the giant Holofernes's from the girdle of Judith" (311), he is possibly recalling a picture by Christofano Allori or the great painting by Paul Veronese.[18] Ahab regards the head as a sculptural masterpiece, "the Sphynx's in the desert," and Ishmael later considers that the sperm whale is "physiognomically a Sphinx" (348)—that is, a hooded mysterious artwork. The physiognomist plays a technical role in portraiture by showing, through descriptions and sketches, the conformations and lines of the face in portraying the subject's character. In the chapter called "The Prairie," Melville has Ishmael consider what can be made of this science in the portraiture of whales. Indicating that Lavater had studied animals as well as men and looked at "the faces of horses, birds, serpents, and fish" for the "modifications of expression discernible therein," he creates a physiognomical sketch of the "anomalous creature," the sperm whale, who does not possess a nose. To emphasize the point that the leviathan must not have a nose, Ishmael has recourse to "landscape gardening, a spire, cupola, monument, or tower of some sort" as well as the sculptural detail of "the nose from Phidias's marble Jove" (345–46).

Moving from the head to the magnificent tail that "analogizes cosmic power in its aesthetic manifestations" (Zoellner 162) brings on an outburst of Ishmael's most impressive art allusion:

> Take away the tied tendons that all over seem bursting from the marble in the carved Hercules, and its charm would be gone. As devout Eckermann lifted the linen sheet from the naked corpse of Goethe, he was overwhelmed with the massive chest of the man, that seemed as a Roman triumphal arch. When Angelo paints even God the Father in human form, mark what robustness is there. And whatever they may reveal of the divine love in the Son, the soft, curled hermaphroditical Italian pictures, in which his idea has been most successfully embodied; these pictures, so destitute as they are of all brawniness, hint nothing of any power, but the mere negative, feminine one of submission and endurance, which on all hands, it is conceded, form the peculiar practical virtues of his teaching. (376)

At least part of the passage may come from Melville's reading of Madame de Staël's novel *Corinne*. Aboard the ship that took him to England in 1849, Melville had heard "another curious discussion between the Swede & the Frenchman about Lamertine [*sic*] and Corinne." His curiosity aroused, he purchased a copy of the novel (*Journals* 9, 144). Like the *Italian Journey,* part of Goethe's autobiographical works that he acquired at about the same time, *Corinne* provides nuggets of information about the arts, for much of the book takes the form of an art pilgrimage in which Lord Nevil is led by his lover, the heroine, to observe Italian artworks.

In the eighth book of *Corinne,* entitled "The Statues and the Pictures," the two travel through Rome, where they view the *Apollo Belvedere,* the *Laocoön,* the foot of an enormous Jupiter, the *Castor and Pollux,* and "among broken statues, the torso of Hercules." These lead them to conjecture that, "as the gods wore our shape, every attribute appears symbolical; the 'brawns of Hercules' suggest no recollections of vulgar life, but of divine, almighty will, clothed in supernatural grandeur" (8:126). In the next chapter they look at paintings, and Lord Nevil is "almost scandalized at seeing that Michael Angelo had attempted to represent the Deity himself in mortal shape." A few lines further on, he and Corinne believe "that religious meditation is the most heartfelt sentiment we can experience and that which supplies a painter with the grandest physiognomical mysteries." The Melvillean passage, subtle and seamless, is woven from fabrics of reading, seeing artworks, and contemplating their pictorial values.

The skeletal whale is also to be comprehended as a work of art. King Tranquo, "gifted with a devout love for all matters of barbaric vertù," is an art collector who has brought together "carved woods of wonderful devices, chiselled shells, inlaid spears, costly paddles, aromatic canoes." Respecting Nature as the greatest of artists, he saves "whatever natural wonders, the wonder-freighted, tribute-rendering waves had cast upon his shores," including the skeleton of a whale. The skeleton, already a work of natural art, forms a chapel, an architectural artwork, its ribs furnished with trophies, its vertebrae carved "in strange hieroglyphics" (449).[19] Its location, in the middle of a wood "green as the mosses of the Icy Glen," places death in the midst of life where, "Through the lacings of the leaves, the great sun seemed a flying shuttle weaving the unwearied verdure." The result is a complex, paradoxical, parabolical objet d'art where "Life folded Death; Death trellised Life; the grim god wived with youthful Life, and begat him curly-headed glories" (450).

Throughout his lengthy word-painting of the leviathan, Melville has alternated between the generality of portraying "the whale" and depicting one particular whale. He fastens upon characteristics that the visual artist would consider in his work. Shape and form are as important and as Ionian as any columns, but the painter would have to give thought to color and chiaroscuro, the shadings of light and dark in a picture. Blackness is predominant in the Spouter-Inn picture, while, in the whaling chapel painting, the blackness of rock and breakers contrasts with the radiance of the sunlit angel's face. The *Pequod,* viewed as a work of marine art, has a darkened complexion relieved by the whiteness of sea ivory and whale teeth. Considering the most prominent feature of Moby Dick, his whiteness, which is hardly a "Venetian tint," Ishmael discourses upon this color, or noncolor, in works of art. Jove, "incarnate in a snow-white bull," is represented in paintings by Titian and Veronese (189). White is present in "the celebration of the Passion of our Lord" and in "the Vision of St. John," two scenes prominent in Italian paintings.[20] The White Steed of the prairies sounds like the subject of a painting, with "the flashing cascade of his mane, the curving comet of his tail" (191). But the white horse, a magnificent exhibit of life, quickly metamorphoses into a picture of death where we "throw the same snowy mantle round our phantoms; all ghosts rising in a milk-white fog," and it is inevitable that Ishmael will be reminded that "the king of terrors, when personified by the evangelist, rides on his pallid horse" (192), a subject familiar enough in Revelations 6:8 and portrayed in Benjamin West's *Death on the Pale Horse,* much admired for what Washington Allston called its "visions of sublimity."[21]

The indefiniteness of white, its noncolor, as of "the charnel-house" or "the monumental white shroud," is "most appalling to mankind" and fuels "the fiery hunt" for the whale. In *Melville and Turner,* Wallace cites the Goethean theory of colors and Charles Eastlake's translation and notes to Goethe's writings as influential in Melville's thinking (396–99). Melville may also be considering a reply to Ruskin's assertion that "truths of colours are the least important of all truths," an idea he develops in *Modern Painters* (sect. 1, chap. 5). Since colors change, and since it is hardly certain that any two persons see the same colors in objects, Ruskin argues that "the artist who sacrifices or forgets a truth of form in the pursuit of a truth of color, sacrifices what is definite to what is uncertain, and what is essential to what is accidental." It can hardly be said that Ishmael neglects form in his chapters on the whale, but, recognizing at all times that his thoughts on color are vague and "so mystical and well nigh ineffable" (188), he still gives it a primary place in his repertory of painterly effects.

MANMAKER

Ishmael takes great interest in such aspects of the art analogy as the function of the artist who doubles as artisan and the transcendental importance of the visual arts as a description of man the microcosm in the macrocosmic world. From the first, he presents characters who attempt to codify their experiences in suitable artworks. The sailor in the Spouter-Inn who carves a ship under sail on his bench, the sailors who examine their carved pieces of scrimshaw, and the landlord who decks his public room to as to make it resemble the whale's head are all trying to give voice to the facts of their existence. The innumerable creators of "monstrous pictures" of whales and "less erroneous pictures" are engaged in similar ventures, as are the savage and the "white sailor savage" who patiently carve bone sculpture "as close packed in its maziness of design, as the Greek savage, Achilles' shield; and full of barbaric spirit and suggestiveness, as the prints of that fine old Dutch savage, Albert Durer" (270).

The *Pequod*'s blacksmith, constantly engaged in the useful task of repairing the weapons of whaling and the metal boat furniture, is a further example. Working with great patience, he shapes forms "as if toil were life itself." Ahab calls him to an artistic task far beyond the usual human need, to create a magic weapon from fabulous materials, from the nailstubs of the shoes of racing horses that "will weld together like glue from the melted bones of murderers" and from the steel of razors barbs "sharp as the needle-sleet of the Icy Sea" (488–89). In this venture, Ahab acts as monitor and art critic, accepting or rejecting parts of the sculptural construct as they are fashioned into portions of the harpoon. An even more pointed example of the artisan as artist is the carpenter, "unhesitatingly expert in all manner of conflicting aptitudes, both useful and capricious" (467). His useful aptitude is easily characterized by his work with stove whaleboats, belaying pins, sprung spars, and clumsy-bladed oars. His capricious aptitude takes other forms, in the fashioning of an exotic birdcage from "right-whale bone, and cross-beams of sperm whale ivory," and the decoration of Stubb's whaleboat oars with stars, painted by the carpenter into an unnamed constellation. The capricious aptitude is the aesthetic side of the carpenter's nature, for, like the primitive natives of Queequeg's island or other places in the South Seas, he embellishes the practical object with the artistic flourish, dispensable for its use but vital for the spirit.

Since the carpenter has such an artistic side to his nature, he tends to regard human and animal parts as the materials for practical and artistic use: "Teeth he accounted bits of ivory; heads he deemed but top-blocks; men themselves, he lightly held for capstans" (467). His reductive view of the human goes too far. Man, created by the greatest of artists, is a beautifully articulated version of the practical but clumsy capstan, and so Ishmael reverses the carpenter's criticism, finding him something like "a common pocket knife," omnitooled and useful but, to an extent, at the mercy of his user (468). Looking deeper, however, Ishmael does not let his simple reversal stand. Although the carpenter seems to work "by a kind of deaf and dumb, spontaneous literal process," he is a mysterious figure, part manipulated tool and part artist. Ishmael admits that the man "had a subtle something that somehow anomalously did its duty." This something may be "essence of quicksilver" or "a few drops of hartshorn," a product of natural or animal magic and thus an "unaccountable, cunning life-principle" (468).

The spontaneous and literal art procedure of the carpenter has its counterbalance in the more conscious artistry of Queequeg. Desperately ill and wanting a coffin that resembles "certain little canoes of dark wood, like the rich warwood of his native isles," Queequeg applies to the carpenter, who chooses "some heathenish, coffin-colored old lumber" to get the desired effect as he builds the coffin. Queequeg, superior as artist, gets well and carves the lid of the coffin, now turned into a sea-chest:

> Many hours he spent, in carving the lid with all manner of grotesque figures and
> drawings; and it seemed that hereby he was striving, in his rude way, to copy parts
> of the twisted tattooing in his body. And this tattooing had been the work of a
> departed prophet and seer of his island, who, by these hieroglyphic marks, had
> written out on his body a complete theory of the heavens and the earth, and a
> mystical treatise on the art of attaining truth. (480–81)

The purpose of all art is the art of attaining truth, and in his endeavors Queequeg
is following the dictates of natural magic. It is hard to tell what Melville read and
studied of this exotic subject, but some of the ideas he touches upon can be
found in Francis Barrett's *The Magus* (1802), a compendium of natural, talismanic, and cabalistical magic, forming "a complete system of occult philosophy," as the main title page assures the prospective reader.[22] Barrett defines natural magic as "a comprehensive knowledge of all Nature, by which we search out
her secret and occult operations throughout her vast and spacious elaboratory
[*sic*]." The Lord, having created the macrocosmic world, made, "in man, likewise, an exact model of the great world . . . in which we may trace in miniature
the exact resemblance or copy of the universe" (1:13). This miniaturization, in
artistic form, of a theory that was once generally understood is part of Queequeg's
outward appearance, couched in a language that he cannot understand. It is a
hieroglphyic in the same sense that the markings on the "visible surface" of the
whale are hieroglphyics. Queequeg, like most artists, is highly skilled in repro-
ducing the talismanic pictures that no longer have any real meaning or substance.

The matter of meaning in art is given further interpretation in the treatment
of the doubloon, a fine artwork that Ahab has nailed to the mainmast. It is not
simply payment for an accomplished act, for Ahab seems "to be newly attracted
by the strange figures and inscriptions stamped on it" and desires to interpret
"whatever significance might lurk in them." Observing him at his new task,
Ishmael conjectures that "some certain significance lurks in all things, else all
things are little worth, and the round world itself but an empty cipher" (430).
The coin is as much a cipher, whether an empty one or not, as the hieroglyphic
markings upon the whale, Queequeg, and the coffin lid. As pieces of numis-
matic art, South American coins contain a bewildering variety of images, "palms,
alpacas, and volcanoes; sun's disks and stars; ecliptics, horns-of-plenty, and rich
banners waving" (431). As he did in painting the whale, Melville proceeds from
the general, offering the varied characteristics of many exemplary coins, for not
all the coins that Ishmael has seen contain all of the signs and symbols that he
here enumerates. Mansfield and Vincent point out that perhaps seven South

American countries are represented in this generous all-embracing description (804).

Beyond such generalizations, Ishmael's ekphrasis of one particular coin of Ecuador reproduces the lettered inscription that places its minting at Quito. The description is a curious one, specific and detailed in some matters and vague in others: "Zoned by those letters you saw the likeness of three Andes' summits; from one a flame; a tower on another; on the third a crowing cock; while arching over all was a segment of the partitioned zodiac, the signs all marked with their usual cabalistics, and the keystone sun entering the equinoctial point at Libra" (431). The reader can easily visualize parts of this miniature artwork, for the mountains with their decorations are vividly rendered; but the phrase "usual cabalistics" betrays some impatience with occult interpretations. The pretensions of cabalistical and zodiacal symbolism offer only "some certain significance" in all things, not a universal or even comprehensible significance.

Whatever its significance, the coin is a work of art possessing beauty and integrity. In her elaborate study of the "ciphered text" of *Moby-Dick*, Viola Sachs relates the novel to a particular work of art, Albrecht Dürer's print *Melencolia* and offers a wide range of talismanic and cabalistic illustrations in her interpretation. The Dürer print, which Melville may have seen by 1851, is something like the Ecuadorian coin, a work of art that can give rise to meditative consideration of the human mystery. Melville dismisses much of the mystery, however, for, after letting Ahab find the coin a kind of looking glass in which a man "but mirrors back his mysterious self" and allowing Starbuck to see religious significance, Flask to see it as nothing more than money, and Pip to indulge in "crazy-witty" interpretation, he gives the last word to Stubb, who compares the doubloon to "the ship's navel" and warns of the consequences of unscrewing your navel (435).

The "omnisciently exhaustive" presentation of the whale leads Ishmael to "magnify him in an archaeological, fossiliferous, and antediluvian point of view" (455), and the quest results in a chapter rich in eighteenth- and ninteenth-century geological evidence and guesswork, art allusions, and cosmological speculation. Ishmael is almost overcome by his announced program, for his thoughts "include the whole circle of the sciences, and all the generations of whales, and men, and mastodons, past, present, and to come, with all the revolving panoramas of empire on earth" (456). The word "panoramas" has a specialized significance. A panorama was a combination of art show and theatrical spectacle attended by large audiences who saw what amounted to an early version of a "moving picture." Melville was well acquainted with these spectacular artistic exhibitions. He knew the work of John Banvard, one of the most famous of panorama painters, and thought that Constantinople in 1856 was a subject for Banvard, who "should paint a few hundred miles of this pageant of moving processions" (*Journals* 65, 406). In *Clarel*, there is a description of "The Latin Organ," which is probably suggested by Banvard's panoramic painting of the Holy Land.[23]

As he proceeded with the composition of *Moby-Dick*, Melville had panoramas on his mind. Since a panoramic painting, sometimes hundreds of feet long, was mounted on spindles and turned so that audiences could view an ever-changing picture, a tale of whaling could easily resemble the panoramas of the subject. The Benjamin Russell-Caleb Purrington panorama "A Whaling Voyage Round the World" was shown in Boston in 1849 at a time when the Melvilles were visiting the Shaws (Carothers and Marsh 319ff), and it seems likely that Melville attended a showing. *The Confidence-Man*, like *Moby-Dick*, could qualify as a panoramic novel. Like Banvard's panorama of the Mississippi, displayed in 1847 and later, it needed a wide stretch of canvas. An 1848 review of the Banvard painting noted that "The romantic scenery, the bold bluffs, the towering hills, and the elevated shot-towers between the mouth of the Ohio and St. Louis, are transferred to the canvas with wonderful force, effect, and truthfulness" (McDermott 28). The Mississippi River was a popular subject for panorama painters. Before doing his own panorama, Henry Lewis took a river tour in 1840, making sketches for his painting.[24]

Moby-Dick is cast as a panorama that encompasses the entire novel, and within it are smaller but still extensive panoramas. The narrator announces one in the first chapter as "WHALING VOYAGE BY ONE ISHMAEL," which could have matched the Russell panorama in many of its details, but would include plot elements that Russell would not have envisioned.[25] Another topic treated in a panoramic manner would have included "Cetology," an unfolding of kinds of whales; to it might be added the account of portraits of whales, monstrous, less erroneous, and correct. In chapter 104 Melville seems to have a paleontological panorama in mind as he lays out his subject, fossils found in Lombardy, England, Louisiana, Mississippi, and Alabama, along with "pre-adamite" traces "upon Egyptian tablets, whose antiquity seems to claim for them an almost fossiliferous character" (457).

Following the mention of Egyptian tablets, Melville offers a remarkable passage of ekphrasis: "In an apartment of the great temple of Denderah, some fifty years ago, there was discovered upon the granite ceiling a sculptured and painted planisphere, abounding in centaurs, griffins, and dolphins, similar to the grotesque figures on the celestial globe of the moderns. Gliding among them, old Leviathan swam as of yore; was there swimming in that planisphere, centuries before Solomon was cradled" (457–58). Melville is fond of describing apartments that house rich and unusual works of art. His juvenile "Fragments from a Writing Desk" features one. Redburn encounters a room filled with art that reminds him of pornographic and obscene pictures. Others will come in works written after *Moby-Dick:* Pierre Glendenning's closet, in which is contained the mysterious portrait of his father; in *Clarel* the apartment of Abdon, the innkeeper (1.2) and the rich apartment of the abbot at Mar Saba (3.23). Melville's descriptions become topographies, made opulent by their keen sense of attendant subjects, the history, myth, and ambiance of a place. Some of these descriptions perform as strong thematic elements in the whole literary work, but the description of the Temple of Denderah, for all its richness, is simply one more item in the long chain of evidence Ishmael cites in his portrait of the whale.

Nevertheless, the passage displays Melville's characteristic technique of tossing off some enigmatic bit of erudition. John Gretchko's essay on the Temple of Denderah identifies a likely source, Vivant Denon's illustrated *Egypt Delineated*, a volume about the "Scenery, Antiquities, Architecture, Hieroglyphics, Costume, Inhabitants, Animals, etc., of that Country," published in 1818 and republished several times subsequently (51ff). In this book, Melville could have seen pictures of the temple and the planisphere and could have read, in Denon's text, about the architectural and sculptural masterpieces found there.[26] With his customary adeptness in reading, observing, and transforming his miscellaneous materials into closely woven texture of his prose, Melville convinces one that Ishmael has some special knowledge to bring to bear upon his exotic subject.

Just as the Egyptological sources reach their best expression in Melville's use of the art analogy, so do his Oriental sources. The earliest of the monstrous pictures of whales involves "the oldest Hindoo, Egyptian, and Grecian sculptures" and describes the "famous cavern-pagods of Elephanta, in India," with its statues. The whale is an incarnation of Vishnu, "learnedly known as the Matse Avatar," and "half man and half whale" is wrong, for the tail does not resemble "the broad palms of the true whale's majestic flukes" (261). Examination of the sources gives further insight into the workings of Melville's visual imagination.[27] A passage like this consists of a melding of bits and pieces, and he willfully falsifies his sources, changing things about to get the effect that he desires. The desire for literal truth does not give him pause. He will be truthful if truth works but will, if necessary, depart from truth if the departure ensures beauty.

This intense concentration upon seeing a world of art in the world of shipboard continues to the end of *Moby-Dick*. In chapter 130, "The Hat," Ahab's "slouching hat" is given what almost amounts to the validity of an artwork as it is stolen by a sea-hawk and Ishmael is made to link its fate to the mythic story wherein "An eagle flew thrice round Tarquin's head, removing his cap to replace it, and thereupon Tanaquil, his wife, declared that Tarquin would be king of Rome" (539). Ahab's fate is predicted by the loss of his hat, stolen and "falling from that vast height into the sea." In chapter 133, "The Chase—First Day," upon the first real appearance of the fabled white whale, Ishmael finds a remarkable art allusion to describe the vision: "Not the white bull Jupiter swimming away with ravished Europa clinging to his graceful horns; his lovely, leering eyes sideways intent upon the maid; with smooth bewitching fleetness, rippling straight for the nuptial bower in Crete" (548). Gretchko has pointed out, in *Melvillean Loomings,* that Melville seems to be alluding to a painting by Titian, *The Rape of Europa,* and ingeniously suggests that this allusion foreshadows the "abduction" of Ahab by the whale (34–37).

In the last agonistic scene of the encounter with the whale, there is a reprise of the Spouter-Inn painting as the *Pequod* sinks so that the men in the lifeboat see "only the uppermost masts out of water." The tiny drama of the sky-hawk who pecks at the flag and is caught by Tashtego's hammer, held to the mast, and dragged, "a living part of heaven," recapitulates in ironic reversal the scene of the sea-hawk and Ahab's hat and mimics, in tableau style, the art symbol of the eagle and flag upon the mast "whose wood could only be American" (571–72). And, as a final act of heavenly grace, Ishmael, art lover and artist possessed of a remarkable word-hoard, is saved by a magnificent objet d'art now converted to daily uses, the coffin buoy whose lid Queequeg has lovingly carved as some part of "a mystical treatise on the art of attaining truth," though its "mysteries not even himself could read."

FIVE

Pierre

"A Stranger's Head by an Unknown Hand"

THE IMMENSE EFFORT OF literary pictorialism in *Moby-Dick* ensured that Melville had learned to use the device with consummate skill in his writings. There hardly seems room for further development of the technique, or even for its further refinement. But composing *Pierre* presented a new and difficult set of problems in composition, and his own attitude toward the book is revelatory. Responding to some remarks that Sophia Hawthorne must have made about the recently published *Moby-Dick,* Melville wrote on January 8, 1852, with scarcely concealed irony, "I had some vague idea while writing it, that the whole book was susceptible of an allegoric construction" and promised that "I shall not again send you a bowl of salt water. The next chalice I shall commend, will be a rural bowl of milk" (*Correspondence* 219)—humorous and somewhat blasphemous wordplay notable for its implication. The letter's playfulness then gives way to a declaration of serious intent in which the composition of the book is like a sea voyage that can conclude in "All Persia & the delicious lands roundabout Damascus" (220).

Pierre is an unanticipated lengthy voyage, for Melville had originally intended what must have been a swift-paced thriller on the model of Bulwer-Lytton, William Gilmore Simms, or the Englishmen William Harrison Ainsworth and George Walker.[1] The book did change during the course of composition, and the result was a novel that garnered unfriendly reviews, some of them savage.[2] More recent critics reflect the difficulties the novel offers. Newton Arvin is dismissive: "So extreme is its badness as an integral work of art that some faint-hearted readers might well wish to be excused from any prolonged discussion of it" (219). A more temperate view is offered by Warner Berthoff: "Its great theme is again muffled by the preposterousness of the story, which is finished out by main force, in haste and self-doubt" (53–54). Henry A. Murray speaks of the book as "a literary monster," its "repellent aspects" balanced by its excellences. Other studies avoid judgments of the whole and concentrate on certain aspects, its Timonism, its relationships with Spenser or Dante, its narrator, or its themes of flux and fixity.³

But whatever final accounting we give of *Pierre*, a study of its ekphrastic prose displays Melville at his virtuosic best, using his hard-earned skills to advantage in embellishing the texture of his tale or developing motifs and plot. Pierre's loneliness, as an only son, and his desire for a sibling as well as for some personal glory "capping the fame-column, whose tall shaft had been erected by his noble sires," is a theme rendered in architectural terms. These terms continue with Pierre's reflection on the ruins of Palmyra, including "a crumbling, uncompleted shaft, and some leagues off, ages ago left in the quarry, is the crumbling corresponding capital, also incomplete" (8). The architectural motif foreshadows the fall of the house of Glendenning, represented here by a splendid but ruined art object that "Time crushed in the egg." Time is the quenchless feuding enemy and the stone cannot compete with it but is "left abased beneath the soil." A "fine military portrait" of General Glendenning, Pierre's grandfather, offers the occasion for an ekphrastic passage that emphasizes its "majestic sweetness" and its "heavenly persuasiveness of angelic speech" that declares "man is a noble, god-like being, full of choicest juices; made up of strength and beauty" (30). Melville's description is enriched by his using an actual family portrait, Gilbert Stuart's painting of Peter Gansevoort, to serve as model for Pierre's revered ancestor. Lucy Tartan is described in painterly terms, in which "her hair was Danae's spangled with Jove's shower" (24). The allusion is largely mythological, but Danae is also a famous art subject. Melville was not to see Correggio's *Danae* until his visit to the Borghese Gallery in Rome on March 5, 1857, but Correggio's picture was well-known from copies and widely distributed prints. Seduced by Zeus, Danae became the mother of Perseus, and later Perseus undertook to defend his mother against King Polydectes of Seriphos, who attempted to force her to marry him. Pierre, an avatar of Perseus, defends his Danae from Glen, a modern Polydectes. Lucy is an enthusiastic artist who does pencil sketches and sits with Pierre to examine pictures: "there's the book of Flemish prints—that first we must look over; then, second, is Flaxman's Homer—clear-cut outlines, yet full of unadorned barbaric nobleness. Then Flaxman's Dante—Dante! Night's and

Hell's poet he" (39, 42).[4] The Flemish prints offer a picturesque version of rural life, in stark contrast to the hellish inferno of Flaxman's Dante illustrations, which will reflect the descent into the city of Dis, where the eventual tragedy will take place.

THE PERFECT MARBLE FORM

Pierre's deceased father is presented through a series of art objects. Learning that Isabel is his sister, Pierre must face the prospect of regarding the parent—whose "shrine seemed spotless, and still new as the marble of the tomb of him of Arimathea"—in a new light, for her letter has "stripped his holiest shrine of all overlaid bloom, and buried the mild statue of the saint beneath the prostrated ruins of the soul's temple itself" (69). His new and perilous regard becomes centered upon a number of art objects, the first a marble statue:

> this shrine was of marble—a niched pillar, deemed solid and eternal, and from whose top radiated all those innumerable sculptured scrolls and branches, which supported the entire one-pillared temple of his moral life; as in some beautiful Gothic oratories, one central pillar, trunk-like, upholds the roof. In this shrine, in this niche of this pillar, stood the perfect marble form of his departed father; without blemish, unclouded, snow-white, and serene; Pierre's fond personification of perfect human goodness and virtue. (68)

The lavish description and the comparison of the shrine to the Mausoleum permit Melville to emphasize the illusions that Pierre has about his father. Through a few careful strokes, he casts doubt almost immediately upon the young man's devotion, painting him as "the eye-expanded boy" who "perceives, or vaguely thinks he perceives, slight specks and flaws in the character he once so wholly reverenced" (68). Since the elder Glendenning is dead, he must be evoked entirely by the revenants of art. Like the elder Redburn, he intrudes, a wraithlike apparition of an unhappy past, slowly made clear to the young man. The persistence of this motif, worked by means of the art analogy, is a central feature of both *Redburn* and *Pierre* and offers the added impact of the autobiographical fact. Through his own art, Melville attempts to exorcise the father, a source of his deepest, most resigned melancholy.

The next pictorial rendering of the father occurs almost immediately, in an elaborate passage describing the painting that Pierre keeps in a locked, round-windowed closet:

In this closet, sacred to the Tadmor privacies and repose of the sometimes solitary Pierre, there hung, by long cords from the cornice, a small portrait in oil,
before which Pierre had many a time trancedly stood. Had this painting hung in
any annual public exhibition, and in its turn been described in print by the casual glancing critics, they would probably have described it thus, and truthfully:
"An impromptu portrait of a fine-looking, gay-hearted, youthful gentleman. He
is lightly, and, as it were, airily and but grazingly seated in, or rather flittingly
tenanting an old-fashioned chair of Malacca. One arm confining his hat and
cane is loungingly thrown over the back of the chair, while the fingers of the
other hand play with his gold watch-seal and key. The free-templed head is sideways turned, with a peculiarly bright, and care-free, morning expression. He
seems as if just dropped in for a visit upon some familiar acquaintance. Altogether, the painting is exceedingly clever and cheerful; with a fine, off-handed
expression about it. Undoubtedly a portrait, and no fancy-piece; and to hazard a
vague conjecture, by an amateur." (71–72)

The details in this carefully structured description are relevant to the novel's
motifs. "Tadmoor privacies" return us to the earlier allusions to Palmyra. Tadmor
is an alternative name for the city, with its broken and uncompleted architecture, symbolic of the family. Privacies have been the overwhelming characteristic of the seemingly happy Glendennings, concealing the sinful past that will
overwhelm the present.

Melville has been accused of using the outworn style of a dying romantic
tradition in *Pierre*, but passages such as this one go far to refute the claim. The
novel is multivoiced and full of vocal mimicry. Melville always knows what he is
parodying. The "casual glancing" and well-imagined critic who might have commented on the painting is skewered by the language that the author creates for
him. There is a rich fund of humor in the mocking ekphrasis, in phrases like
"grazingly seated in," "free-templed head," and the critically opaque "morning
expression." Melville wants us to see how foolish such a substitute for authentic
art criticism can sound. His target could be any of the current newspapers and
journals of the period. A likely candidate for his satire is *The Literary World*,
which printed much about the visual arts in articles about exhibitions, poems
about artists, reviews of books about the arts, and articles that undertook to
provide art tours. The magazine displayed a deep interest in the Art-Union and
printed lengthy and usually bad criticisms of exhibited paintings as well as full-
page advertisements of the Union's offerings.[5] A typical critical note appears in
the issue of November 6, 1847:

No. 144. "Our Father who art in Heaven." H. P. Gray. A sweet picture that appeals so directly to the heart that criticism seems set at defiance. What little faults of drawing there may be, pass unnoticed when we stand before it, and feel the calm and holy spirit that pervades the composition in every part, so full of expression, so delicate in sentiment. There is beautiful color here, and an elaborate finish that does not in the least detract from the breadth of the picture. The accessories are charmingly painted. Pictures such as this will elevate the public taste, and fulfil the great mission of Art to raise the mind of man out of the depths of his lower nature. (330)

As a serious student of the visual arts, determined to understand them and make them part of his battery of literary devices, Melville must have been struck by the amateurism, sentimentality, and limp diction of such prose, an irresistible object for his caricature.

As Henry Murray indicates, Melville is describing a portrait of his father, executed by John Rubens Smith (1775–1849), who lived in New York and Philadelphia and worked as a drawing teacher, engraver, and painter. Melville might well have read some of Smith's interesting publications, including *A Compendium of Picturesque Anatomy* (1827) and *A Key to the Art of Drawing the Human Figure* (1831).[6] Of most importance, however, is what the passage contributes to the novel. We learn that the portrait is a companion to another picture of Pierre's father, one not locked away but freely and openly displayed in the Glendenning home. Mrs. Glendenning has found the first portrait "namelessly unpleasant and repelling" and "could not abide this picture which she had always asserted did signally belie her husband." The portrait that she does approve of shows "a middle-aged, married man, and seemed to possess all the nameless and slightly portly tranquilities, incident to that condition when a felicitous one" (72–73). The description of this larger portrait fits the painting of Allan Melvill by Ezra Ames (1768–1836). The hidden portrait, like the hidden life of the elder Glendenning, does not offer the felicitous picture of middle-aged comforts and timidities.[7]

Comparison of the two portraits leads the narrator to explain how Pierre has acquired the little picture, a gift when he reached the age of fifteen, from his father's sister. She retains a miniature that portrays her dead brother. To Pierre's insistent questions, she answers with the story of the painter, Ralph Winwood, a cousin, and the French emigrant lady who attracted the attentions of Pierre's father and then disappeared. Ralph has painted his cousin's portrait by slyly getting the self-absorbed man to sit without being aware of his role; "stealing his portrait" is the vivid phrase that Aunt Dorothea uses.

In the scheme of the novel, the use of Ralph Winwood as well as real artists like John Rubens Smith and Ezra Ames has an important role. Melville's earlier novels stand upon a solid basis of internationalism, emphasized by the exoticism of *Typee, Omoo,* and *Mardi,* the mix of national character types in *White-Jacket,* and, in *Moby-Dick,* the astonishment of the "outlandish," even on the streets of New Bedford with its "nondescripts from foreign parts." By contrast, *Pierre,* the "rural bowl of milk," is American, regional, and provincial. It is imagined "that in demagoguical America, the sacred past hath no fixed statues erected to it, but all things irreverently seeth and boil in the vulgar caldron of an ever-lasting uncrystalizing Present" (8). The art of America is part of that vulgar caldron of the uncrystalizing Present, its chief exhibits copies or prints of great European art or phony artworks with revered European names attached to make them attractive or the work of the art unions, a mix of paintings by genuine artists such as Cole, Allston, Durand, West, and a few others and the amateurish dabs and daubs distributed to Union members and overpraised by whatever passes for art criticism. Melville seems intent upon making a case in favor of this raw America but also demonstrates the two levels of response to American art. The portrait of the young Glendenning is the work of an amateur. The portrait of the older Glendenning, fit for exhibiting openly in one's home and, later, in museums, is the work of a professional.

The lengthy passage discoursing upon the two portraits comes to an end with Pierre reflecting upon what they tell him: that, perhaps, Ralph Winwood knew of Glendenning's liaison with the Frenchwoman and of Isabel, its issue; and that the two portraits in their differences make up one full picture of a man. Here Melville introduces what Hagstrum designates as *ecphrasis,* a situation in which an art object is given voice. Pierre is made to imagine the voice of his portrayed father emanating from the paintings and saying "Consider in thy mind, Pierre whether we two paintings may not make only one. Faithful wives are ever overfond to a certain imaginary image of their husbands; and faithful widows are ever over-reverential to a certain imagined ghost of that same imagined image" (83). This double vision, mirrored in the two portraits, becomes merged for Pierre, who can react only by recalling the appropriate verses from the twenty-fifth canto of *The Inferno,* which portrays the fusion of Agnello and a serpent in the seventh bolgia of Circle VIII, a horrid metamorphosis at which the watchers exclaim, in words that Melville quotes, "Ah! how dost thou change, / Agnello! See! Thou art not double now, / Nor only one" (85). The fusion is not complete, either, for Agnello or for Pierre's father, despite the latter's effort to convince his son that the two portraits offer a true depiction. Melville possesses a keen visu-alizing talent and could imagine vividly the scene of Agnello's transformation;

but he would be greatly aided by John Flaxman's illustrations of Dante's infernal torments, even though none of Flaxman's pictures illustrates this scene. The reading of Dante, in the Bohn edition of 1847, which Melville acquired in 1848, and the impact of the Flaxman *Oeuvre Complet* (Paris 1833), apparently acquired in 1849, stirred his imaginative rendering of Pierre's inner hell.[8]

Melville's experience in dealing with the art analogy grew out of his determined efforts to learn about the sister arts. In 1847 he became a member of the New-York Gallery of Fine Arts and, no doubt, took advantage of his membership to visit its exhibitions. He had the advantage of personal contact with artists and was able to view their works from a particular, personal point of view. The portraits of his grandfather, father, and mother, executed by Gilbert Stuart, E. L. Henry, and Ezra Ames, conveyed much about character painting and adducing the worth of a person from the display of physical appearance. In 1847 Melville himself sat for a portrait by Asa Weston Twitchell and could therefore see the results of physiognomical representation applied to him. During the visit to London in 1849–50, he associated with artists; during the 1856-7 journey to Europe, he visited the studios of several artists in Italy.[9]

Pierre's reactions to the portraits of his father demonstrate his inability to come to terms with his new knowledge. He cannot bear to look at the "no longer enigmatical, but still ambiguously smiling portrait" and turns it to the wall of his closet (87). He cannot go to his mother, whom he depicts in her "immense pride;—her pride of birth, her pride of affluence, her pride of purity, and all the pride of high-born, refined and wealthy Life, and all the Semiramian pride of woman." As a result, he feels "himself driven out an infant Ishmael into the desert, with no maternal Hagar to accompany and comfort him" (89). The reference to Ishmael and Hagar links Pierre to the Ishmael of *Redburn* and *Moby-Dick,* and, perhaps, to Salvator Rosa's painting of the subject. The unspecified allusions may be either to literary works or to artworks.

Murray discusses the literary backgrounds of the Semiramis allusion, citing Spenser, Byron, Calderon, Voltaire, and Rossini (456). Particularly valuable is the Rossini notation, a production of his *Semiramide* at Palmo's theater in New York in June 1847, for Melville may well have attended performances of the musical drama. More important, however, is the linking of the proud queen with Melville's interest in such varied subjects as Babylon, Nineveh, Chaldeans, and magi. By the time he visited the British Museum on November 16, 1849, and saw "big arm & foot—Rosetta stone—Nineveh sculptures—&c" (*Journals* 19), he had very likely read of Henry Layard's excavations at Nineveh, for *White-Jacket* alludes to them. There is no evidence that he knew Layard's *Nineveh and Its Remains* (1848–49), which contained illustrations, but magazine stories called attention to Layard's work and his study *The Monuments of Nineveh*, "illustrated in One Hundred Plates."[10] The subject fascinated Melville. James B. Fraser's *Mesopotamia and Assyria* (1845), a volume in Harper's Family Library, would have given him information for his allusion to Nineveh in *Redburn*. The pictorial elements for a portrait of the fabled Semiramis—who "is said to have built the city of Babylon and its hanging gardens, founded Nineveh, and conquered Persia, Libya, and Ethiopia" (Murray 456)—offer a splendid precursor to compare to Pierre's overly proud mother.[11]

As an exiled Ishmael, Pierre can hardly tell his mother all about Isabel. He can just about manage a question for Mr. Falsgrave, the minister, another character who is visualized in painterly terms. Breaking a roll for Mrs. Glendenning, the minister "acquitted himself on this little occasion, in a manner that beheld of old by Leonardo, might have given that artist no despicable hint touching his celestial painting" (99). Melville's model here is Leonardo's *Last Supper,* in which the Lord gravely breaks bread with his friends. Falsgrave, "an image of white-browed and white-handed, and napkined immaculateness," cannot properly answer Pierre's earnest question about the proper relationships between a legitimate son and an illegitimate child and, thus, hardly acquits himself as well as the figure in Leonardo's painting. When Pierre has presented his presumably hypothetical case and been answered by the minister's alliterations and pomposities ("Millions of circumstances modify all moral questions"), there occurs a scene involving some highly symbolic art objects. Falsgrave's napkin, "surplice-like," falls away revealing "a minute but exquisitely cut cameo brooch, representing the allegorical union of the serpent and dove" (102). Melville was probably well acquainted with the arts of cameo and pendant design, since his father, as an importer of European art objects, must have brought to America any number of examples. The iconography of dove and serpent is familiar, though perhaps not as familiar in cameos, which more often seem to be used for portraiture. Enameled pendants, on the other hand, often bear mythical and biblical illustrations—David with the head of Goliath, Leda and the swan, St. George and the dragon. In his great need, Pierre cannot expect aid from Falsgrave and adopts the serpent symbol of the cameo as the basis of his thinking. The thought of his future, "in great part and at all hazards dedicated to Isabel," is "icy-cold and serpent-like" as it crawls "in upon his other shuddering imaginings" (104).

Sensitive to what he read, Melville often responded to it with laughter. The language of ekphrasis in magazines and books of the time stirred him to parody, and the picturesque landscape of Walter Ulver's farm is as richly confusing as it is improbable:

Where he stood was in the rude wood road, only used by sledges in the time of snow; just where the outposted trees formed a narrow arch, and fancied gateway leading upon the far, wide pastures sweeping down toward the lake. In that wet and misty eve the scattered, shivering pasture elms seemed standing in a world inhospitable, yet rooted by inscrutable sense of duty to their place. Beyond, the lake lay in one sheet of blankness and of dumbness, unstirred by breeze or breath; fast bound there it lay, with not life enough to reflect the smallest shrub or twig. Yet in the lake was seen the duplicate, stirless sky above. Only in sunshine did that lake catch gay, green images; and these but displaced the imaged muteness of the unfeatured heavens.

On both sides, in the remoter distance, and also far beyond the mild lake's further shore, rose the long, mysterious mountain masses; shaggy with pines and hemlocks, mystical with nameless, vaporous exhalations, and in that dim air black with dread and gloom. At their base, profoundest forests lay entranced, and from their far owl-haunted depths of caves and rotted leaves, and unused and unregarded inland overgrowth of decaying wood—for smallest sticks of which, in other climes many a pauper was that moment perishing; from out the infinite inhumanities of those profounder forests, came a moaning, muttering, roaring, intermitted changeful sound: rain-shakings of the palsied trees, slidings of rocks undermined, final crashings of long riven boughs, and devilish gibberish of the forest-ghosts. (109)

This is a fascinating, strange bit of pictorialism. The elements portrayed in the first paragraph are characteristically Melvillean. The lake, in its blankness and dumbness, mirroring the blank, dumb sky, is much like the tranced, watery vistas of other writers, the silent, mirroring tarn at Poe's house of usher, the lakes and streams of Shelley's *Alastor,* and others.

As the description proceeds, however, Melville dips into the language of Gothic hyperbole, piling on visual and aural images till they collide and collapse. His models are in the romantic sensational literature of the previous generation, the language, say, of *Frankenstein,* which Melville had taken care to acquire and read. In Mary Shelley's portrayal of the mountains, there are "shattered pines," a "thunder sound of the avalanche," the cracking of "accumulated ice, which, through the silent working of immutable laws, was ever and anon rent and torn" (chap. 10).

David S. Reynolds has made an excellent case for the vast number of sensational writings, "dark adventures" and "subversive fiction," available to Melville during the 1840s. He cites especially the stories of George Lippard, George Thompson, Laughton Osborn, and Richard Kimball. Without focusing upon what Melville is sure to have known, Reynolds speculates that "Melville and Hawthorne were almost certainly aware of Kimball's *St. Leger* (1849), a novel that created a great sensation" (193–95). Reynolds shifts the basis of scholarly interest in Melville's reading from the works of acknowledged masters to best-sellers, crowd-pleasing fictions that gloried in bloodletting, incest, mystery, and extravagant adventure. Since Pierre fits exactly into this pattern and, in fact, spends much of its strength in satirizing and mimicking such fictions, the emphasis is rightly taken.

However, the horrors of the landscape that Pierre observes, its lakes of blankness reflecting the indifference of nature, its air "black with dread and gloom," its forest-ghosts full of "devilish gibberish," only one aspect of Melville's art of parody. This is the horrific sublime of Burke, carefully overstated to push it into the realm of comedy. The contemporary critics who spoke ill of the prose in *Pierre* were missing the point. The prose is not bad; it is doing precisely what Melville intended for it to do, though the risk of parody is that the audience may mistake it for its target. Melville's comic vision once more intrudes, as he moves his picture, in the blink of an eye or the turn of a paragraph, from the horrific sublime to a pastoral calm. The movement is from Salvator Rosa or Henry Fuseli to John Constable. Nor do Pierre's reflections help the description, for, looking at the decaying wood in the forest, he is stung by social concerns. The wood is going to waste, while "for smallest sticks of which, in other climes many a pauper was at that moment perishing." This from Pierre, eater of large breakfasts.

Another aspect of Melville's landscape painting here is its insistence upon the sentimental side of romantic art, the portrayal of rusticity and rural beauty. His "moss-incrusted" farmhouse is picturesque:

> At one gabled end, a tangled arbor claimed support, and paid for it by generous gratuities of broad-flung verdure, one viny shaft of which pointed itself upright against the chimney-bricks, as if a waving lightning-rod. Against the other gable, you saw the lowly dairy-shed; its sides close netted with traced Madeira vines; and had you been close enough, peeping through that imprisoning tracery, and through the light slate barring the little embrasure of a window, you might have seen the gentle and contented captives—the pans of milk, and the snow-white Dutch cheeses in a row, and the molds of golden butter, and the jars of lily cream. (110)

These are the standard accessories for pictures of rural simplicity and calm. The dairy shed is a particularly comic touch, with its gentle captives—the milk, cheeses, and cream (where one might have expected the captives to be the cattle).

Melville's parody of the picturesque is stoutly anchored in the literary practices of the late eighteenth and early nineteenth centuries and should be related to literary pictorialism. John Bryant, summarizing the work of William Gilpin,

Archibald Alison, and Richard Payne Knight, discovers the picturesque in "that which we associate in the mind with framed pictures . . . a visual habit, a painterly way of seeing the world and transforming nature into a coherent landscape" (147–48). Familiar with landscape paintings and prints, Melville owned examples of the work of Constable, Landseer, Wouverman, Poussin, and other topographical studies. This "painterly way" of seeing a portion of the world as a framed picture offers the author, aware of his audience's probable knowledge of such views, the chance to create, in his ekphrastic prose, a kind of landscape that no one artist could have painted. The passage demonstrates Melville's distrust of the pathetic fallacy and the keenness of his mimicry. The elms have a sense of duty, the lake is bound by its bed, and the entranced forests mutter and roar. The arbor claims support and the cheeses and creams stand as "gentle captives." With a sure hand, he points out the most ridiculous excesses of this genre and touches them with his mockery.

The story that Isabel tells Pierre has some elements in common with the story the creature tells in *Frankenstein,* and Isabel herself is somewhat like Safie, the "Arabian" in the creature's narrative. Safie has had a difficult past, she plays the guitar, and she sings strange songs. Mary Shelley carefully avoids the necessity of quoting Safie's lyrics, simply noting that they are "entrancingly beautiful." Melville, of course, tops this by quoting Isabel's lame lyrics, and the word "mystery" uses up six of her song's ten words. In the description of her song "the waltzings, and the droppings, and the swarming of the sounds," the word "droppings" is artfully ambiguous (126).

The delineation of Isabel makes use of art analogy, portraying her unruly mass of hair as covering and muffling her face like the "saya of Limean girl." Visiting Peru and reading about it, Melville was much taken with the subject of "saya y manto," the first being a petticoat or skirt and the second a mantle or veil used to conceal the face.[12] Pierre sees Isabel's veiling herself in her hair in terms of religious art. She is like a girl "at the dim mass in St. Dominic's cathedral." Moreover, "To Pierre, the deep oaken recess of the double casement, before which Isabel was kneeling, seemed now the immediate vestibule of some awful shrine, mystically revealed through the obscurely open window, which ever and anon was softly illuminated" (149). Pierre, deprived of the marble niche where he had worshiped his father, discovers a wooden niche, cathedral-like within the confines of Ulver's red farmhouse, where he can worship the sister he had hoped for. The ambiguity—perhaps the irony—of the scene resides in the clash between the hushed portrayal of religious art and the eroticism of Isabel's displaying herself with hair like the "saya," the petticoat, partially concealing her face, rather than the "manto," the far more usual mantle of concealment.

Having decided to go away with Isabel and Dolly, Pierre, at the Black Swan Inn, looks once more at the chair-portrait of his father:

> Face up, it met him with its noiseless, ever-nameless, and ambiguous, unchanging smile. Now his first repugnance was augmented by an emotion altogether new. That certain lurking lineament in the portrait, whose strange transfer blended with far other, and sweeter, and nobler characteristics, was visible in the countenance of Isabel; that lineament in the portrait was somehow now detestable; nay, altogether loathsome, ineffably so, to Pierre. He argued not with himself why this was so; he only felt it, and most keenly. (196)

The psychology of aesthetic and moral perceptions engages Melville's attention here, and he is quick to establish the ways in which knowledge and the emotions control what the viewer of a work of art sees. The little painting has not changed since Pierre last studied it, but he has. The passage underlines some of the meanings of the novel's subtitle by its use of the word "ambiguous." The ambiguity of the portrayed father's smile allows Melville to probe Pierre's developing ideas about the world he has, so unprepared, found himself facing. In the next paragraph, there is a rich fund of ideas about the powers of the visual arts:

> In the strange relativeness, reciprocalness, and transmittedness, between the long-dead father's portrait, and the living daughter's face, Pierre might have seemed to see reflected to him, by visible and uncontrollable symbols, the tyranny of Time and Fate. Painted before the daughter was conceived or born, like a dumb seer, the portrait still seemed leveling its prophetic finger at that empty air, from which Isabel did finally emerge. There seemed to lurk some mystical intelligence and vitality in the picture; because, since in his own memory of his father, Pierre could not recall any distinct lineament transmitted to Isabel, but vaguely saw such in the portrait; therefore, not Pierre's parent, as any way rememberable by him, but the portrait's painted self seemed the real father of Isabel. (197)

The portrait has a reality beyond the reality of the actual world. It depicts, with greater truth than the available facts, what Pierre should have known, and its "painted self," in Melville's telling phrase, is now more real than any memory of the vanished father. It is the function of a portrait to give substance to an evanescent and nearly forgotten past and to bring before the observer a personage otherwise lost to negligent memory. Ralph Winwood's little portrait of the elder Glendenning is an example of what the artist who painted better than he knew could accomplish. It stirs Pierre to a significant soliloquy, in which he declares

Khasneh, or Treasure House, Petra. From Colonel Wilson, ed., *Picturesque Palestine, Sinai and Egypt,* 2 vols. (New York: D. Appleton, 1883). Courtesy of the Howard-Tilton Memorial Library, Tulane University.

Raphael, *Saint Cecelia Listening to the Singing of Angels*. From N. D'Anvers, *Raphael* (London: Sampson Low, Marston, n.d.). Courtesy of the Howard-Tilton Memorial Library, Tulane University.

Claude, *Seaport*. From Owen J. Dullea, *Claude Gellee le Lorrain* (New York: Scribner and Welford, 1887). Courtesy of the Howard-Tilton Memorial Library, Tulane University.

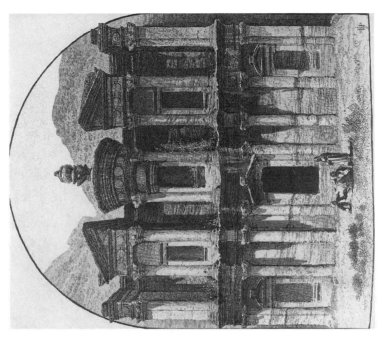

El Deir, Petra. From Colonel Wilson, ed., *Picturesque Palestine, Sinai and Egypt*. Courtesy of the Howard-Tilton Memorial Library, Tulane University.

Title page from Archibald Duncan, *The Mariner's Chronicle* (Boston: Charles Gaylord, 1834).

Albert Durer, *Death's Head Coat of Arms*. From *The Works of Eminent Masters, in Painting, Sculpture, Architecture, and Decorative Arts*, 2 vol. (London: Cassell, 1854).

Lady Macbeth. From *The Dramatic Works of William Shakespeare, with a Life of the Poet, and Notes, Original and Selected*, vol. 3 (Boston: Hilliard, Gray, 1837). Courtesy of the Howard-Tilton Memorial Library, Tulane University.

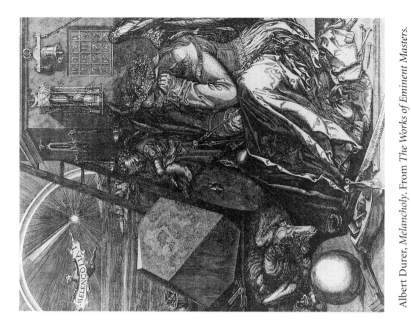

Albert Durer, *Melancholy*. From *The Works of Eminent Masters*.

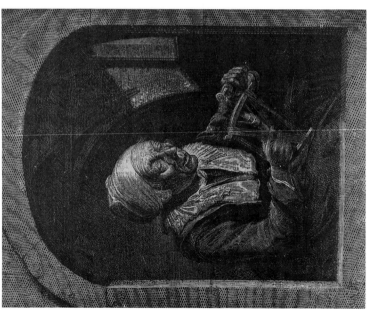

Gerard Dow, *His Mother*. From *The Works of Eminent Masters*.

Adrian Von Ostade, *A Painter in His Studio*. From *The Works of Eminent Masters*.

William Van der Velde, *A Fresh Breeze*. From *The Works of Eminent Masters.*

Joseph Vernet, *View of Pausilippo*. From *The Works of Eminent Masters.*

that he will not "mummy" his memory into such a memorial as the painting. His "Hamletism," hinted at in the lengthy passage about the Memnon Stone, comes to the fore. Like Hamlet, he will set right the time that is out of joint, but first, as Hamlet does, he must fix the present in his mind by destroying all memorials of the past.

When Pierre and his companions move into the old Church of the Apostles that has been turned into a boarding house, Melville offers a painterly description of the building, its stone construction, and its tower. The brick building at the rear of the church receives a detailed account, with its colonnades and the "dismantled, rusted, and forlorn old railing of iron" that encloses what was once a burial ground (265–66). That Melville was interested in prints showing buildings of various sorts is emphasized by Wallace's account of the Reese collection, much of which consists of pictures of churches, homes, and abbeys.[13] Churches appear in the Liverpool landscape of *Redburn* (chaps. 36, 41) and in the treatment of the Whaleman's Chapel in *Moby-Dick* (chap. 7). These descriptions tend to be rather general; in the chapel that Ishmael visits, more is made of the memorial tablets and the pulpit than of the structure itself. Redburn designates himself "an admirer of church architecture," and Melville's 1849–50 visit to Europe gave him the opportunity to examine architectural views. As his journal records, he was keen to seize upon his chance and visited Canterbury Cathedral, St. Swithin's, and St. Magnus Martyr. He went "down to the Temple-Church to hear the music," visited Westminster Abbey, and took note of St. Giles and St. Dunstans (*Journals* 16, 17, 20). In France, he went to Notre Dame (31), St. Roche, and "an old church near by," possibly St. Etienne-du-Mont. In Cologne, he saw the cathedral and its tower as well as the Jesuits' church.[14]

With this extraordinarily large cache of observations and impressions, Melville composed *Moby-Dick,* and, although the novel did not offer many opportunities for him to use his enlarged knowledge of church architecture, he did manage to refer to the Cologne cathedral and insert allusions to some of the secular architecture he observed, notably the Hotel de Cluny. Gordon V. Boudreau looks closely at Melville's use of Gothic architecture in *Moby-Dick,* especially at the handling of archways made of whalebones, the whalebone chapel in "A Bower in the Arsacides," and Father Mapple's church in New Bedford ("Of Pale Ushers" 67–72). The fullest experience Melville had during his earlier books was in observing and describing the structure of ships, and he made good use of this experience in *Moby-Dick.*

The Church of the Apostles once had its day in what had been a fine residential district, but "change and progress had rolled clean through its broad-side and side-aisles" (266). Melville's description of the changes in the church, its being divided into stores and offices, is a devastating reminder of the differences between the old and new worlds. In Europe he had seen many churches, some of them ancient, preserved with care and affection and still used for their original and appropriate functions. By contrast, in New York a church barely a hundred years old is converted to secular and vulgar occupations. The offices have become "a roost for gregarious lawyers," a place of perches for unusual fowls. The bird imagery continues in the description, as upper stories of the building house "ambiguously professional nondescripts" who take rooms and "like storks in Holland, light on the eaves" where they sit "and talk like magpies." Looking for dinners, they are "like lean rows of broken-hearted pelicans" (267). Ruskin believed that architecture is "an art that shelters human life" (Landow 107), and Melville's images underline his strong feeling about the inhuman uses of a human art.

His knowledge of architecture, already strengthened by his assiduous study of churches and other structures, could have been supplemented by a reading of Ruskin's *The Seven Lamps of Architecture* (1848). The book was reviewed in *The Literary World* in July, and, as part of Evert Duyckinck's library, it was available to Melville (Wallace, *Melville and Turner* 330–31). The first volume of Ruskin's *The Stones of Venice* appeared in 1851, and Melville could have profited not only from Ruskin's aesthetic theories but also from the moral and ethical conclusions of the volumes. In *Seven Lamps,* Ruskin observed that "we can command an honest architecture: the meagreness of poverty may be pardoned, the sternness of utility respected; but what is there but scorn for the meanness of deception." The architecture of the Church of the Apostles is surely honest, but its poverty and loss of a moneyed congregation resulted in its being handed over to the new owners, who ruin its honesty by converting it to new uses. The "venerable merchants and accountants," pretending distress at the necessity, have decided "that the building could no longer be efficiently devoted to its primitive purpose" (266). The operative word is "efficiently." Even a church must pay its way by doing its job, whatever that might turn out to be, in an efficient manner.[15]

What seems to be of importance in this venture into pictorialism is the moral conclusion to be drawn from the church that has been transmogrified into a commercial structure. It is no longer a church of the Divine Unity but only a church of the Apostles. Divinity has departed and been supplanted by the "virtuous expediency" of Plotinus Plinlimmon's thesis. The birdlike grotesquerie of its tenants is matched by the "indigent philosophers," some of whom are "Teleological Theorists, and Social Reformers, and political propagandists of all manner of heterodoxical tenets." Hence, each is "styled an Apostle" (268), though they can hardly be what Christ had in mind when he designated, from his disciples, the original apostles.

In treating Lucy's fascination with art, Melville depicts that favorite subject of visual artists, the artist's studio. She has an "expertness in catching likenesses, and judiciously and truthfully beautifying them" and wants to sketch some of the remarkable heads of the church's tenants. She is greatly satisfied by the room arranged as her studio. An artist's studio once before, it has some advantages, for "one window had been considerably elevated, while by a singular arrangement of the interior shutters, the light could in any direction be thrown about at will" (330–31). Her theory of a "beautifying atmosphere" such as the water of a lagoon where "the roughest stone, without transformation, put on the softest aspects" has echoes in Archibald Alison's *Essays on the Nature and Principles of Taste,* which notes that "the greater part of those bodies in Nature, which possess Hardness, Strength, or Durability, are distinguished by angular forms," whereas curves indicate softness and delicacy. Roughness is an essential element in the picturesque, but Lucy's art would turn the picturesque into the beautiful. She will take striking, perhaps rough, heads and, "by steeping them in a beautifying atmosphere," soften their outlines. This Tartanesque version of the sublime, the picturesque, and the beautiful contradicts the heroic vision of Pierre (himself a rough stone), who is likely to see the world in its rugged and sublime aspects, as in the Memnon Stone and the natural sculpture of Enceladus.

In a glancing way, Melville relates the passage on Pierre's book to literary pictorialism:

As a statue, planted on a revolving pedestal, shows now this limb, now that; now front, now back, now side; continually changing, too, its general profile; so does the pivoted statued soul of man, when turned by the hand of Truth. Lies only never vary; look for no invariableness in Pierre. Nor does any canting showman here stand by to announce his phases as he revolves. Catch his phrases as your insights may. (337)

Unlike the oil painting or engraving, the statue can be viewed from many points of view, each offering a different vista for contemplation and thus offering more of the inner sense of a figure or bust than a portrait in oils. The revolving pedestal was used in nineteenth-century showings of sculpture, notably in exhibits of Powers's *Greek Slave*. Melville's simile allows him to characterize Pierre from a number of vantage points, some of them contradictory. Pierre is a thwarted Titan, his thews "forestallingly cut by the scissors of Fate." He is seen "as a moose, hamstrung." He is an atheist who "wrote down the godliest things" (339). Melville's depiction of the malady that Pierre suffers when his eyes begin to fail is, perhaps, suggested by the appearance of eyes in sculptured busts: "again the pupils of his eyes rolled away from him to their orbits. He put his hand up to them, and sat back in his seat. Then, without saying one word, he continued there for his usual turn, suspended motionless, blank" (341). This blankness matches the usual blankness of sculpted busts.

THAT BOLD TROPHY OF HIGH ART

The Enceladus episode, crucial to Melville's conception of Pierre and of the entire novel, represents a most impressive and intricate use of literary pictorialism. He prepares us for it by portraying Pierre's thoughts in the sections of the novel immediately following the matter of Lucy's artistic ambitions. Aware that Glen Stanly and Frederic, "two boiling bloods," are likely to take violent steps to prevent Lucy's staying at the Church of the Apostles, and certain that they are planning some action, Pierre has to "look forward to wild work." Thinking of "all the ambiguities which hemmed him in," including the loss of happiness and "his one only prospect a black, bottomless gulf of guilt," his hatred of Glen and Frederic could lead only to murder.

The murder of Stanly does not seem to have an adequate objective correlative. Newton Arvin attempts to find it in Pierre's emotional absolutism and destructive violence, "burning the father's picture to ashes, driving the mother to madness and death, shooting and killing the cousin, bringing death to the fiancee and the half sister, and at last gulping poison oneself" (203–4). Arvin locates Melville's models in "the old novel of sensibility, the Gothic romance, the novel of romantic sophistication, and even Elizabethan tragedy," citing "Mrs. Radcliffe or Susanna Rowson . . . Charles R. Maturin or Disraeli" as possible originals for Melville's outrageous plot. There is a closer possible source, however, in William Gilmore Simms's *Beauchampe; or The Kentucky Tragedy* (1842). The perceptive comment of Mansfield and Vincent that "whatever Melville read he piratically made his own, extending, deepening, and embellishing his thefts so that no literary judge can but approve and applaud" (570–71) applies well in the case of Simms.

The "Kentucky Tragedy" achieved fame in American literature in treatments by Poe, Thomas Holley Chivers, Robert Penn Warren, and a number of playwrights. It was the sort of story that Melville would have enjoyed and used as he used the Colt-Adams case and the story of Monroe Edwards in "Bartleby." In 1825, Jeroboam O. Beauchamp stabbed Colonel Solomon Sharp to death in Frankfort, Kentucky, to avenge the dishonoring of his wife. The crime and trial were sensational and much written about. In prison, awaiting execution, Beauchamp wrote his confession, which was published as a pamphlet after his death. He and his wife attempted suicide in his cell. She died, but he survived long enough to be hanged.[16]

Simms's novel follows the original tale closely, elaborating it with rationalizations to justify the murder. After Beauchampe has finally been told by his wife that his friend, Colonel Sharpe, is the man who dishonored her, Simms asserts that "the world will not willingly account this madness. It matters not greatly by what name you call a passion which has broken bounds, and disdains the right angles of convention" (*Beauchampe* 320; chap. 32). Later, he asks the question, "Was Beauchampe any more sane—we should phrase it otherwise— was he any less mad than his wife?" Beauchampe, Simms's character, had, like the real Beauchamp, pledged to kill the man, but believed that this implied a duel. Sharpe refuses to fight, an unthinkable dilemma for a Kentucky gentleman like Beauchampe, who now has no alternative but to murder his adversary. Simms accepts unquestioningly the code of honor.

Melville is not given such an option, however, and finds motivation in his treatment of the Enceladus story. This passage revives the ancient literary device of the dream-vision, a "phantasmagoria of the Mount of Titans" (342). Among rocky shapes near his home, Pierre has a vision of "Enceladus the Titan, the most potent of all the giants, writhing from out the imprisoning earth." He then compares this vision to an artwork:

> Not unworthy to be compared with that leaden Titan, wherewith the art of Marsy and the broad-flung pride of Bourbon enriched the enchanted gardens of Versailles;—and from whose still twisted mouth for sixty feet the waters yet upgush, in elemental rivalry with those Etna flames, of old asserted to be the malicious breath of the borne-down giant;—not unworthy to be compared with that leaden demi-god—piled with costly rocks, and with one bent wrenching knee protruding from the broken bronze; not unworthy to be compared with that bold trophy to high art, the American Enceladus, wrought by the vigorous hand of Nature's self, it did go further than compare;—it did far surpass that fine figure molded by the inferior skill of man. (345–46)

Melville again places Nature as artist in competition with human artistic creation and discovers it to be superior in its conceptions and execution. "Marsy gave arms to the eternally defenseless," he says, "but Nature, more truthful performed an amputation, and left the impotent Titan without one serviceable ball-and-socket above the thigh" (346). In his visit to Versailles, on December 6, 1849,

Melville recorded seeing a "Titan overthrown by thunderbolts &c" (*Journals* 34). Horsford cites, among items viewed in the visit, the Paul Veronese painting of Jupiter hurling thunderbolts and the *Bassin d'Encelade* of Gaspard Marsy (1625–1681). In his careful study of the art of Versailles, Gerald Van Der Kemp describes the Enceladus fountain as a "huge lead sculpture" that "represents the giant crushed by the rocks of Mount Olympus which he had attempted to scale with his companions to reach heaven" (206–07).

Conjoining painting with sculpture, Melville can give the scene a genuine fullness of expression. Enceladus, the rebellious giant, was partially buried under Mount Etna, and Marsy's sculpture depicts the event. But under Melville's hand, Pierre does not "fail still further" to elucidate the vision that has presented itself in this phantasmagoria:

> Old Titan's self was the son of incestuous Coelus and Terra, the son of incestuous Heaven and Earth. And Titan married his mother Terra, another and accumulatively incestuous match. And thereof Enceladus was one issue. So Enceladus was both the son and grandson of an incest, and even thus, there had been born from the organic blended heavenliness and earthliness of Pierre, another mixed, uncertain, heaven-aspiring, but still not wholly earth-emancipated mood; which again by its terrestrial taint held down to its terrestrial mother, generated there the present doubly incestuous Enceladus within him; so that the present mood of Pierre—that reckless sky-assaulting mood of his, was nevertheless on one side the grandson of the sky. (347)

Richard Brodhead quotes this passage with the comment that it "makes the myth of Enceladus figure forth the dynamics of Pierre's moral anguish" and, as well, "the dynamics of his psychological experience, showing how his relation to his mother breeds in him an ambiguous mixture of sexual desire and reverential love" (187–88). Pierre, Michael Rogin suggests, is "punished not for his own sin of incest, but for his family's" (181).[17]

Pierre, recovering from what he has witnessed, now resolves "by an entire and violent change, and by a willful act against his own most habitual inclinations, to wrestle with the strange malady of his eyes, this new death-fiend of the trance, and this Inferno of his Titanic vision" (347). The Titanic vision is an Inferno because Pierre, drenched in Dante, combines the classical vision of Enceladus with the medieval Dantean tableau of the Giants who stand around the edge of the central pit of Hell. In the Cary translation of *The Inferno*, which Melville owned, the passage reads "of one already I descried the face, / Shoulders, and breast, and of the belly huge / Great part, and both arms down along his ribs" (31.42–44). Dante is describing Nimrod of Nineveh, builder of the Tower of Babel, who brought a confusion of tongues to the world. Other Giants in Dante's catalog are Ephialtes, Briareus, and Antaeus. Dante took advantage of the medieval confusion of Titans and Giants and combined their rebellions and punishments. Though Enceladus is not mentioned by Dante, he is one of the rebellious Titans and would have been punished as the others were. Nathalia Wright discusses this passage in the light of Pierre's rebellion against divine authority, an action in which he imitates the folly of the Giants and Titans; she enumerates some striking parallels—"The equivalent of Ephialtes in Latin is *incubus;* the moss on the head of the rock Enceladus is an 'undoffable incubus'"—and relates the blindness of Ephialtes to Pierre's eye trouble ("Pierre" 176–78n.36). Flaxman's illustrations have been discussed by Schless, who points out that thirty-eight of the drawings are devoted to *The Inferno*. Schless does not treat this passage from *Pierre*, but his discussion of the City of Dis, accompanied by the appropriate Flaxman illustration, demonstrates the kinds of pictorial inspiration that Melville would have drawn from his study of the artist's work (74–76).

It is the "reckless, sky-assaulting mood" of Pierre that sets him apart from such heroes as Beauchampe. They play out an earthbound fantasy of the gentleman's honor while he rebels against the divinity and against his fate. In *Moby-Dick* Ahab accepts the same terrible odds, saying "I'd strike the sun if it insulted me. For could the sun do that, then could I do the other." A vaulting, godlike ambition, doomed by its own nature, is one of the similitudes between Pierre and Ahab, but Ahab's rage is against a godlike creature who can punish him directly, while Pierre assaults another man, easily gunning him down, and thus an important ingredient of the epic pattern is lost.

Nevertheless, working with the Flaxman drawings, Melville must have been struck by the illustrations that the artist had provided for Aeschylus. The hero of *Prometheus Bound*, another sky-assaulting Titan, receives a punishment similar to that visited upon Enceladus. Melville's treatment of the Enceladus rock— partly excavated by "young collegians" and leaving "stark naked his in vain indignant chest to the defilements of the birds, which for untold ages had cast their foulness on his vanquished crest" (345)—parodies the activities of the eagles who tear at the vitals of the bound Prometheus.

The phantasmagoric vision of an American Enceladus finds its double in Pierre's face and features, as the art of the portrait or of sculptured portraiture doubles and magnifies human or godlike physiognomy. The physiognomical researches of Lavater, Gall, and Spurzheim, among others, play an important role in establishing both a moral and an aesthetic basis for the depiction of a face. Melville knew Lavater's writings well. In London, on November 21, 1849, he "bought Lavater's Phisiognomy in Holborn, for 10 shillings (sterling)" (*Journals* 24). The link between Lavater's studies of physiognomy as a science and as the art of portraiture is to be found in the works of Henry Fuseli (1741–1825), painter and close friend of Lavater. Two portraits of Fuseli appear in the 1789 edition of Lavater's *Physiognomy*, and one, from a drawing by Sir Thomas Lawrence, has been said to offer an accurate reading of the painter's character, a prime purpose in physiognomical research. In his own art, Fuseli "followed the precepts of Lavater in expressing by attitude, gesture, or other movements of the limbs or features, the passions or emotions which he wished to delineate in his characters." His pictures were often depictions of Shakespearean scenes and mythology, and his "Milton Gallery" consisted of forty pictures from that poet's work. His posthumously published *Lectures on Painting* (1830) were republished in 1848 by Bohn, as part of *Lectures on Painting, by the Royal Academicians, Barry, Opie, and Fuseli,* and Melville may well have seen this volume. They would have offered him a basis for his portrayal of Enceladus. In the first lecture, Fuseli speaks of expression in the work of ancient artists, notably Apollodorus, pointing out "that as all men were connected by one general form, so they were separated each by some predominant power, which fixed character, and bound them to a class." As an example, Fuseli cites "the figure of Ajax wrecked, and from the sea-swept rock hurling defiance unto the murky sky" (Fuseli 357).[18]

Gall and Spurzheim had a bad influence upon physiognomy, for their work led to the development of phrenology, a laughable pseudoscience, whereas physiognomy might have continued to offer aesthetic guidelines for the noble art of portraiture. It is noticeable that Melville took a somewhat jesting attitude toward phrenology, while his comments based on physiognomy are more serious, even though he had once called it "a passing fable." His lecture on "Statues in Rome," delivered about six years after publication of *Pierre,* seems to be based almost entirely on physiognomical considerations. In Sealts's carefully assembled version of the lecture, Melville points out that his "object is to paint the appearance of Roman statuary objectively and afterward to speculate upon the emotions and pleasures that appearance is apt to excite in the human breast." His characterizations of sculptured busts and forms partake of the language of physiognomy. Demosthenes "resembles a modern advocate, face thin and haggard and his body lean." Socrates "reminds one much of the head and rubicund phiz of an Irish comedian." Julius Caesar's head is much like that of a railroad president, and Seneca has "a face more like that of a disappointed pawnbroker." Nero's "delicate features are only those of a genteelly dissipated youth." In chapter 79 of

Moby-Dick Ishmael seriously considers the physiognomical aspect of the whale and finds that "the Sperm Whale is an anomalous creature" who must be surveyed from the point of view of "the full front of his head," for "this aspect is sublime."

The American sublime is much on Melville's mind as he ponders and writes about Enceladus. American artists may not be able to execute sculptural forms with the power of Marsy's Titan, or, if we consider other statues that impressed Melville, the *Laocoön, Apollo Belvedere, Farnese Hercules,* or *Antinous*. Still, in the American wilderness, Nature far surpasses, in truth and power, the fabricated works of human artists. An apparent jumble of rocks rearranges itself, if the eye of the beholder be willing, into sphinxes, "the Cheopian pyramid," or the Titanic "form defiant, a form of awfulness." Keenly aware of the imitativeness of much of the American art that he observed, Melville was especially sensitive to the artistic qualities of inimitable Nature.

A STRANGER'S HEAD

Pierre, Isabel, and Lucy visit a "gallery of paintings, recently imported from Europe, and now on free exhibition preparatory to their sale by auction." This is a familiar scene for Melville, who saw the exhibits of firms like Goupil, Vibert & Company frequently advertised and subjected to commentary in *The Literary World*.[19] Studying the fictional exhibit's catalog, "Among the long columns of such names as Rubens, Raphael, Angelo, Domenichino, Da Vinci, all shamelessly prefaced with the words 'undoubted,' or 'testified,' Pierre met the following brief lines:—'No. 99. A stranger's head by an unknown hand'" (349). Like Melville, Pierre is incensed by the effrontery of art dealers who deliberately mislead their patrons, for "the whole must be a collection of those wretched imported daubs ... christened by the loftiest names known to Art" (349–50).

Writers on art matters tried constantly to put Americans on their guard against fakery. In *The Literary World* for April 22, 1848, a notice, ironically entitled "Pictures by Old Masters," pointed out that many pictures on the market were "third-rate copies, picked up from the picture dealers of the continent, and introduced to the Americans with all the pompous epithets of connoisseurship" (228). But Pierre sees some merit even in the fakes, which might be "yet unfulfilled perfections of the future" (350). Melville uses both his printed sources and his own observations about art matters. In the same story in *The Literary World,* the writer notes that a catalog of "the gallery recently opened in the Lyceum Building, 563 Broadway," contains some of the most famous names in painting, and it is a matter of secondary importance to establish the originality of all these works, since, in almost every instance, they are so marked with the characteristics of those to whom they are ascribed, that they adequately represent the school of each artist . . . . Cuyp's landscape glows with the sentiment of the hour . . . . Vandyke's Prince Maurice in armor is a noble specimen of his unequalled school of portraiture. The "Lot and His Daughters," attributed to Rubens, is a piece of coloring which our young artists would do well to contemplate patiently. (228)

This may be so, Melville seems to be saying, but he cannot let the observant Pierre accept such an optimistic view, for as he

walked along by the thickly hung walls, and seemed to detect the infatuated vanity which must have prompted many of these utterly unknown artists in the attempted execution by feeble hand of vigorous themes; he could not repress the most melancholy foreboding concerning himself. All the walls of the world seemed thickly hung with the empty and impotent scope of pictures, grandly outlined, but miserably filled. The smaller and humbler pictures, representing little familiar things, were by far the best executed, but these, though touching him not unpleasingly, in one restricted sense, awoke no dormant majesties in his soul, and therefore, upon the whole, were contemptibly inadequate and unsatisfactory. (350)

Pierre's Titanism, like Ahab's Promethean ambition, is in the great line of Goethe's Faustian excess. Ishmael discovered that "man must eventually lower, or at least shift, his conceit of attainable felicity" (*Moby-Dick* 416), but Ahab and Pierre are "sky-assaulting" giants. For Pierre, the "smaller and humbler pictures" represent the smaller and humbler, and therefore the "contemptibly inadequate and unsatisfactory" life.

At this point in the narrative, Melville's pictorial strategy is to avoid ekphrastic description of details in any of the pictures that Pierre is observing. The allusions to Rubens, Raphael, Michelangelo, Domenichino, and Da Vinci allow the reader to make whatever he will of the kinds of paintings and of fakes that are being displayed. The names are the staples of art guides and traveler's guidebooks. But the centerpiece of the art gallery scene is a pair of recognitions. In her encounter with the mysterious painting "by an unknown hand," Isabel at once recognizes that the stranger's face in the painting is familiar, for "only my mirror has ever shown me that look before." The effect is complex, since in perceiving her father's lineaments in the European painting, she also sees her own and Pierre's. At the same time, Lucy, separated from the others, observes a famous work of art, a copy of "that sweetest, most touching, but most awful of all feminine heads—the Cenci of Guido." The two pictures, facing one another across the gallery, seem "pantomimically talking over and across the heads of the living spectators." the *Beatrice Cenci* reminds the viewer of "the two most horrible crimes . . . possible to civilized humanity—incest and parricide" (351), while the "Stranger" excites the contradictory feelings of Isabel and Pierre about their relationship. The *ecphrasis* of the pictorial scene—that is, the implication that the pictures facing one another carry on a colloquy—is subtly rendered. Of what would they converse? Incest and parricide are the presumed topics, along with speculation about the definitively blonde Cenci, "double hooded, as it were, by the black crape" of her crime. Melville is fascinated by the deceptive nature of the art of portraiture, that can demonstrate innocence in the face of guilt and thus create "that sweetest, most touching, but most awful of all feminine heads."[20]

From this scene, the novel hastens to its tragic conclusion. Goaded by the letter of Glen Stanly and Frederic Tartan, Pierre rushes, armed, into the street. His encounter with the two men and his murder of Stanly are treated in a very brief scope, less than a page of the story. The remainder of the tale takes up only a short section, about two and a half more pages. It is no doubt this economy of scenic narration that has caused problems for readers and critics. Berthoff's remark that the story is "finished out by main force, in haste and self-doubt," serves well as a critique of Melville's unusual technique—or, perhaps, his supposed lack of technique—at this point in his narrative.

But an alternative suggestion about his procedure takes us back to the conclusion of William Gilmore Simms's *Beauchampe*. When Orville Beauchampe murders Colonel Sharpe, the scene is rendered in few words: "The sharp edge of the dagger had answered the shocking secret—whatever might have been its character—and the terrible oath of the husband was redeemed!—redeemed in a single moment, and by a single blow" (333). Having disposed of the most dramatic scene in the novel in one sentence, Simms then gives some leisurely pages to explaining why he has not lingered over the murder:

> A murder in a novel, though of very common occurrence, is usually a matter of a thousand thrilling minutiae. In the hands of a score of modern romancers, it is surprising what capital they make of it! How it runs through a score of chapters!—admits of a variety of details, descriptions, commentaries, and conjectures! Take any of the great raconteurs of the European world—not forgetting Dumas and Reynolds—and see what they will do with it! How they turn it over, and twist it about, as a sweet morsel under the tongue. (335)

Simms goes on to satirize the "dreary details," the "particulars of search and discovery," and the "poor devil," who, while innocent, looks guilty. This is one way of writing a novel, and "one might think it a tolerably good way, indeed, were it not that most people find it abominably tedious." He then concludes his explanation with a cautionary and self-congratulatory statement, to the effect that "We make short a story which, long enough already, we apprehend, might, by an ingenious romancer, be made a great deal longer" (335–37). Such an appeal to the reader's common sense might have proved irresistible to Melville, who, in any case, was having trouble with the length in his own novel.

It is helpful to compare the conclusions of Simms's and Melville's tales. Simms had to deal with a trial and incarceration, a suicide and an attempted suicide, the execution of Beauchampe, and some later events, but he has six more chapters for these events, and so, while he can skimp description of the trial, despite the good material available in pamphlets and books about the case, he can give himself room to philosophize about love and honor. Melville never takes his story as far as a trial but has his suicides occur in the city jail on the evening of the murder. The contemporary accounts of the "Kentucky Tragedy" could have served him well if he had chosen, or been allowed, to make use of them in an expansive way.

It is impossible to say with certainty that Melville knew Simms's novel. There is no record of his having owned or read it. One teasing possibility emerges. *Beauchampe* was published as a two-volume novel in 1842. When it was reissued in 1856, the second volume, dealing with the murder and the trial, was published as a novel under the title *Charlemont*. In 1856 Melville was writing *The Confidence-Man,* the thirty-fourth chapter of which is the Cosmopolitan's story "of the gentleman-madman," Charlemont. The coincidence is provocative but hardly conclusive. But the similarities between the two books show that Melville knew quite well what kind of novel he wanted to write in order to engage the novel-reading public. Beyond that, he demonstrated vigorously that he could find in a lurid plot a suitable vehicle for a tragedy of heroic and even noble proportions.

SIX

Clarel

"Dwell on Those Etchings in the Night"

*C*LAREL, "A POEM AND PILGRIMAGE," is Melville's most carefully considered book. Its composition engaged him for years, and its wide reaches, far beyond the scope of his brief stay in Palestine, are filled with the results of his reading and study and with echoes of accounts of other travelers and pilgrims. As Walter Bezanson has amply demonstrated, Melville used a number of books that he acquired in the years after his pilgrimage: William Henry Bartlett's *Forty Days in the Desert* and *Walks About the City and Environs of Jerusalem,* William McClure Thomson's *The Land and the Book,* and Arthur Penrhyn Stanley's *Sinai and Palestine in Connection with Their History.* He may have used John Murray's guide for Syria and Palestine and Eliot Warburton's *The Crescent and the Cross* and quite possibly some other sources (*Clarel* 704–05, 706ff.). Allusions and insertions indicate his gathered knowledge when he pauses, for instance, "to impart / A chapter of the Middle Age" (1.34.73–74), a record of "The Travels of Bishop Arculf in the Holy Land, Toward A.D. 700." As Bezanson indicates (*Clarel* 752), Melville probably took as his source the printing of Arculf's travels from Thomas Wright's *Early Travels in Palestine* (London: Henry G. Bohn, 1848), another of those inexpensive books that he must have encountered as he "swam through libraries." If he read Wright, he had before him, in addition to the account of Arculf's journey, a pageant of travels through the Holy Land from the eighth through the seventeenth centuries. Reading through these successive travel accounts, he found a varied set of impressions and attitudes and might have reacted to a predominantly reverential approach to the scene by taking pleasure, for instance, in the travel notes of Henry Maundrell (1697), who cast a skeptical eye on the impressions of previous travelers and often found them wanting in accuracy. The story of the apples of Sodom, Maundrell wrote, "induces me to believe that there may be a greater deceit in this fruit than that which is usually reported of it," and he cited "my Lord Bacon" in noting that false ideas are kept up "because it serves for a good allusion, and helps the poet to a similitude." Maundrell found that the Dead Sea would not buoy up his body as others had reported. He doubted the usual reports of the age of the olive trees in Gethsemane and observed, ironically, that most of the actions reported as occurring in the Holy Land seemed to take place in grottoes (Wright 454–55, 471, 479). But, however Melville read them, the main value of these early travel records is that they provided him, again and again, with descriptions of the places he himself had seen in a land of stones and monuments—the Church of the Holy Sepulcher, the Church of the Nativity, the Dead Sea, the Wailing Wall. Where he had set his foot, others, centuries before, had also passed. He therefore wrote much of *Clarel* under the influence of the idea, expressed at the end of the poem, of a procession of travelers, like figures upon a frieze. Like him, they passed and paid tribute to the desert wastes, the stones, the churches and grottoes, the fragments of art, wisdom, and folly that made up such a pilgrimage.

The most striking impression that Melville had of his visit must have been the "diabolical landscapes" of Judea (*Journals* 89). He had seen nothing quite like this since his journey to the Galapagos Islands, and, in his writings, he would seek to establish the likenesses between those arid islands and this dessicated world. He was struck by what he called the "Barrenness of Judea," spoke of the "bones of rocks," and found in the scene the "mere refuse & rubbish of creation" (83). A passage that combined serious and whimsical observations dealt with the "Stones of Judea" (90). Melville speculated, "Is the desolation of the land the result of the fatal embrace of the Deity? Hapless are the favorites of Heaven" (91). His observation reflected the idea, widely held during the century, of a land cursed and made desolate by God.

It seems likely that this intense feeling about the barren land that he saw impressed itself upon Melville's consciousness for the same reason that it affected many other pilgrims. Naomi Shepherd suggests that "Palestine had to compete with a powerful rival: its own image in European art and literature" (17) and that painters, contradicting what they would have seen in the Holy Land, which they never visited, often used elements of European scenery as backgrounds for the painting of biblical events. The paintings that Melville and his contemporaries admired depicted their events against imaginary settings that clashed harshly with the reality one saw on the site, for they were settings that might be full of luxurious trees and bodies of water. Clarel's earliest impressions of the Holy Land, teased by what he has seen of it in inaccurate pictures, include "the scorch of noon / Thrown off by crags" and the towers of Jerusalem "Like the ice-bastions round the Pole" (1.1.53–60). The visual, and hence the strong intrusion of the visual arts, plays its crucial role in such a pilgrimage. Melville came to his depiction of the Holy Land well armed with the visual conceptions of artists to agree with or to contradict by his own impressions. Many of the travel books produced in profusion during the first half of the nineteenth century were illustrated. William Henry Bartlett, who produced the pictures for *Walks about the City and Environs of Jerusalem* and *Forty Days in the Desert*, two of the books that Melville acquired, was chiefly an illustrator "intent on topographical accuracy" (Shepherd 100). Bartlett (1809–1854), a prolific and widely traveled artist, made three trips to Palestine as well as four tours of America and Canada, and Melville may have previously known the pictures that he produced for N. P. Willis's *American Scenery* in 1840. Bartlett's illustrations would serve as an aid, should there be any need of one, for Melville's extraordinary visual imagination. Sir David Wilkie and Horace Vernet also visited the Holy Land to paint the scenes there.[1]

When the pilgrims of the poem move out into the desert regions, the poet has a ready description:

> Sands immense
> Impart the oceanic sense:
> The flying grit like scud is made:
> Pillars of sand which whirl about
> Or arc along in colonnade,
> True kin be to the water-spout. (2.12.38–43)

The colonnades of dust are the evanescent architectural landscape of a desert scene and match the description that Melville marked in his copy of Bartlett's *Forty Days in the Desert* where the "loose shifting hills" are "lashed up by the whirlwind into dense tremendous clouds of sand, obscuring all prospect . . . relieved on the dark stormy sky, formed a sublime spectacle" (Cowen 1:169). Melville adds the movement of a caravan proceeding, "long drawn, dispirited," and finds in it the simile of a dismasted fleet retreating from battle (44–50). The description is, as Shirley Dettlaff points out, an excellent example of the Burkean sublime in its immensities of vista (218).

Landscape painting, a central concern of ekphrasis, allows Melville to shift from the omnipresent, dispirited scenery of Judea to pictures of his native land that reflect its generous vegetal growths on prairies and rivers. Looking at the "walls of wane" in Jerusalem and the pool of Hezekiah, Clarel thinks of another desolate scene in which

> No tarn
> Among the Kaatskills, high above
> Farm-house and stack, last lichened barn
> And log-bridge rotting in remove (1.1.163–70)

can be more lonesome than the place he is viewing. In the canto describing the life of Nathan, father of Ruth, there is a setting in Illinois, the "vast space" that challenges the space of the desert. What Nathan "daily beheld" is a new land seen as an old one:

> Three Indian mounds
> Against the horizon's level bounds
> Dim showed across the prairie green
> Like dwarfed and blunted mimic shapes
> Of Pyramids at distance seen
> From the broad Delta's planted capes
> Of vernal grain. In nearer view
> With trees he saw them crowned, which drew
> From the red sagamores of eld
> Entombed within, the vital gum
> Which green kept each mausoleum. (1.17.57–67)

The "prairie green" of the American Midwest is a stark contrast to desert landscape, and the poetry luxuriates in finding analogies that contradict, seeing the Indian mounds as "mimic shapes" of the pyramids of Egypt, the "vernal grain" of the midcontinental river in contrast to the Nile, and the burial grounds of Indian sagamores as a counterpoint to the tombs of Pharaohs. But an oncoming night, as the poet sings, is

> Like sails convened when calms delay
> Off the twin forelands on fair day,
> So, on Damascus' plain behold
> Mid groves and gardens, girdling ones,
> White fleets of sprinkled villas. (1.18.1–5)

The colors of the retreating day "Thy wall, Angelico, suffuse, / Whose tender pigments melt from view— / Die down, die out, as sunsets do" (29–31). Watching the onset of night, we are back in the painterly world of Fra Angelico's Florence. Melville probably did see the famous frescoes of Fra Angelico, though he left the event unrecorded in his journal. Hawthorne, coming to Italy after Melville, recorded on April 12, 1858, that he saw in Rome "some beautiful frescoes by Fra Angelico," discovered after having disappeared. They were "of sacred subjects, both on the walls and ceiling, a good deal faded, yet pretty distinctly preserved."

Nathan's Illinois landscape is immediately reinforced by the details of a nearby scene that features "Bones like sea corals; one bleached skull / A vase vined round and beautiful / With flowers" (68–71). The picture is a still life, a product of Nature, the supreme artist. In "Neither Believer nor Infidel," William B. Dillingham quotes the passage as an example of "nature's lack of reverence for man" (511), but surely nature has no reason to revere man or any of its other creations. Nathan is made aware of its power, for as he looks, he feels "with bated breath / The floral revelry over death" (71–72). When Paul Cezanne came to use skulls as objects in still life paintings, substituting them for fruits, vegetables, or dead game, the pictorial result was powerful and strange. Nathan's vision of death in such natural surroundings makes it only a part—perhaps not the most important part—of an immense and timeless pageantry.

Melville offers a powerful ekphrasis of the Dead Sea by associating it with Keats's poetic description of the Grecian urn. "The legend round a Grecian urn," he tells us, "the sylvan legend" is that of a vessel which certainly possesses the "Ionian form" that he considers requisite to beauty. Details of the "Venetian tint" may have been erased where "decay / Have wormed the garland all away, / And fire have left its Vandal burn," but he can assert that "beauty inextinct may charm / In outline of the vessel's form" (2.29.1–6). With this vision of the form of beauty before him, he looks at "Sodom, shore and sea" and finds that the form is there and that the "valley's sweep repays the glance, / And wavy curves of winding beach." As far as form is concerned, the sea might be as beautiful as Lake Como, Melville might have said; but he reverses the analogy, insisting that "Fair Como would like Sodom be / Should horror overrun the scene" where all that might be sylvan and blooming "is charred and crunched and riven." The sylvan parts of Keats's "flowery tale" of youth "beneath the trees" and of the carving of "brede / Of marble men and maidens overwrought / With forest branches and the trodden weed" are firmly before the mind of the poet writing of the "horror" of Sodom. Eye and mind suffer from comparing the scene on Keats's urn with the overpowering impression of the Dead Sea's precincts. It is a place that "Scarce seems of earth whereon we dwell," and this terrible vision leads to the ironic conclusion that "framed within the lines of heaven / The picture intimates a hell" (7–19). This pictorial diptych underlines Melville's forceful contention that "J. C. should have appeared in Taheiti" (*Journals* 158) and Rolfe's assertion, late in the poem, that "Tahiti should have been the place / For Christ in advent." The pilgrims have been considering "How wrought the sites of Bethlehem / On Western natures," and Rolfe's "musings" of Tahiti include "That vinewreathed urn of Ver, in sea / Of halcyons," a scene far removed from the Palestinian waste land (4.18.31–43).

Melville's brief experience of the Dead Sea contributes greatly to his description. The sea would have been Lake George, "all but verdure," and the "foam on beach & pebbles like slaver of mad dog." He tasted the bitterness of the water and saw a rainbow over the sea, raised because "heaven, after all, has no malice against it." A picnic would have been a fitting subject, with "nought to eat but bitumen & ashes with desert of Sodom apples washed down with water of Dead Sea" (*Journals* 83). When he came to jot down some ideas for imaginative works of prose or poetry, "bitterness" was the term that most engaged his thought and becomes, almost, a visual image: "Bitterness—Dead Sea. (Bitterness of Death)" (158).

This passage, descriptive of a "calcined" landscape, is like the portrayal, by Agath, the timoneer, of Narborough Isle, one of the Galapagos chain. Questioned by Vine as to whether he has seen any landscape that might "compare / With Judah here," Agath unfolds a description of "that isle which haunteth me." This is a set piece, and the poet makes it more so by claiming license in his rendering of what the "rude" timoneer actually says. The scene, burning and volcanic, is "leaden," "dull," and "sealed," and its "beach is cinders." The rocks form "A broken field of tumbled slabs / Like ice-cakes" and shape themselves into a place of worship, where they are "much worn down / Like to some old, old kneeling-stone / Before a shrine" (4.3.10–35). The sense of a shrine, something created, usually artistically, for a worshipful purpose, continues: "Paved with jet blocks those terraces, / The surface rubbed to unctuous gleam / By something which has life, you feel" (50–52). The timoneer has an overwhelming impression of Nature itself creating art, for he, it seems, is a living, breathing art object himself, his arm a "living fresco," with its tattooed crucifixion "A thing of art, vermil and blue" (4.2.50). The Narborough Isle ekphrasis revisits Melville's painterly world of Salvator Rosa and the "heaps of cinders" in the Spenserian landscapes of "The Encantadas." The fourth sketch of that work portrays "the grim and charred Enchanted Isles," placing Narborough "in the black jaws of Albermarle like a wolf's red tongue in his open mouth." In the first sketch, Melville had speculated on the "desolateness" of the islands, which could not evoke the sympathetic thoughts that cemeteries and ruins, "associated with humanity," might offer. He asserts that "even the Dead Sea, along with whatever other emotions it may at times inspire, does not fail to touch in the pilgrim some of his less unpleasurable feelings." In the fact of the visit to the Dead Sea, it is hard to find "less unpleasurable feelings."

THE PILGRIMS NEXT: WHOM NOW TO LIMN

Although landscape plays a crucial role in Melville's conception of the Holy Land that he visited, by offering "inscapes" to match the externality of a barren world, he conceived his poem as a number of set pieces, monologues, dialogues, and colloquies of his pilgrims. The literary portraiture in *Clarel* is vital to the successful realization of Melville's intentions, and he creates an impressive gallery of characters, often associating them with artworks. The beginning of the pilgrimage sounds somewhat like the prologue to *The Canterbury Tales,* but he makes a point of calling attention to the differences between his pilgrims and Chaucer's; there will be no franklin or squire, for instance, and there will be no "morris-dance / Of wit and story good as then" (2.1.10–11). (A morris dance, or Moorish dance, is one in which a story is acted out by costumed dancers.) Melville follows the lead of Chaucer's prologue by offering well-drawn preliminary depictions of several of his pilgrims as they embark on their horseback journey, and then, at least in some instances, of going to greater length within the later portions of the poem to establish each one's essence, or being.

Clarel himself is lightly drawn in the poem, but we know at once how he differs from such robust young men as Redburn and Ishmael. The "face he lifts— in features fine, / Yet pale, and all but feminine" (1.1.15–16) has more in common with Harry Bolton than with Redburn. As a student rather than one who has independently taken to the sea, he has

> a mind
> Earnest by nature, long confined
> Apart like Vesta in a grove
> Collegiate, but let to rove
> At last abroad among mankind. (106–10)

Association with the goddess of the hearth, and, perhaps with the Vestal Virgins who worship at her temple, may account for the feminine element in his nature and appearance. And, like the Vestal Virgins who have broken their vow, he is immured, as the poem opens, in the room of his inn, which is of "Masonry old, late washed with lime— / Much like a tomb new-cut in stone" (2–3). He is not given the chance, as Redburn and Ishmael were, of reviewing and recounting his tale after the passage of years. It is natural that he would seek, as Harry Bolton did in Redburn, a robust nature to fill a masculine element in his life, and he finds it in Rolfe. His name, Clarel, is unusual, and he may take both his name and situation from the pictorialism of heraldry, where it is associated with the armorial device of six martlets (Burke 198). Ruskin speaks of "The most brilliant, and . . . most effective of the arts—Heraldry," and surely an effective way of characterizing the young student is by offering him under a coat of arms that bears the martlet, the symbolic bird portrayed without feet and representing, perhaps, the younger son who has no footing in the inheritance of family property. Melville, fascinated by the art of heraldry, knew well the arms of his own family (*Clarel* 839–40) and used armorial devices as artworks often in his writings.

For Melville's depiction of Derwent, Chaucer's "A Knyght ther was, and that a worthy man" becomes a source of parody. "A priest he was—though but in part," is the observation, bolstered by a glance at Derwent's "prosperous look / That bordered vanity" and his "Fair color as from ruddy heart" (2.1.26–29). Since the Englishman is a combination of "cavalier and monk," Chaucer's satirical treatment of his monk is a subtext to Melville's portrait. Melville concentrates on his priest's worldly attitude, in which "Thought's last adopted style he showed." Derwent is very much "A priest of the club—a talking man," and Melville uses such physical details as the cloth cape and "cleric coat" as "emblems of that facile wit, / Which suits the age" (30–56). Bezanson perceptively draws attention to Derwent's resemblance to characters in other Melvillean works "who practice their law, medicine, or theology so professionally as to endanger their response to experience" and cites the lawyer-narrator of "Bartleby" and the minister, Falsgrave, in *Pierre* as good examples (*Clarel* 621).

In the canto of argument with Clarel, Derwent attempts to lessen the influence of other pilgrims upon the young man

> Our comrades—frankly let me say—
> That Rolfe, good fellow though he be,
> And Vine, methinks, would you but see,
> Are much like prints from plates but old. (3.21.286–89)

The simile is an attractive one, for much-used old plates would yield blurry prints rather than sharp pictures for the student to use in studying their approaches to religious belief. But Melville immediately cancels out such a happy

assessment of Derwent's art knowledge by posing him against a genuinely powerful work of art, a medallion at the monastery of Mar Saba,

> a shield of marble nigh,
> Set in the living rock: a stone
> In low relief, where well was shown,
> Before an altar under sky,
> A man in armor, visor down,
> Enlocked complete in panoply,
> Uplifting reverent a crown
> In invocation. (3.22.19–26)

There seems to be no actual source for the medallion (811), so that the description given it is, like that of Keats's urn, an ekphrasis of an invented artwork,
limned in careful detail without the burden of having to adhere to the factuality
of the real:

> This armed man
> In corselet showed the dinted plate,
> And dread streaks down the thigh-piece ran;
> But the bright helm inviolate
> Seemed raised above the battle-zone—
> Cherubic with a rare device:
> Perch for the bird of Paradise.
> A victor seemed he, without pride
> Of victory, or joy in fame:
> 'Twas reverence, and naught beside,
> Unless it might that shadow claim
> Which comes of trial. Yes, the art
> So cunning was, that it in part
> By fair expressiveness of grace
> Atoned even for the visored face. (27–41)

Melville's treatment of the piece of marble is imaginative. It might be difficult to
show the "dread streaks" on the armor, but perhaps the source is Chaucer's knight,
who "wered a gypon / Al besmotered with his habergeon." The helm's device,
"perch for the bird of Paradise," is a cross that, raised above the scene of battle, is
an indication of a Christian victory. Derwent's mood, as he views the medallion,
gives a sense of his superficiality. At first, he is "Charmed by the marble's quiet

mood / Of beauty" (43–44), but when he becomes convinced that the figure is not Achilles, then "straightway / He felt the charm in sort decline" (68–69). Derwent cannot recognize the figure of a Crusader in the low-relief sculpture, and his narrowness would make him, in any event, skeptical of the Crusades. The marble shield comes as close as anything can to disturbing Derwent's imperturbable mediocrity of vision, though he is very nearly able to shrug off the unsettling effect of this artwork, with its "unglad mystery," so strange to him, by conceding, "in his further range," that "travel teaches much that's strange" (3.23.1–5).

Derwent is again placed in close proximity to art when he resolves to visit the abbot, "the archimandrite." Here, he brings "to pass the thing / That he designed: which was to view / The treasures of this hermit-king." The blind old man prizes what he shows:

> Small shrines and reliquaries old:
> Beryl and Indian seed-pearl set
> In little folding-doors of gold
> And ivory, of triptych form,
> With starred Byzantine pictures warm,
> And opening into cabinet
> Where lay secured in precious stone
> The honeycombed gray-greenish bone
> Of storied saint. (3.23.78–86)

Although the abbot's treasures are worthy of reverence, and Derwent does offer it, he maintains a silent skepticism that the old man perceives. They engage in a dialogue about the miraculous powers of the relics, and Derwent's response to them, as might be expected, is "bland" as he asks, "Have miracles been wrought / From these?" But his superficial religious belief keeps him in suspension between faked reverence and ironic disbelief, so the art objects do not have the proper effect upon his spirit.

It is hardly possible that two personages could be less alike than Derwent and Vine, though they share a common lineage in their names. The Derwent is a British river, probably Wordsworthian, shallow, perhaps, but beautiful as a work of natural art and at the center of the Melvillean myth where "meditation and water are wedded forever" (*Moby-Dick* 4). And Vine is part of some deep mystical traditions: on the eve of his crucifixion, Christ says to his disciples, "I am the vine, ye are the branches: He that abideth in me, and I in him, the same bringeth forth much fruit" (John 15.5). Melville links Vine with laurel, mistletoe, and the Golden Bough, all sublime symbols of veneration. While Derwent is characterized by the device of placing him close to artworks, it is Vine's physical appearance in the pilgrim company, with his centrality to the poem's meanings, that evokes a powerful ekphrasis of sculpture and painting, for Vine himself is a work of art. In Clarel's first view of him, at the Sepulcher of Kings, before the journey of the pilgrims begins, he is posed against the frieze that mirrors both the Hellenic joy of Theocritus and the Hebraic grief of a text of Joel. He is vividly presented: "A low wind waves his Lydian hair; / A funeral man, yet richly fair— / Fair as the sabled violets be" (1.28.41–43). Vine's Lydian hair is in the style of carvings and friezes of the Lydians, the ancient Aegean peoples of Sardis and Smyrna, and thus art and man become joined in Melville's poetic view:

> The frieze and this secluded one,
> Retaining each a separate tone,
> Beauty yet harmonized in grace
> And contrast to the barren place. (44–47)

The next canto of the poem, "The Recluse," adds measurably to the portrait of Vine. Clarel first envisions him as the most potent of all figures in Melville's mythic iconography:

> If use he served not, but forbore—
> Such indolence might still but pine
> In dearth of rich incentive high:
> Apollo slave in Mammon's mine?
> Better Admetus' shepherd lie. (1.29.17–21)

Apollo had killed the Cyclopes, armorers to Zeus, and as punishment was first banished to Tartarus and then, upon a plea for mercy from Leto, his mother, was made to serve King Admetus of Pherae for a year in his sheepfolds. The Apollonian qualities of Vine are suggested both by his physical beauty and by his name, which may refer to the laurel wreath that crowns the head of Apollo in statues. The statue of the *Apollo Belvedere* features, as a support to the figure's form, a tree trunk embellished with laurel leaves. A further association is suggested by the allusions to mistletoe and the Golden Bough. In Turner's painting of *The Golden Bough*, the Apollonian Aeneas receives the sacred bough from the Cumaean Sibyl. A framed engraving of Turner's painting, part of Melville's collection of prints (Wallace, *Melville and Turner* 49, 613), is central to Melville's concept; Aeneas receives the bough, which Virgil compares to the mistletoe in winter, giving forth new leaves. In his portrait, the poet asserts Vine's "gifts unique," which, like the plant, "grow, / As on the tree the mistletoe" (1.29.4–6). Bezanson calls attention to the passage from the *Aeneid*, to the Turner print, and to the use of the mistletoe analogy (*Clarel* 745). With such apparent gifts in his person, it is no wonder that Vine "gleamed the richer for the shade / About him, as in sombre glade / Of Virgil's wood" (56–58). Like the Virgilian Aeneas, he is entering the underworld of his own enigmatic being. This allusion links Vine with Hawthorne, for Melville was no doubt well aware that his friend was often referred to as an "Apollo." The Hawthorne home in the Berkshires contained a bust of Apollo, and friends like William Ellery Channing wrote of Hawthorne as an Apollo figure.[2]

Melville further develops his verbal portrait of Vine by associating him with Christian legend and art. Though the poet denies that he is describing a saint, nevertheless Vine's

> charm of subtle virtue shed
> A personal influence coveted,
> Whose source was difficult to tell
> As ever was that perfumed spell
> Of Paradise-flowers invisible
> Which angels round Cecilia bred. (1.29.22–27)

A number of paintings celebrate Saint Cecelia. Melville's journal for March 30, 1857, reports his seeing Raphael's *St. Cecelia in Ecstasy* in Bologna, and he owned a print of Domenichino's *St. Cecelia* (Wallace, "Berkshire" 83, fig. 9). The "Paradise-flowers" are most likely the lily and rose, which symbolize the saint's purity and martyrdom. Melville almost surely knew the story of St. Cecelia from Chaucer's "Second Nun's Tale." This paradoxical ekphrasis of Vine, ranging from the masculine pagan Apollonian to the feminizing Christian saint, is part of Melville's taxonomy of human beauty. The beauty of Billy Budd, for example, is that "which the Greek sculptor in some instances gave to his heroic strong man, Hercules." In *Redburn*, Harry Bolton is "one of those small, but perfectly formed beings," his complexion "a mantling brunette, feminine as a girl's." Vine is between these extremes. As mature as the Apollo, as delicate as the fabled saint, he is no saint but possesses "the ripe flush, Venetian mould" (29) that Melville had noted in Venice in "the rich brown complexions of Titian's women drawn from nature, after all (Titian was a Venetian)" (*Journals* 119). And, in further paradox, Vine is "in sort Carthusian / Though born a Sybarite" (39–40).

For a final bit of portraiture in the canto, Melville draws deeply on Virgilian myth and its representation in pictorial terms. Vine is again drawn away from the monkish life:

> Cloisters? No monk he was, allow;
> But gleamed the richer for the shade
> About him, as in somber glade
> Of Virgil's wood the Sibyl's Golden Bough. (55–58)

Melville's language is painterly. "Gleamed," "shade," and "somber" strongly imply the shadings of chiaroscuro and characterize the shadings and rich light of Vine's complex character. Bezanson calls attention to the appropriate passage in Virgil's *Aeneid* and associates the description with J. M. W. Turner's *Lake Avernus, the Fates, and the Golden Bough* (*Clarel* 745). Wallace indicates that Melville probably saw Turner's painting in 1849 and perhaps again in 1857 and then, at some subsequent date, acquired J. T. Willimore's engraving of the painting ("Ambrose Group" 34–35). Aeneas, guided by the Sibyl of Cumae, receives the Golden Bough as a talisman and enters the underworld at Avernus. Richly reinterpreting the myth, Melville places Vine in a personal, perhaps hellish, underworld that seems to be of his own making.

When Clarel next sees Vine, he is a member of the group of pilgrims, though he is lagging behind the others and looking back, as if pursued. Indeed, he is pursued—by "reminiscence folded over," perhaps, or by "some deep moral fantasy." The projection of his character and visage is, again, complex, for there is "in face a dusk and shiver," as if he "heard amazed" and

> saw the phantom knight
> (Boccaccio's) with the dagger raised
> Still hunt the lady in her flight
> From solitude to solitude. (2.1.239–45)

The story, from *The Decameron,* puts Vine in the position of Boccaccio's young man, a witness to a continuously reenacted scene of horror and violence in which a knight, who has committed suicide for love, pursues his lover, disembowels her, and feeds heart and entrails to his dogs (*Clarel* 761). The tale has some points in common with the often-reenacted scene of Actaeon and the naked Artemis, a favored mythological subject for painters. If Vine is intended, partially, as a Melvillean portrayal of Nathaniel Hawthorne, the story has points of reference with Hawthornesque tales. Goodman Brown is the unwilling witness to the supernatural scene in the forest. Reuben Bourne's expiation for his failure to bury Roger Malvin comes as a result of his participating in, and being a witness to, the almost ritualistic murder of his son. Vine, as a character, is in part a portrait drawn from Hawthorne, in part a figure from classical sculpture, and he takes some of his form and color from religious legendry and from Titian's golds and browns.[3]

But the most revealing of all the portraits of Vine occurs in the third book of the poem, where Clarel observes him:

> He wore that nameless look
> About the mouth—so hard to brook—
> Which in the Cenci portrait shows,
> Lost in each copy, oil or print;
> Lost, or else slurred, as 'twere a hint
> Which, if received, few might sustain:
> A trembling over of small throes
> In weak swoll'n lips, which to restrain
> Desire is none, nor any rein. (3.7.17–25)

By the time he wrote this passage, Melville must have read Hawthorne's remarks on the Guido Reni portrait of *Beatrice Cenci* in the *Italian Notebooks,* as well as the description in chapter 7 of *The Marble Faun*. Hilda has studied the portrait, since permission has not been given for it to be copied. Hilda's picture shows "a sorrow that removed this beautiful girl out of the sphere of humanity, and set her in a far-off remote region, the remoteness of which—while yet her face is so close before us makes us shiver as at a spectre." The expression is lost or slurred because, in the language of Hawthorne's Miriam, "Everywhere we see oil-paintings, crayon-sketches, cameos, engravings, lithographs, pretending to be Beatrice, and representing the poor girl with blubbered eyes, a leer of coquetry, a merry look as if she were dancing, a piteous look as if she were beaten, and twenty other modes of fantastic mistakes."

Clarel, withdrawing from the other pilgrims, has "passed among the crags" and seen "there / Like David in Adullum's lair— / Could it be Vine, and quivering so?" (13–16). David is in the cave Adullam (1 Sam. 22) because he is fleeing the wrath of Saul and has had to feign madness to escape death. In his Bible, Melville had marked some relevant passages in Samuel. David relieved Saul of his evil spirit by playing the harp (16.23), a subject treated by Browning in his poem "Saul." After the battle with the Philistines and David's slaying of Goliath, he is greatly praised and Saul is "very wroth" and "displeased," suspicious that David may get his kingdom, so that he "eyed David from that day and forward" (18.9). In the next verse that Melville marked (18.15), because David has acted wisely and "the Lord was with him," Saul "was afraid of him." The passage about David at Adullam is not marked. Melville has Vine seek a hiding place because he, like Clarel, is moved by the cry of Jesus crucified and, apparently, forsaken (Mark 15.34). If Vine wears the nameless look of Beatrice, it is because, according to the apocryphal story, she is portrayed in the painting on the night before her execution and is likewise forsaken. Christ on the Cross is the subject of much iconography, His anguish a larger thing than Vine's. Real anguish and real fear can be conjured up from Old and New Testament exempla and from Renaissance legendry, but not from Vine's nineteenth-century "small throes."

As Vine represents the internalized, doubting, hypersensitive temperament of the artist, Rolfe is depicted in an opposite light, a man, in Bezanson's words, who "is an experienced world-traveler, mariner, and intellectual who quickly assumes leadership among the pilgrims" (631). To Clarel's view,

> Trapper or pioneer
> He looked, astray in Judah's seat—
> Or one who might his business ply
> On waters under tropic sky. (1.31.4–7)

The depiction of his physical characteristics is vivid and intricate, a mingling of art and myth, for he is, in some part, a living work of art:

> He rose, removed his hat to greet,
> Disclosing so in shapely sphere
> A marble brow over face embrowned:
> So Sunium by her fane is crowned.
> One read his superscription clear—
> A genial heart, a brain austere—
> And further, deemed that such a man
> Though given to study, as might seem,
> Was no scholastic partisan
> Or euphonist of Academe,
> But supplanted Plato's theme
> With daedal life in boats and tents. (1.31.9–20)

On his brief sojourn in Greece as he returned from Palestine in 1857, Melville did not record seeing Sunium, crowned with its fane, though he might have caught some glimpse of it around February 8. Since his allusion is literary and artistic, a probable source for it is a book he acquired in 1871, Christopher Wordsworth's *Greece: Pictorial, Descriptive, and Historical* (1844), which, along with text, featured "three hundred and fifty engravings on wood and twenty-eight on steel, illustrative of the scenery, architecture, and costume of that country." Wordsworth provides an engraving of the site and describes the ruins of the structure that he identifies as a temple of Minerva at Sunium. It stands "like the Portico or Vestibule of Athens," the whiteness of its marble visible from a great distance, to remind the traveler approaching it from the south, "by the fair proportions of its architecture, and by the decorations of sculpture and of painting with which it was adorned, that he was coming to a land illustrious for its skill in the most graceful Arts." Attica was thus "a sacred Temenos, whose boundaries were Seas and Mountains, and whose Propylaea was the Temple of Minerva on the promontory of Sunium" (128). Like the white marble temple of Minerva, the goddess of wisdom, the marbled brow of Rolfe is the propylaeum, or entrance, to the temple of his "brain austere."[4] Davis perceptively notes that "Rolfe joins religious desire with aesthetic and sensuous appreciation" (144). Melville captures both in his portrayal of the brow as the locus of both wisdom and the beautiful architectural realization of devotion.

The marble of brow above the embrowning earth and rock is a "noble superscription" of the proper fusion of heart and head, the distinguishing trait that sets Rolfe off from Vine. In "Ethan Brand" Hawthorne had drawn the archetypal personage whose intellect had overborne his heart, the seat of feelings, so that it "had withered,—had contracted,—had hardened,—had perished." When Brand, so branded, throws himself despairingly into the kiln to perish, his heart retains its shape, as though made of marble. Rolfe, equipped with a marble brow, escapes such a characterization with his "genial heart," which continues to give him what Hawthorne called a "hold on the magnetic chain of humanity." If Melville is providing, in Vine, a parodic portrait of Hawthorne, he is probably offering a parodic portrait of himself in Rolfe to establish the differences between the two men. He finds himself, like Rolfe, "Too frank, too unreserved, may be, / And indiscreet in honesty" (24–25).

Rolfe's "daedal life" sets him off from the other pilgrims. Aspects of the word "daedal" include its hints of artistry, aesthetic cunning, and insistence upon the labyrinthine. Rolfe is an artist in his word-painting and in his understanding, in his description of Petra, of what art does. "Mid such a scene / Of Nature's terror, how serene / That ordered form," he says. Daedal also means "of the earth," an important element in Rolfe's complex character, for it softens the hardness of his marble intelligence and brings the necessary leavening of the coldness by adding the fertility of the soil.

Clarel tries to estimate the two men as he "glanced from him to Vine; / Peers, peers—yes, needs that these must pair." They are "Exceptional natures, of a weather / Strange as the tropics with strange trees, / Strange birds strange fishes, skies and trees" (41–42, 45–47). Rolfe has within him some "tinge of the soil— / Like tarnish" in his look to match what, in his character, is a "touch of the unto-ward / In aspect hinting nothing froward" (27–31). The "untoward" is some-thing refractory in one's nature, and "froward" is stubborn, contrary, and obsti-nate; Rolfe, paradoxically, is one but not the other. The soil, too, although it relieves him of the classical hardness of marble, has its own taint. Like all Melvillean characters, he has a tarnish somewhere in his nature, though he is closest, in the poem, to a complete personality.

Bezanson characterizes Ruth as "Less a person than a symbol of vestal love" (*Clarel* 632), and, thus, she is a suitable foil for Clarel, who was "long confined / Apart like Vesta." Melville, with his usually subtle onomastic sense, has given her the name of the Old Testament book and personage, the woman who, with her mother-in-law, Naomi, goes to Bethlehem after the deaths of her husband and his father. There she remarries and bears a son who will be an ancestor of David. The biblical story suggests what Goethe had called "the loveliest little idyll that tradition has transmitted to us," and Clarel's courting of his Ruth should be an idyllic and attractive portion of the poem. It does not turn out that way, how-ever, and the love story is at first underplayed and then made tragic in a curi-ously muted manner. Melville's treatment of what ought to be a central fact of Clarel's life becomes a pessimistic comment on the tragic consequences of love.

When Clarel, in company with Nehemiah, visits the "Wall of Wail," he first sees Ruth. She is thus shown poised against a huge masterpiece of architectural art, an "Ararat / Founded on beveled blocks how wide, / Reputed each a stone august / Of Solomon's fane" (1.16.88–91), and, even in such an impressive set-ting, she resembles a precious work of art, for "She looked a legate to insure / That Paradise is possible / Now" (163–65). With her "Eve-like face," she must resemble the artworks that Melville saw in Rome. Looking at the Vatican fres-coes based upon the designs of Raphael, which Melville recorded seeing on March 2, 1857, "The Loggie—piazzas—sky between columns—Adam & Eve—The Eve—" (*Journals* 108). Christian and pagan elements intermix in the portrait in Ruth's "Nereid eyes with virgin spell." Her nereid eyes and other characteristics con-trast with those of her mother. Nathan, Ruth's father, met "A Jewess who about him threw / Else than Nerea's amorous net / And dubious wile. 'Twas Miriam's race" (1.17.203–05). Agar, "A sibyl, but a woman too," does not practice the wiles of Nerea, or Nereis, or Eurybia, the sea nymph who, as Doris, mothered, with Nereus, the fifty nereids. But Ruth nevertheless inherited, if not from her mother then from elsewhere, something of the nereid quality. As Perseus fascinates Melville as an archetype of the vividly pictorial, so do the nereids so often associated with him. They enter into Melville's painterly thinking, in this case from such pictures as Guido Reni's *Perseus Rescuing Andromeda*. Cassiopeia, mother of Andromeda, boasted that her daughter and she were more beautiful than the nereids. When the sea nymphs complained to Poseidon, he sent the sea monster that Perseus must slay in order to rescue Andromeda.

Ruth's portrait continues in a deepening sense of paradox. She seems a dove, it is true, but "deeper viewed, / What was it that looked part amiss? / A bit impaired? what lack of peace?" Even at this early stage there is a feeling of fated mystery about the girl that will play its way out in later portions of the poem. Still, Melville quiets these intangible feelings by the delicately coloristic depiction of the girl's features:

> Hebrew the profile, every line,
> But as in haven fringed with palm,
> Which Indian reefs embay from harm,
> Belulled as in the vase the wine—
> Red budded corals in remove,
> Peep coy through quietudes above;
> So through clear olive of the skin,
> And features finely Hagarene;
> Its way a tell-tale flush did win—
> A tint which unto Israel's sand
> Blabbed of the June in some far clover land. (178–88)

Melville's portrait of Ruth, like those of Lucy Tartan and Isabel, is a promising development and seems to signal a softening element in the generally harsh picture of the world that Clarel has entered. He has been "bereft while still young, / Mother or sister had not known." But his love for Ruth and the welcome into her family allow Melville the use of some religious pictorialism. Noticing "What charm to woman may belong / When by a natural bent inclined," he concludes that "On earth no better thing than this— / It canonizes very clay," and apostrophizes the eternal female and maternal with "Madonna, hence thy worship is" (1.39.16–26). In Bologna, on March 30, 1857, Melville recorded his visit "To the Gallery. The Madonna of the Rosary." As Horsford notes, he could have seen

Madonnas by Lodovico Caracci or Zampieri Domenichino (*Journals* 116, 499). In his copy of Valery's *Travels,* which he seems to have been using as a guidebook during this tour, Melville marked the descriptions of a number of paintings, including the Domenichino *Madonna,* "with its shower of roses, and the sublime old man's head" (Cowen 2:711).

Melville's satirical portraiture is reserved for the unnamed pilgrim known simply as a "banker of the rich Levant" who lives in "Thessalonica, / Which views Olympus" (2.1.105, 111–12). Like Chaucer's franklin, he is vividly realized: "Parisian was his garb, and gay. / Upon his saddle-pommel lay / A rich Angora rug, for shawl / Or pillow" (119–22). The banker is a generalized realization of a servant of Mammon (*Clarel* 616–17). His place in the poem is as a foil to a religious ascetic such as Nehemiah. A heavy smoker, he is visibly uncomfortable on the journey—" Florid overmuch and corpulent, / Labored in lungs, and audibly" (2.12.19 –20). Rolfe generously changes horses with him and then, in reflecting upon this representative of Mammon, places him in an unusual connection with examples of the visual arts:

> Ill would it accord
> If nabob with asthmatic breath
> Lighted on Holbein's Dance of Death
> Sly slipped among his prints from Claude.
> Cosmetic-users scarce are bold
> To face a skull. (28–33)

The Claudian landscapes, attractive and soothing, would have offered the old banker an unpleasing jolt if Holbein's unsavory depiction of death turned up among them.

The banker has no name, but as Ekaterina Georgoudaki has shown, he is closely based on Djékis Abbot, whom Melville had met on his journey. His journal for December 7, 1856, records a visit to "Abbots place enclosed by high thick stone wall," where he viewed conspicuous signs of wealth and was "Served with sweetmeats & liqueurs & coffee" (*Journals* 55–56). As usual, Melville's journal entry is only a hint of all he has observed; he will depend on his capacious memory to enliven his portrait.

For all that he is associated with art, the banker simply considers artworks another possession. Irritable about his companions on the pilgrimage, he regards them as "Pedants and poor! nor used to dine / In ease of table-talk benign —/ Steeds, pictures, ladies, gold, Tokay, / Gardens and baths, the English news, / Stamboul, the market" (2.10.187–91). Prints of Claudian landscapes or even of

Holbein's allegory of death, statues in his garden, and an architectural master-piece of a house are the signs of wealth and power. Even the possession of a prospective son-in-law in Glaucon, his young companion on the pilgrimage, lends stature to his economic superiority. The pilgrimage itself is not under-taken, as it is with others, from a deep desire to see the outward forms of reli-gious feeling. He has "dull time to kill" and, with the young man, "Scarce through self-knowledge or self-love / They ventured Judah's wilds to rove" (2.1.173–76).

Mortmain is first characterized by his name, for "so in whim / Some moral wit had christened him" (2.1.190–91). To be christened is more than to be named or nicknamed. This person is baptized with the name of "dead hand," a fitting cognomen to his system of theological belief. In *The Spirit Above the Dust,* Ronald Mason perceptively suggests that Mortmain "is a more intellectual, more disil-lusioned Bulkington" who finds no comfort in idealism and detachment, until finally he "asks no more than oblivion, and oblivion is all he gets" (237). Here is a striking indication that, in some ways, *Clarel* may be thought of as a reconsid-ered *Moby-Dick,* developing and amplifying ideas proposed in the novel. Melville conspicuously withholds details of portraiture of Mortmain in the long descrip-tion given of his background (2.4) but makes him into an artist of sorts in "The Inscription" (2.31). Derwent discovers a rock on which Mortmain has "Traced in dull chalk" a kind of picture—"a cross; three stars in row / Upright, two more for thwarting limb / Which drooped oblique" (22–24). He is somewhat like the carpenter in *Moby-Dick* who paints vermilion stars on Stubbs's paddle. The pil-grims attempt to make sense of his rather crude device, created in "passion's whim," as Vine puts it, musing "in silent heart." It might be the representation of the Southern Cross, Clarel believes, and is seconded by Rolfe. But like painters who will not let the image speak for itself, but, in the manner of Turner, append verses to explain the pictorial, Mortmain has resorted to verse. Bereft of Turner's pictorial skill, he is a somewhat better poet. He sees the "device" in the language of coats of arms. The stars are "emblazoned," as it were in the skies, and, as "symbols vain," have simply "declined to heraldries" (53–59). As we have seen with the hieroglyphs of Queequeg's religion, when the living qualities of a belief have "declined" into artistic representation, meaning has somehow been lost, as it may have been done in the case of "Orion's sword." If this is so, then "In con-stellations unadored, / Christ and the giant equal prize" (70–71). Bryan C. Short discusses Mortmain's song as one of those that "reaffirm the significance of a faith" or "conveys the attractiveness of the dead symbol" (563). But, instead, his rough scrawling on the rock seems to confirm his status: *"By one who wails the loss, / This altar to the Slanting Cross"* (46–47).

In the canto, "Mortmain Reappears" (2.34), we are given a sense of the Swede's actual appearance. The pilgrims, eager enough to see him, nevertheless "shrank or fell adroop" at sight of him, and with good reason. He is portrayed in menacing terms:

> Like Hecla ice inveined with marl
> And frozen cinders showed his face
> Rigid and darkened. Shunning parle
> He seated him aloof in place,
> Hands clasped about the knees drawn up
> As round the cask the binding hoop—
> Condensed in self, or like a seer
> Unconscious of each object near,
> While yet, informed, the nerve may reach
> Like wire under wave to furthest beach. (2.34.10–19)

The frozen spewings of the Icelandic volcano, once active and fiery but now immovable, match the name of Mortmain and his face, "Rigid and darkened." While around it, as Sabine Baring-Gould wrote in his travel book, *Iceland* (1863), "clustered the white heads of the mountain asphodel" (190). Asphodel, as the mystic sign of Agath, is life below the death of fire. Melville thus sets up a contrast between the two men by his use of pictorial techniques.

Agath, the "pilgrim-timoneer," is a human work of art—carved, wrinkled, and tattooed. His "weird and weather-beaten face, / Bearded and pitted, and fine vexed / With wrinkles of cabala text" (3.12.32–34), like the tattooed face of Queequeg, is embellished with a once-meaningful symbolical and now cabalistic set of lines and forms that heralds an occult and esoteric theosophy too withdrawn from human considerations to be seen otherwise as art. He possesses "a beauty grave" bald except for "a silvery round / Of small curled bud-like locks which bound / His temples as with asphodel" (42–44).

The simile of the asphodel is resonant with myth, poetry, and the pictorial. In the eleventh book of the *Odyssey*, the great journey into the underworld to seek knowledge from Tiresias, Odysseus encounters Achilles, who first expresses his pain at being dead and then asks news of his son Neoptolemus. Odysseus praises the young man's actions in the Trojan Horse:

> This made the soul of swift Achilles tread
> A march of glory through the herby mead,

> For joy to hear me so renown his son;
> And vanish'd stalking.

The translation is Chapman's (11.731–34) and is emphatically marked in Melville's copy (Cowen 2.53). Chapman's version does not mention the asphodel, but Melville would have known that it is the flower of the Elysian fields. In Milton's *Comus* he could have read "To embathe / In nectared leaves strewed with asphodel" (838), and his favorite Thomas Browne spoke, in *Hydriotaphia*, of how "The dead are made to eat Asphodels about the Elysian meadows." A more recent reminder would have been Tennyson, who wrote in "The Lotos-Eaters" of "some, 'tis whispered—down in hell / Suffer endless anguish, others in Elysian valleys dwell, / Resting weary limbs at last on beds of asphodel" (168–70). Agath's arm is "a living fresco," as Derwent calls it. It is "A thing of art, vermeil and blue, / A crucifixion in tattoo, / With trickling blood-drops strange to see." This portion of the pictograph, with its bright red and blue on a field of white, the man's arm, would greatly resemble a medallion or coat of arms. But Derwent's characterization of the entire illustration as fresco is justified because of the complexity of the incised images:

> Above that emblem of the loss,
> Twin curving palm-boughs draping met
> In manner of a canopy
> Over an equi-limbed small cross
> And three tri-spiked and equal crowns:
> And under these a star was set:
> And all was tanned and toned in browns.
>   In chapel erst which knew the mass,
> A mullioned window's umber glass
> Dyed with some saintly legend old,
> Obscured by cobwebs; this might hold
> Some likeness to the picture rare
> On arm here webbed with straggling hair. (4.2.50–65)

The ekphrasis is doubly proposed in the backgrounds offered for the embellishments. The old man's arm, "tanned and toned in browns," rivals the "window's umber glass" of the chapel that Melville adds as the other element of his simile. The elaborate symbolism of palm boughs, cross, crowns, and star is lost on Agath, who believes that it "by some / A charm is held 'gainst watery doom" (95–96). But it is a signal to the others, who interpret or question it as they will. Derwent's interpretation is the most conventional, as might be expected. The palm signifies Judea, the crowns are those of the magi, the star is that of Bethlehem, and the "cross scarce needs a word, agree" (131–36). Rolfe, more learned, more interpretative, and more historically attuned, links the tattoo with the marks of pilgrims who have made the journey to Calvary (*Clarel* 821–23), as well as with the artistic renditions of Crusaders who bore the artwork upon armor or body. As Rolfe justly concludes, it is another form of religious art that has lost its significance, and "Losing the import and true key, / Descends to boatswains of the brine" (124–25). Agath, like Queequeg, is a living work of art who cannot speak the message of his pictographs.

HUGE BE THE BUTTRESSES

Architecture, as a powerful and impressive art form, plays a significant role in the poem, casting its spell over pilgrims and tourists. In Palestine one is overwhelmed by buildings built on ruins and, often, built of ruins. As any pilgrim must, Clarel makes his expected visit to that most revered shrine, the Church of the Holy Sepulcher, where he sees, "in sculptured stone, / Dim and defaced" the depiction of "the march / Of Christ into another gate— / The golden and triumphal one, / Upon Palm's Morn." This exhibition of the entrance's sculptured stone entrance should be compared to Melville's ironic description in his journal entry: "Much elaborate sculpture once graced what is now visible of the original facade; but Time has nibbled it away, till it now looks like so much spoiled pastry at which the mice have been at work" (*Journals* 89). Bartlett's *Walks about the City and Environs of Jerusalem,* one of Melville's often-used sources in his composition of the poem, provides an engraving of the church that offers a more neutral picture, perhaps in keeping with the more neutral language of the poem. The picture shows hardly any of the defacement of the entryway (*Clarel* 714).

Several of the architectural features of the city are visited and alluded to but without much attempt at pictorial depiction. The Golden Gate (1.10.75–104), David's Tower (1.11.65–77), and the Ecce Homo Arch (1.13.20–30) are each given their place and do add a portion of the movement in the poem, but they remain unclear, as a guidebook notation might. Melville is not intent upon giving equal weight to all the historically interesting features of the pilgrimage. However, his pictorial sense operates briefly but effectively in his description of "The Wall of Wail." Clarel and Nehemiah follow a group of pilgrims and, in a "sunken yard / Obscure, where dust and rubbish blow," they observe the wall,

> Massed up immense, an Ararat
> Founded on beveled blocks how wide
> Reputed each a stone august
> Of Solomon's fane. (1.16.85–92)

This impressive piece of architecture links art and history, and the illustration provided in Bartlett's *Walks about the City and Environs of Jerusalem* (*Clarel* 733), which Melville acquired before writing the passage, gave him the chance to pursue his "object, the saturation of my mind with the atmosphere of Jerusalem, offering myself up a passive subject, and no unwilling one, to its weird impressions" (*Journals* 86).

Full ekphrastic description is given to "The rifled Sepulcher of Kings" when Ruth and Clarel, as new young lovers, visit this "waste where beauty clings." The sepulcher, itself a work of art, is embellished with the works of artists:

> Hewn from the rock a sunken space
> Conducts to garlands—fit for vase—
> In sculptured frieze above a tomb:
> Palm leaves, pine apples, grapes. These bloom,
> Involved in dearth—to puzzle us—
> As 'twere thy line, Theocritus,
> Dark Joel's text of terror threading:
> Yes, strange that Pocahontas-wedding
> Of contraries in old belief—
> Hellenic cheer, Hebraic grief.
> The homicide Herods, men aver,
> Inurned behind that wreathage were. (1.28.25–36)

The passage is full, even clotted, with the results of Melville's observation, reading, and thought. The line of Theocritus, embodying Hellenic cheer, is not made clear from the context, but Joel's "text of terror" and an example of "Hebraic grief" might be the passage that Melville marked: "Egypt shall be a desolation, and Edom shall be a desolate wilderness, for the violence against the children of Judah, because they have shed innocent blood in their land" (Joel 3:19). Melville enriches this canto by using the opportunity to introduce Vine in this stony atmosphere of vine leaves and ruins, for Vine surely combines the contrarieties of Hellenic and Hebraic.

The most spectacular example of architectural ekphrasis in the poem occurs in the canto "Of Petra." Melville had met a "Petra party" (*Journals* 80), but Clarel and the pilgrims will not ride south to see the long-deserted city, and so Derwent asks Rolfe for a description. The features in Rolfe's monologue are those mentioned by other visitors to the Red City. Above the "purple gloom" of the cliffs, the natural beauty of oleanders mixes with the "rosy stain" of the rock that forms "porch and pediment in crag." Rolfe expresses his astonishment: "One starts. In Esau's waste are blent / Ionian form, Venetian tint" (2.30.18–19).

We have seen Melville create ekphrastic representations of existent artworks that he has observed and have noted how he can create descriptions of imaginary art objects. Here he moves into new reaches of rhetorical pictorialism in evoking a real masterpiece of architecture that he has never seen. For this accomplishment, as Bezanson has carefully documented it, he was dependent upon the description of Petra in Arthur Stanley's *Sinai and Palestine.* Stanley is insistent upon the array of colors at the site: "All the describers have spoken of bright hues—scarlet, sky-blue, orange, etc. Had they taken the courage to say instead, 'dull crimson, indigo, yellow, and purple' their account would have lost something in effect, but gained much in truth. Nor really would it have lost much any way. For the colours, though not gaudy,—or rather because they are not gaudy,— are gorgeous" (Cowen 2:611). Stanley thus provides the elements of Melville's "Venetian tint," an effect noted during his stay in Venice. The journal entry for April 6, 1857, reports his response to the scene of a "shining lagoon through windows draped with rosy silks . . . silver censers" a scene with a "Great gorgeousness of effect" (119). The beautiful women that he sees, with skins of "clear, rich, golden brown," are like those of Titian's, with their "rich brown complexions." He notes St. Mark's "at sunset, gilt mosaics, pinnacles," and "precious marbles, from extreme age," that "look like a mosaic of rare old soaps." No wonder the splendid colors cause him to reflect, "Rather be in Venice on a rainy day, than any other capital on fine one" (119–20). Something of this buoyancy of colors gets into the description of Petra.

In addition to his reading and marking in Stanley, Melville also marked relevant passages about Petra in his copy of Bartlett's *Forty Days in the Desert.* Bartlett is always conscious of previous explorers. Setting out on his "formidable" journey he is especially aware of "a feeling of melancholy" while standing "within a stone's throw too of the grave of poor Burckhardt" (Cowen 1:163). He later praises Burckhardt's account, the "accurate notes of Irby and Mangles" and Count Leon de Laborde and M. Linant, who obtained "materials for the splendid work which first introduced Petra to the European public," and knows the "lively account" of John Lloyd Stephens. El Deir is "a remarkable architectural facade" with a "most singular . . . very mysterious appearance" (167). He notes "the wonderful contrasts of the colouring, the variety of the overhanging foliage of the wild fig, the crimson-flowered oleander, and the trailing bright-green plants, with the plan of light and shade among the rocks." With triple side-lines, Melville marked a passage descriptive of the whole scene of edifices, where "The mass of crags out of which they are hewn is also most picturesque, rising in numerous jagged points and clefts" (168). Bartlett's experience as an artist is demonstrated in his remarks about the colors of the rocks, a passage that Melville partially marked:

> The general tinting of the sandstone mountains environing the city is very fine; the broad rich red and grey tones such as the artist revels in; but, in addition, the surface of the rocks is veined after the manner of watered silk, with a most inde-scribably and startling variety of hues—white, saffron, orange, vermillion, pink, crimson, and violet, in endless shades and tints, in some places forming combina-tions really beautiful. (168)

He marked another passage on El Deir, which offers, "from its vastness and the wildness of its situation, an impression almost of awe." Bartlett's artistic eye takes note that "it is very defective in its style, for it is ponderous without gran-deur, and elaborate without elegance" (168). Perhaps this is what Rolfe means by the door "sculptured in elfin freak."

The "Ionian form" is present in poetic phrases limning the shapes of Petra, the "porch and pediment in crag." The dizzying heights surrounding these great architectural entryways to temple and tomb mark the sublimity of the deserted city, where

> Mid such a scene
> Of Nature's terror, how serene
> That ordered form. Nor less 'tis cut
> Out of that terror—does abut
> Thereon: there's Art. (41–45)

The passage, splendidly depicting a fabulous work of art, presents a problem, that of function within the large structure of the poem. The word "abut" is par-ticularly relevant, since the elaborately carved fronts of the Khasne and other cliff constructions promise more than is behind them in the caves. Bezanson cites the themes of the passage as "that the charm of expectation surpasses ful-fillment, that art is an ordered form on the rim of the abyss, and that all solicita-tions for final meanings remain unanswered"; he makes the point that the canto is "an episodic intrusion" that "may have been added at any time" (*Clarel* 784).

Shirley Dettlaff makes the passage an essential part of Melvillean aesthetics, point-ing out that, while "the serenity of ordered form can co-exist with the terror of nature's chaos," there is not a complete transformation—"the carved buildings create only a momentary relief from inhospitable surroundings" (215–16).

However, Melville's ekphrasis plays a functional part in the poem. The Petra canto is embedded in a discussion initiated by Derwent and Rolfe at the shore of the Dead Sea. To the south of the pilgrim's route is Mount Hor and "prohibited Seir / In cut-off Edom" (2.29.78–79). Nehemiah then brings up the curse of God upon Edom, "None there pass through—no, never, never," a paraphrase of the biblical "none shall pass through it for ever and ever" (Isa. 34:10). The theme is further established in Ezekiel 35:3 in the words of God, "O mount Seir, I am against thee, and I will make thee most desolate." After the rediscovery in 1812 of Petra, the deserted city in Edom, its long desolation was interpreted by some as the desolation foretold by the Lord. In the discussion, Margoth and Derwent disagree with the predominant theory. "My friend Max Levi, he passed through," Margoth says (85), and Derwent remarks that one must

> make allowance meet
> For Orientalism's display
> In Scripture, where the chapters treat
> Of mystic themes. (98–101)

"Ay, Keith's grown obsolete" (104), claims Margoth (referring to the writings of Alexander Keith, the most prominent of the writers who argued for the curse of God and the desolation of Edom [*Clarel* 783–84]). Rolfe, as someone who has passed through Petra, is a vivid proof of the ineffectiveness of the curse.

Stanley, Melville's chief source for the Petra canto, does not enter into the argument of God's curse upon the city. It is clear that Melville knew of Keith's argument, and he may have known another book that described the Red City. John G. Kinnear's *Cairo, Petra, and Damascus in 1839* (London 1841), written as a series of letters, contains an interesting account of Petra. Kinnear, accompa-nied by the artist, David Roberts, discovered that, when he first saw the city, his "expectations were far more than realised." The passage continues

> It is certainly one of the most wonderful scenes in the world. The eye wanders in
> amazement from the stupendous rampart of rocks which surrounds the valley to
> the porticoes and ornamented doorways sculptured on its surface. The dark yawn-
> ing entrances of the temples and tombs, and the long range of excavated cham-
> bers, give an air of emptiness and desolation to the scene. . . . But in the valley

itself, the patches of green corn among the ruins, the stream bordered with oleander and willow, the sweet sound of running water, and the cry of the cuckoo and
partridge, were all delightful and refreshing after the silence and dreary solitude
of the Desert. (132)

Kinnear sees and describes all the outstanding sites, the Khasne, El Syk, the
"convent," or "El Dier," as he calls it in contradiction of other writers who settle
for "El Deir." He concludes with an earnest consideration of the prophetic curse
and disagrees by citing the passage of pilgrims through the country and "a
party of merchants" who "bivouacked beside us one night" and told of passing
through annually. Moreover, the streams and land have not turned into pitch,
nor the dust into brimstone, as the prophecy had claimed. Kinnear's explanation is that the prophecy has a "double application, to the visible and to a mystical Edom, as the prophecies against Babylon are applied in a secondary sense
to Rome, the mystical Babylon" (156–57). Kinnear's use of "mystical" for the
prophecies is seemingly echoed in Derwent's "mystic themes" in Scripture.

Derwent's innocent-sounding skepticism extends beyond the prophecies in
the Petra canto. To Rolfe's "a dream the Edomite," he makes the rejoinder that

> dreamers all who dream of him—
> Though Sinbad's pleasant in the skim.
> Paestum and Petra: good to use
> For sedative when one would muse. (60–64)

A skim is superficial, and so are the wonderful adventures of Sinbad. Paestum,
the ruined Greek colony of Sybaris famed for its temples, is as minatory as Petra
but does not bear the burden of the Lord's curse. The lesson is driven home in
the next canto when the cross and stars are discovered chalked upon a rock with
a "mystical" verse about "symbols vain once counted wise, / And gods declined
to heraldries" (2.31.52, 58–59). The versifier then questions the Cross,

> When, ages hence, they lift their eyes
> Tell, what shall they retain of thee?
> But class thee with Orion's sword?
> In constellations unadored,
> Christ and the Giant equal prize? (67–71)

The Cross, not nearly as marvelous a pictorial apparition as the city of Petra,
nevertheless adds its point about the skeptical religious view.

The matter of Petra and the Cross is part of a problem enunciated by Rolfe, who earlier stated that "All's now revised: / Zion, like Rome, is Niebuhrized" (1.34.18–19). Barthold Niebuhr's *History of Rome* "sought to winnow out factual history from the long accumulations of myth and legend" (*Clarel* 753). In turn, George Grote's *History of Greece,* in its earlier chapters, sought to Niebuhrize Grecian myth and history, as John Stuart Mill's *Edinburgh Review* essay pointed out. Zion, as Rolfe observes, is being Niebuhrized and so, as he may have added, is the great mythic city of Petra. The author of the verses shown with the Cross certainly wonders if Christianity will become as much a myth as the Greek myths.

By attaching to the lengthy third part of the poem, with its thirty-two cantos, the name of "Mar Saba," Melville gives this architectural gem its rightfully central place in the poem, and its ekphrasis extends over many lines of poetry. The ninth canto approaches the subject prelusively by evoking monasteries in a great range of other places and times—one in the Alps, a "desert convent of the Copts" in Egypt, one near Mount Olympus, others in the Grand Chartreuse, Vallambrosa, and Montserrat (3.9.1–32). Saba, however, is unique; as "the loneliest," which "with an eagle's theft / Seizeth and dwelleth in the cleft" of the high mountainous region. The Greek monastery is graced by a splendid heraldic standard, "With mystic silvery brede divine, / St. Basil's banner of Our Lord . . . Stained with the five small wounds and red" (53–57). The monastery church, "the minster," is rich in embellishment, "Gilded with venerable gold," and possessed of riches in "Plate of Byzantium, stones and spars, / Urim and Thummin, gold and green"; the Old Testament is read aloud "From parchment, not plebeian print." Even Derwent, suspicious as always of whatever clashes with his rather utilitarian Anglican world, finds the church "A goodly fane" (1–30, 53).

The monastery is impressive from every vantage point. Clarel, on the watch-towers with Derwent, has a view of "All the mountain-land . . . poised as in a chaos true, / Or throe-lock of transitional earth" (3.21.11–17). Leaving the tower, he chances to see into a crypt where, posed on benches, "Sat the dim conclave of the dead, / Encircled where the shadow rules, / By sloping theaters of skulls" (3.24.52–54). As a souvenir of Mar Saba, Melville owned a watercolor given by the artist, Peter Toft, in 1882, of *The Holy Palm of Mar Saba Palestine* (Wallace, "Berkshire" 86; Marovitz 101). Writing before this event, Melville places the palm in the center of his meditations. As Sanford Marovitz notes, the palm has some such function as the doubloon in Moby-Dick, allowing "four principal speakers [to] address the palm in monologue from as many different vantage points" (102). Vine, who confesses that "I but love the past," sees the scene as accomplished picture: "Mar Saba, thou fine long-ago / Lithographed here" (3.26.15, 20–21). Mortmain dies while viewing the palm, his "filmed orbed fixed upon the

Tree," an eagle's feather lightly resting on his lips. In death, he is seen architecturally, "undermined / In frame; the brain a tocsin-bell / Overburdensome for citadel / Whose base was shattered" (3.32.30–42).

In Bethlehem, the pilgrims visit the Church of the Star. Led by a monk whose appearance has sculptural significance—"the feet, the face / Alike in lucid marble grace" (4.13.26–27)—they pass through "long-drawn double colonnades: / Monoliths two-score and eight" (41–42), to the star in the pavement that marks where the Magi once stood, and then by way of "a rock-hewn stair," to the "place of the Nativity." Here, Melville's ekphrastic touches combine into a fully realized picture:

> Dim pendent lamps, in cluster small
> Were Pleiads of the mystic hall;
> Fair lamps of silver, lamps of gold—
> Rich gifts devout of monarchs old,
> Kings catholic. Rare objects beamed
> All round, recalling things but dreamed:
> Solomon's talismans garnered up,
> His sword, his signet-ring and cup.
> In further caverns, part revealed,
> What silent shapes like statues kneeled;
> What brown monks moved by twinkling shrines
> Like Aztecs down in silver mines. (114–25)

The pilgrims are startled by the discordance of perception implied by the dissimilarity of a richly embellished grotto and the Nativity tale of "the Stable mean and poor." They are inclined to question the idea of a Nativity taking place in a cave, with the sort of skepticism that Maundrell had expressed in the seventeenth century and Harriet Martineau echoed in the nineteenth century by quoting Maundrell. Other richly embellished objects leave Derwent in a state of frivolity, though "open levity 'twas not" (199). The situation of the manger, "marble lined," with draperies including a "damask one of gold and white / Rich flowered with pinks embroidered bright" might be cause for levity, but the pilgrims are moved by the sight of "herdsmen in the shaggy coat" who worship at the shrine.

SHRINES AND RELIQUARIES OLD

Throughout the poem, Melville describes works of art or makes use of them in allusive passages. One of the most suggestive of these occurs in a powerful speech by Celio. Of the passage, Bezanson says, "One of the better dramatic sequences of the poem is his eloquent defiance of Christ at the Arch of Ecce Homo" (*Clarel* 618). In his edition of *Clarel,* Bezanson has characterized Celio as embittered by the deformity of his body and noted that he has "the hope of extracting some new talisman from Judah's ancient secret." As he stands at the Arch, Celio makes a lengthy speech, part of which is as follows:

> Anew, anew,
> For this thou bleedest, Anguished Face;
> Yea, thou through ages to accrue,
> Shalt the Medusa shield replace:
> In beauty and in terror too
> Shalt paralyze the nobler race—
> Smite or suspend, perplex, deter—
> Tortured, shalt prove a torturer. (1.13.92–99)

The iconography of the Medusa Shield is a lengthy and complex one. Melville must have encountered Joseph Forsyth's description when he acquired Forsyth's account of travels in Italy in the early 1800s, just after Napoleon's plunder of that country's art treasures. Touring the Vatican, Forsyth commented on the loss to the French of the *Apollo* and mentions the statue of Perseus that "stands fronting the cast of the departed Apollo and seems to challenge comparison." His description of the Perseus would have greatly interested Melville: "Perhaps the hero is too delicate and smooth for a mortal warriour; he has the soft beauty of a Mercury, or an Antinous. Instead of turning in horrour from the petrifick head, he eyes it with indignant complacency." A footnote describes the aegis of Minerva, where "the Gorgon is generally a flat, round, gaping face; on the vases, called Etruscan, it has the tusk of a boar; but Canova's Medusa has classick authority for its soft and feminine beauty" (Forsyth 195–96). It is clearly not the Medusa of Canova that Melville has in mind but the Gorgonian one as his exemplary horrific sublime.

One of the most impressive uses of artworks occurs in the canto of *Clarel* entitled "Prelusive," in a passage of more than thirty lines given to a description and comment on "Piranezi's rarer prints." These are very likely the set of Carceri (*Clarel* 789–91), "rarer" because they were not easily available in America and because Melville did not encounter them during his art pilgrimages in Europe. The Lathers collection of engravings, accessible to Melville, had works, not identified, of Piranesi (Cohen, "Lathers" 23), and Melville might have seen illustrated books not specified in any of his writings.

The ekphrasis is carefully arranged to make the most of the "Interiors measurelessly strange" that impress the poet:

> Stairs upon stairs which dim ascend
> In series from plunged Bastiles drear—
> Pit under pit; long tier on tier
> Of shadowed galleries which impend
> Over cloisters, cloisters without end;
> The height, the depth—the far, the near;
> Ring-bolts to pillars in vaulted lanes,
> And dragging Rhadamanthine chains;
> These less of wizard influence lend
> Than some allusive chambers closed. (2.35.5–14)

As the poet reminds the reader, it will be better for him not to read the next canto if he, "green or gray retain / Childhood's illusion, or but feign" (38–39), for the next canto will destroy whatever illusions he may have. The next canto, "Sodom," is a lucid and lengthy exposition of the Pauline text, Paul's "mystery of iniquity," the text from 2 Thess. 2:7 that often engages Melville's attention. Most of "Sodom" is given over to the exposition, with examples, of man's labyrinthine iniquity, and this exposition is left to Mortmain, the "dead hand" of the church. The prelusive canto is meant to prepare us for that, for, like Piranesi's labyrinthine stairs, pits, galleries, and cloisters, like the ringbolts and chains, like man's "penetralia of retreat— / His heart, with labyrinths replete" (35.21–22), the finally insoluble mystery that "the greatest enemy to man is man" is put forth in its most vivid pictorial terms.[5] It is of great interest that Melville's labyrinth is that of Piranesi's prison rather than the Daedalian labyrinth of Minos, a classical allusion one might have expected him to use.[6]

In the "Sodom" canto, Mortmain uses brilliant and evocative exempla to support his (and Melville's) disturbing indictment of humanity's inhumanity: "Burkers," who, like resurrectionist William Burke, kindly suffocates victims in order not to ruin the cadavers for dissection; Medea, the mass murderer; Jael, the murderer of Sisera. It is because of such examples that Melville visualizes, in the prelusive canto, the method of engraving used in Piranesi's work, the "touches bitten in the steel / By aqua-fortis" (34–35). Aqua-fortis, the nitric acid used in steel engraving, is also the ancient "strong water," its corrosiveness the bitter water of the Dead Sea.

In Bethlehem, the pilgrims are called to attention by Derwent, who points out an object for them to examine. It turns out to be "an ancient monument—

Rude stone; but tablets lent a charm" (4.20.8–9). Melville offers a detailed account of the three tablets that the pilgrims observe:

> In one
> The Tender Shepherd mild looked down
> Upon the rescued weanling lost,
> Snugged now in arms. In emblem crossed
> By pastoral crook, Christ's monogram
> (Wrought with a medieval grace)
> Showed on the square opposed in face.
> But chiefly did they feel the claim
> Of the main tablet; there a lamb
> On passive haunches upright sate
> In patience which reproached not fate;
> The two fine furry fore-legs drooping
> Like tassels; while the shearer, stooping,
> Embraced it with one arm; and all
> The fleece rolled off in seamless shawl
> Flecked here and there with hinted blood.
> It did not shrink; no cry did come:
> In still life of that stone subdued
> Shearer and shorn alike were dumb. (10–28)

As Bezanson notes, there does not seem to be an existent monument for Melville's observation or in the travel literature (*Clarel* 827). So the ekphrasis has the freedom of not being tied down to a precise description of an existent artwork, and Melville is allowed to dispose the pictorial elements in the most effective manner for his needs. Bezanson perceptively calls attention to the near paraphrase of Isa. 53:9: "he is brought as a lamb to the slaughter, and as a sheep before his shearers is dumb, so he openeth not his mouth." In the dumb show of the carving both shearer and shorn are arrested in movement.

Near the end of the poem, Melville composes the description of a procession in the *Via Crucis,* finding the grouping "As 'twere a frieze" (4.29.26). He is thus able to give to the movement the stasis and formality of a carved entablature, rich with varied life:

> Bowed water-carriers; Jews with staves,
> Infirm gray monks; over-loaded slaves;
> Turk soldiers—young, with home-sick eyes;

> A Bey, bereaved through luxuries;
> Strangers and exiles; Moslem dames
> Long-veiled in monumental white,
> Dumb from the mounts which memory claims;
> A half-starved vagrant Edomite;
> Sore-footed Arab girls, which toil
> Depressed under heap of garden-spoil;
> The patient ass with panniered urn;
> Sour camels humped by heaven and man,
> Whose languid necks through habit turn
> For ease—for ease they hardly gain.
> In varied forms of fate they wend—
> Or man or animal, 'tis one:
> Cross-bearers all, alike they tend
> And follow, slowly follow on. (4.34.27–44)

This impressive and artfully arranged grouping of citizenries should, as Clarel recognizes, move him closer to belief. But he is unable to discern "A message from beneath the stone" (53).

Although Clarel "Vanishes in the obscurer town" (56) and from the sight of the reader and seems unable to wrest the conclusion that he has so obviously sought in his pilgrimage, Melville, as narrator, does not quite permit such a moral defeat. Instead, he brings together a grouping of art allusions:

> The ancient Sphinx still keeps the porch of shade,
> And comes Despair, whom not her calm may cow,
> And coldly on that adamantine brow
> Scrawls undeterred his bitter pasquinade.
> But Faith (who from the scrawl indignant turns)
> With blood warm oozing from her wounded trust,
> Inscribes even on her shards of broken urns
> The sign o' the cross—*the spirit above the dust!* (4.35.4–11)

The shards of broken urns formed a predominantly gloomy image for Melville the traveler in Italy. In the poem "The Ravaged Villa," he speaks of the "sylvan vases" broken into shards and the way in which, "flung to kiln, Apollo's bust / Makes lime for Mammon's tower." Faith has the fragile and breakable urn for its armory, while Despair is adamantine, inflexible, and unbreakable. The pasquino, a statue of ancient Rome, served as a posting place for satires, lampoons, and ridicule. The sign of the cross mingles with the coat of arms of the Melville family (*Clarel* 839–40) to provide as hopeful a conclusion as possible: "Even death may prove unreal at the last, / And stoics be astounded into heaven" (25–26).

SEVEN

The Visual Imagination

"Wanderings after the Picturesque"

I N THE QUARTER-CENTURY between *Pierre* (1852) and *Clarel* (1876), Melville wrote both fiction and poetry in which he found partial and sometimes fitful uses for the intensities of ekphrastic composition. There are, of course, good reasons for his interrupted progress. Descriptions of art and the creation of a painterly element are not always required in literary works, and it seems that special conditions are called for to bring them into being. The protagonist or narrator of a tale and the speaker in a poem must demonstrate knowledge of the sister arts, love for their beauties and signification, and an awareness of how these fuse with the resources of the literary imagination. Melville's creation of such personages as Redburn, Ishmael, Pierre, and Clarel, who often seem fixated upon artists and works of art, offered the most likely prospects for this fusion, and his ample reaches of learning and artifice ensure the success of the results. As director of all utterances in the poems, he could depend upon the convention of an erudite narrativity to deal with all aspects of pictorialism.

In the three years following the publication of *Pierre*, Melville concentrated his best efforts in creating the short story, the novella, and the literary sketch. Having lavished the best of his imaginative sense of the art analogy during the previous three years upon *Moby-Dick* and *Pierre*, he was able to consider how to make the most effective use of what his practice had taught him and, while no doubt driven to magazine publication by economic exigencies, to make the shorter forms yield what they could in the way of pictorial opportunities.

The five literary works that constitute *The Piazza Tales* (1856) were carefully chosen from a larger number of short pieces written in the three-year period after the disastrous failure of *Pierre* with the public. In their selection and placement we see Melville's deliberate effort to create a cohesive and coherent group of short pieces rather than a volume of what might have simply been "tales and sketches." As a way of holding the volume together, he establishes a painterly scene and situation in his prose introduction, "The Piazza," which implies that with his skills he can create a genuine unity of view. After all, the landscape itself invites landscape painters; in fact, the area is "A very paradise of painters" (1). The narrator intimates that using his "panoramic piazza" will allow him to "feast upon the view" of the natural world about him. Like a bench in a picture-gallery, the piazza affords the "time and ease" for him to enjoy these "galleries hung, month after month anew, with pictures ever fading into pictures ever fresh" (2). The narrator concludes, after Marianna's tale, by finding his piazza to be a "box-royal" or an "amphitheatre" from which he can view, as artworks, a variety of scenes. The situation is an appealing one, promising another narrator who, like Redburn and Ishmael, loves art and who will view each of the scenes he paints in the stories with an eye that recognizes their kinship with engaging and beautiful art objects. On his piazza, he is "haunted by Marianna's face, and many as real a story" (12). "The Piazza" embodies a noble concept in its insistence on making a collection of shorter pieces into a coherent and cohesive whole and will serve as exemplar for the volumes of poems, *Battle-Pieces, John Marr and Other Sailors, Timoleon,* and the one or two or possibly even three unpublished and incomplete volumes left at his death. He seems to be driven always by an impressive urge toward the integrity of incorporation and embodiment. The integrity of this volume of prose pieces as a unified composition depends largely upon the validity of his apologia in "The Piazza."

The first story in *Piazza Tales*, "Bartleby, the Scrivener," does not really permit its narrator, an elderly lawyer, to see things in a distinctively ekphrastic way. There are hints in his description of his chambers, which he calls "deficient in what landscape painters call 'life,'" and he can here be said to be depicting an architectural artwork. But the description is brief and, from the viewpoint of rendering an objet d'art in prose, quite unsatisfactory. The lawyer's allusion to the Wall Street area as being "deserted as Petra" is effective, as is the immediately following allusion to what must be a painting, or at least an engraving, of "Marius brooding among the ruins of Carthage" (27–28). The employment of the Tombs, or "the Halls of Justice," offers Melville the opportunity to elaborate on the oddity of that structure, secure in its Egyptological imitativeness and gloomy authority, but he declines to make use of its possibilities.

Several scenes of "Benito Cereno" offer excellent situations for the narrator of Captain Delano's misfortunes. As a piece of naval architecture, the *San Dominick* receives impressive ekphrasis. The ship's tops and forecastle are given sufficient notice, as are the quarter galleries: "these tenantless balconies hung over the sea as if it were the grand Venetian canal" (49). Best of all, the "shield-like stern-piece" is demonstrably an artwork, "intricately carved with the arms of Castile and Leon, medallioned about by groups of mythological or symbolical devices; uppermost and central of which was a dark satyr in a mask, holding his foot on the prostrate neck of a writhing figure, likewise masked" (49). The great impact of Melville's ekphrasis, so strategically placed in the story, is its ability, in retrospect, to recall the entire symbolic significance of the tale.[1] In addition, the climactic scene of revelation, the removal of the canvas covering of the beaked forepiece with its gruesome skeleton, as if it were a work of art first revealed, is a powerful ekphrasis that mingles the hideous matter of death with the uncommon beauty of the human frame as art.

The sketches that make up "The Encantadas" offer perhaps the most inviting prospects for Melville's sophisticated pictorialism. He prepares for such a vision by using, in complete consciousness of its appropriateness, the pseudonym, "Salvator Tarnmoor," with its echoes of "Salvator Rosa" and the blasted landscapes of that Neapolitan artist's best work. The islands are beautifully described in the author's most ingenious prose, which without referring to artworks renders them vividly as desolate, solitary, parched, uninhabitable cinders. This presentation of island landscape proceeds realistically in the first sketch, where the extinct volcanoes are shown "looking much as the world at large might, after a penal conflagration" (126). The ekphrasis of Rock Rodondo exhibits its architectural design; the rock looks like the campanile of St. Mark and has a base resembling broken stairs and a tower that rises "in entablatures of strata" (134). The shells and calapees of the Galapagos tortoise are presented as tinted sculptures. "Medallioned and orbed like shields, and dented and blistered like shields that have breasted a battle," the shells remind one of the great shield of Achilles, though, instead of depicting the scenes of life and death in ancient Greece, these beautiful objects expand into a transfiguration, as "Roman Coliseums in magnificent decay" (131). Part of their magnificence comes from their apparently antediluvian presence; they seem, as the narrator puts it, "newly crawled forth from beneath the foundations of the world," where they resemble the Hindu artistic representations of the tortoises that hold up the planet. From this representation of the artistic sublime, the armory of the beasts lapses into useful and comedic artwork, as the sailors fashion "the three mighty concave shells into three fanciful soup-tureens, and polished the three flat yellowish calapees into three gorgeous salvers" (133). The factuality of much of the writing in "The Encantadas," as magnificently equipped as it is for the work of a sketchbook writer or a traveler, intent upon making the reader see and, perhaps, even feel, the grimness of the scenes before him, lacks the last degree of fictive originality. In its final parts, the structure of the work breaks down into anecdote and loses the energy evolved from the sketches devoted to the tortoises or to the unfortunate Hunilla, whose ride into "Payta town" on "a small gray ass" affords a striking ekphrasis of "the jointed workings of the beast's armorial cross" (162). Perhaps Melville, aware that his skills were not being given full range, decided not to complete what might have been a long book and almost certainly would have become a less interesting one.

Given the nature of the plot and setting of "The Bell-Tower," it is inevitable that ekphrastic treatment is a necessary element in the tale. The tower, in the pride of its construction, is not so described, but its ruin is an artwork of the combined labors of man and Nature. It seems "the black stump of some immeasurable pine," and the part still standing, "one steadfast spear of lichened ruin," evokes a beautiful apostrophe: "From that tree-top, what birded chimes of silver throats had rung. A stone pine; a metallic aviary in its crown" (174). The "great state-bell" is somewhat like the fabulous shield of Achilles, embellished with "mythological devices" and fashioned from tin, copper and "much plate." The figure that eventually kills Bannadonna is an impressive creation of art: "It had limbs, and seemed clad in a scaly mail, lustrous as a dragon-beetle's. It was manacled, and its clubbed arms were uplifted, as if, with its manacles, once more to smite its already smitten victim" (182). By means of brief ekphrases and their symbolic values, Melville is able to communicate the subject of his tale, the hubris of the artist who assumes, as Richard Chase notes, "that the task of Prometheus can be accomplished by mechanical means" (xi).

Melville's effort, by persuasion and almost minimal example, to impose structural effects, or at least to prescribe them, in a volume where they are, perhaps, not readily apprehensible to his audience, signals a highly refined and somewhat elusive pictorial sensibility. It is obvious that he has a clear conception of what a "piazza tale" is intended to be, and, since he does not admit other stories, presumably he does not consider them "piazza tales." But what he has left out presents the materials for an engaging discussion of the sensibility that persists in seeing pictures. The brief sketch "I and My Chimney" is well qualified to be considered. Viewed as the narrator views it, the chimney is surely an artwork. It is, for example, situated near the village of New Petra, a contemporary avatar of the magnificent architectural masterpiece in the Near East that Melville accepted into his repertory of pictorial images and continued to use with great skill for many years. The narrator comments on pieces of architecture and the effect of chimneys on them, from the palace of Versailles to his own rather wide house. "The architect of the chimney," he asserts, "must have had the pyramid of Cheops before him; for, after that famous structure, it seems modeled" (355). The chimney is a crippled artwork, some fifteen feet of its summit having been removed with the gable roof that had once supported it (356).

Several stories written during this period take the form of the diptych. James Duban's study of "Poor Man's Pudding and Rich Man's Crumb" indicates the manner in which the author is able to make use of this ancient and honorable exemplum of the decorative arts, to establish contrast between two different pictures observed by the narrator. As Duban notes, "Melville was drawing on a well-established pictorial tradition, but he bent that tradition to serve the ends of plaintive social commentary" (277).[2] The reader loses, almost at once, the sense that the author is really dealing with pictures, even though the two parts of the narrative are entitled "Picture First" and "Picture Second." The result seems to be that the sketches have the pictorial imposed upon them in a superficial way, without much literary profit.

Another diptych, "The Two Temples," with its emphasis upon the architecture of interiors, offers promising materials for ekphrases. In the tower of the first temple, the narrator encounters "three gigantic Gothic windows of richly dyed glass," which add a spectrum of vivid colors, "flaming fire-works and pyrotechnics" to the scene (304). Light and color dominate the scene: "the whole interior temple was lit by nought but glass dimmed, yet glorified with all the imaginable rich and russet hues" (306). The second "temple," a London theater, offers the prospect of an audience as painterly subject: "like beds of glittering coral, through the sea of azure smoke, there, far down, I saw the jewelled necks and white sparkling arms of crowds of ladies in the semicirque" (313). Sanford Marovitz deals in great detail with Melville's use of the architectural, not only in this piece but in a whole range of his writings.[3] Marovitz finds that Melville's use of directional imagery "increases the pictorial effectiveness of his architectural settings as accessories to the intellectual drama in which characters and ideas are dynamically engaged," and he comments effectively on "the subtle use of light/dark imagery" in the creation of architectural pictorialism (103). As a final diptych, "The Paradise of Bachelors and the Tartarus of Maids" poses contrasting scenes in the most extreme terms. The apartment visited by the narrator in the first sketch is given only brief description, but the factory that is the Tartarus is finely conceived in a number of ekphrases. In an impressive natural setting that features "a Dantean gateway," "Plutonian, shaggy-wooded mountains," and the Blood River, the paper-mill gains authority from its "frame of ponderous iron, with a vertical thing like a piston periodically rising and falling upon a heavy wooden block" (328).[4]

THE ANGUISH NONE CAN DRAW

Curiously, perhaps, Melville does not seem to have availed himself of the excellent advantages of ekphrasis in *Israel Potter* or *The Confidence-Man*. The sources of his "Revolutionary narrative of the beggar" did not offer much sanction for the creation of an inward, art-loving character, and there was much in the way of physical action and adventure to float Israel's story without the intrusion of pictorialism. The case of *The Confidence-Man* might have been different, since the river views and landscape of the novel could have been rich in pictorialist opportunities. Melville's observation of panoramic paintings of the Mississippi River might well have suggested to him the value of introducing the art analogy into his narrative. But the tale, as he envisaged it, did not leave much room for elaborate ekphrasis. As Christopher Sten has demonstrated in *The Weaver-God, He Weaves*, setting, perhaps the richest material for exploitation, is "transient, public, dreamlike." The river of John Banvard's literal panoramic painting is not the river of Melville's circular tale whose "narrative inscribes a plot that repeats itself almost endlessly yet seems to go nowhere" (285–86). The description of Cairo, Illinois, in chapter 23 is certainly promising material, bolstered by the chapter's promise, in its title, that it will deal with "the powerful effects of natural scenery." But little happens in that direction. Possibly the scene is too transient and dreamlike, for the reader is treated instead to the cogitations of a character about "human subjectivity" and "the crafty process of social chat." The very nature of Melville's narrative intent undercuts almost any attempt at such conventional novelistic devices as careful ekphrases of personages, ship's architecture, or the panoramic unrolling of an enormous stretch of canvas painted all over with marvelous views of the Mississippi.

When he turned to poetry, after publication of *The Confidence-Man*, Melville was able to translate at least some of his pictorial skills to the new medium. Several of the poems in *Battle-Pieces and Aspects of the War* (1866) are interesting examples of the ekphrastic technique. In "The Portent," the execution of John Brown is depicted as if the poet's view of it is a magazine illustration, but one that could never have appeared in the magazines of the time. There were many magazine illustrations of the event in 1859, but they restricted themselves to showing Brown ascending the steps of the scaffold or standing on the trapdoor of the gallows, his face hidden by the cap, while the executioners fixed the rope and prepared him for the execution. By rendering a portrayal of the execution itself, in which the man is "Hanging from the beam, / Slowly swaying," with the executioner's cap hiding "the anguish none can draw" (*Collected Poems* 3), Melville presents an infinitely more powerful picture for the reader than any that the artistic conventions of the time would have allowed. Here, Melville once more uses art as a prelusive device. The poem and its illustration of Brown as "meteor of the war" indicate the tenor of the volume. The poet's views of the war in the poems that follow will be those of a somewhat distant observer rather than an active participant, and he will have to depend on published accounts of scenes and engagements, along with the many pictorial renditions of the conflict.[5]

"The Temeraire," is, in part, the ekphrasis of an actual painting, Turner's *The Fighting Temeraire,* an engraving of which Melville owned (Wallace, *Melville and Turner* 54–55). But the poet also concentrates upon pictorial effects not evident in the Turner picture in the lines "On open decks you manned the gun / Armorial." The allusion is somewhat cryptic, and he feels called upon to contribute a prose note, part of which reads "Some of the cannon of old times, especially the brass ones, unlike the more effective ordinance of the present day, were cast in shapes which Cellini might have designed," a statement that supports his use, in earlier lines of the poem, of such art terms as "garniture, emblazonment, / And heraldry" (37, 449). These significant words exhibit the artistic endeavor of early naval architecture. *Garniture* is decoration or embellishment with beautiful details; *emblazonment* is rich ornamentation of heraldic devices or armorial bearings; and *heraldry,* a term resonant with connotation, encompasses both garniture and emblazonment upon arms and armor.

Two poems in the volume refer specifically to pictures. Melville makes sure that the reader cannot mistake the source of "The Coming Storm" by attaching an epigraph identifying his source as a painting by Sanford R. Gifford and noting that he has seen it at the April 1865 exhibition of the National Academy. In the poem, however, there is little attempt at ekphrasis; the poet concentrates on speculating about the feelings of Edwin Booth, the owner of the painting. The assassination of Lincoln by John Wilkes Booth had taken place only two weeks before the opening of the exhibition, which, in fact, had been scheduled for April 14 and had to be postponed. On the other hand, "Formerly a Slave" is the ekphrasis of a picture by Elihu Vedder that Melville saw at the same 1865 exhibition. Poetic language matches the visual imagery in the first line, "The sufferance of her race is shown," and in the final pair of lines, "Her dusky face is lit with sober light, / Sibylline, yet benign" (101). A certain poetic inexperience is exhibited by the rather clumsy phrasing of "is shown," which occurs in this poem as well as in "The Portent." A similar problem occurs in "On the Photo-graph of a Corps Commander," which tries valiantly to incorporate the art of photographic portraiture into the poet's lexicon of the art analogy but is de-feated by language like "Here you see" and "A cheering picture. It is good / To look upon a Chief like this." A more poetic solution occurs in "Commemora-tive of a Naval Victory," which evokes "The hawk, the hound, and sworded nobleman / In Titian's picture for a king" to describe suitably the sailors who have won the victory.

Several of the commemorative poems toward the end of the volume use monuments, themselves a form of elegiac art, to comment on aspects of the war. The most effective poem may be "An Uninscribed Monument on One of the Battle-Fields of the Wilderness." The monument itself speaks, an example of what Jean Hagstrum would designate *ecphrasis*, "that special quality of giv-ing voice and language to the otherwise mute art object" (18n.34).

ART'S MERIDIAN

In "Rip Van Winkle's Lilac," a combination of prose sketch and poem that Melville intended for the projected but unpublished volume *Weeds and Wildings*, a painter is imagined as speaker and representative of the pictorial viewpoint. He is "a certain meditative vagabondo, to wit, a young artist," who, "in his summer wan-derings after the Picturesque," has discovered the ruined house where Rip once lived and is busy painting it (*Collected Poems* 287). The site is now "a greenly ruinous home," or, perhaps, in alternative readings, a "green wreck," or even a "ruinous abode," attractive to the artist mainly as a ruin.[6] He has a certain point of view to express about the picturesque, and he gets the opportunity when engaged in some verbal fencing with the "gaunt, hatchet-faced, stony-eyed indi-vidual, with a gray sort of salted complexion like that of a dried cod-fish," an unfortunately conventional sort of character who derides his selection of a paint-erly theme and would prefer that he paint "something respectable, or, better, something godly," like the church on the nearby hill. "Disreputable" is this citizen's word for both Rip and his house. The painter's rejoinder is pert and fitting: "what should we poor devils of Bohemians do for the picturesque, if Nature was in all things a precisian, each building like that church and every man made in your image" (289). The artist might possibly have considered that Nature is al-ways a precisian, even in its creation of ruined wrecks of houses, but he does not do so because Melville is trying out a different idea. The church on the hill, with its aspiring steeple, is posed against the mountains that "looked placidly down," though in a cancelled passage they may have looked "sublimely" down.

Terms like "picturesque" and "sublime" work together a bit later in the account of the artist. "The lean visitor" on his "albino" horse seems merely a picturesque, odd-looking figure, a parody, perhaps, of Ichabod Crane astride old Gunpowder. But as he leaves, he passes "in an elevated turn of the hilly road," and "man and horse, outlined against the vivid blue sky," are framed into a memorable picture for the artist before disappearing "as if swallowed by the grave." This visionary scene gives a serious turn to the occasion: "'What is that verse in the Apocalypse,'" murmured the artist to himself, now suspending the brush and ruminatingly turning his head sideways, "'the verse that prompted Benjamin West to his big canvas?—*I looked and beheld a pale horse, and his name that sat on him was Death*'" (289). It is only the angle of vision as the rider "obliquely crossed the Bohemian's sight" that transforms a picture merely eye-catching in its oddity into the sublime. The pale horse of Benjamin West is a secure part of Melville's lexicon of paintings and appears as part of the terrible vision of whiteness in *Moby-Dick* where "even the king of terrors, when personified by the evangelist, rides on his pallid horse" (192).

In the poem "At the Hostelry," which he may have intended as part of an unrealized "Frescoes of Travel," Melville offers "an inconclusive debate as to the exact import of a current term significant of that of the manifold aspects of life and nature which under various forms all artists strive to transmit to canvas" (*Collected Poems* 317). Under such an expansive rubric, the picturesque encompasses just about any pictorial subject; and, in fact, Melville has the Dutch painter, Jan Steen, express this view of art:

> to this I hold,
> Be it cloth of frieze or cloth of gold,
> All's picturesque beneath the sun;
> I mean, all's picture; death and life
> Pictures and pendants, not at strife—
> No, never to hearts that muse thereon.
> For me, 'tis life, plain life, I limn—
> Not satin-glossed and flossy-fine (*Collected Poems* 329)

Jan Steen is exaggerating a bit, no doubt, although, for a painter all should probably be, at least potentially, picture. Melville is using the term "picturesque" in its most general meaning as something not necessarily striking or unusual but, rather, picturable or suggestive of a picture. Dugald Stewart had defined the term in this way: "Picturesque properly means what is done in the style, and with the spirit of a painter." It is clear that, as the argument develops in Melville's poem, there is much room for all sorts of painterly content in the paintings of the artists who speak. Spagnoletto's "Flaying of St. Bartholomew" and "Laurence on the gridiron" (318) are satisfyingly picturesque. Swanevelt, the Dutch painter, converts the horrific sublime into the picturesque:

> Like beauty strange with horror allied,—
> As shown in great Leonardo's head
> Of snaky Medusa,—so as well
> Grace and the Picturesque may dwell
> With Terror. (319)

In contrast with the Medusa, the "Arcadian woods in hue" of Claude, the Van Dyck portraits, the "boors at inns, / Mud floors—dark settles—jugs—old bins" of Teniers, the seascapes of Van de Velde, and the sprightly kitchen scenes of Gerard Dow (*Collected Poems* 320–26) are also good examples of the picturesque, which thus becomes a term to encompass the sublime, the homeliness of genre art, the narrativity of religious and mythological paintings, the psychology of portraiture, and the "enchanting" and "romantic landscape" of some valley or wood.

Melville's desire to place every sort of picturable event under the comprehensive terminology of the picturesque seems to have been a fairly late development in his thinking about the arts. For at least a brief time, he had considered other possibilities. In *Pierre,* he seems to be speaking for himself in Book 20 when he puts forth a tentatively comprehensive division of his topic:

> If the grown man of taste, possesses not only some eye to detect the picturesque in the natural landscape, so also, has he as keen a perception of what may not unfitly be here styled, the *povertiresque* in the social landscape. To such an one, not more picturesquely conspicuous is the dismantled thatch in a painted cottage of Gainsborough, than the time-tangled and want-thinned locks of a beggar, *povertiresquely* diversifying those snug little cabinet-pictures of the world, which, exquisitely varnished and framed, are hung up in the drawing-room minds of humane men of taste, and amiable philosophers of either the "Compensation," or "Optimist" school. They deny that any misery is in the world. . . . (276–77)

Quoting this passage in *That Cunning Alphabet,* Richard S. Moore points out Melville's concern with "the disjunction between aesthetic vision and reality as well as the clash between moral issues and aestheticism" (187). By the time of the painters' symposium in "At the Hostelry," he seems to have arrived at some sort of compromise, in which the ugly can be seen as the beautiful.

But the compromise is not complete and not a solid part of the poet's think-ing. The term "picturesque" had always been wrestled about, quite often to match the critic's vision of the painterly. In reading William Hazlitt's *Table Talk*, Melville must have encountered the brief essay "On the Picturesque and Ideal," in which the author set out some terms: "The natural in visible objects is what-ever is ordinarily presented to the senses; the picturesque is that which stands out, and catches the attention by some striking peculiarity; the ideal is that which answers to the preconceived imagination and appetite in the mind for love and beauty" (Sealts #266a). Under such a program, Rubens is the most picturesque of painters but almost the least ideal; Rembrandt is picturesque and Correggio and Claude are ideal, while Van Dyke is natural. "A country," Hazlitt contends, "may be beautiful, romantic, or sublime, without being pic-turesque." Melville seems to accept Hazlitt's categories in the first stanza of "The Attic Landscape" when he says,

> Tourist, spare the avid glance
> That greedy roves the sight to see:
> Little here of "Old Romance,"
> Or Picturesque of Tivoli. (*Collected Poems* 245)

The ruins of Tivoli, including Hadrian's villa and a temple dedicated to Vesta, are merely romantic or picturesque or even beautiful, without the "Pure outline pale" that Melville celebrates in the poem's second stanza.

Writing poems that make use of the visual arts in varied ways, Melville con-tinued to read about the subject in his latter years, and his studies seem to underline his sense that the debate over the picturesque continued "inconclu-sive." In a memoir about Melville, Arthur Stedman spoke of his "interest in all matters relating to the fine arts," but most of the art books he acquired "are among those volumes lacking his autograph and notation of his date of pur-chase" (Sealts 130–31). The range is gratifying—pottery, porcelain, "other Ob-jects of Vertu," the ceramic arts, ancient costume—as well as painterly studies of Gainsborough, Constable, Claude, Ruisdael, Hobbema, Cuyp, Potter, Meis-sonier, Corot, Daubigny, Dupré, Millet, Rousseau, Diaz, Rembrandt, Wilkie, Turner, Reynolds, and Cruikshank. The little volumes by Frank Cundall (1891) and John William Mollett (1881, 1882, 1890) offered helpful summaries of the works of painters and provided illustrations of some of their works, but there are no markings or marginal comments to indicate that Melville was still study-ing the subject and acquiring new insights. In his introduction to *Clarel*, Walter Bezanson suggests that Melville was "an avid skimmer of current journals and newspapers" (611); and, in writing about his later life and reading, Merton Sealts points out that "As in earlier days, Melville continued to read newspapers and magazines; according to a family tradition . . . he subscribed to the New York Herald because it contained the best shipping news" (127). If, as is likely, he did read the magazines regularly, he must have come across much about the visual arts that would have interested him. There were, for instance, reviews of the spring exhibitions at the National Academy of Design in *The Nation, Galaxy, Frank Leslie's Popular Monthly,* and *Appleton's Journal.* For a time in the 1870s, the *Atlantic Monthly* ran a regular column on art, and through all of Melville's later years, the magazine printed articles on various subjects.[7] A short article by William Howe Downes on "Elihu Vedder's Pictures" in the June 1885 issue of the *Atlantic Monthly* made the point that "Vedder is, more frankly and thoroughly than any other American painter, an idealist; in this age of naturalism and realism he has set his face squarely in the contrary direction" (842). Downes spoke of the designs Vedder had drawn for the recent edition of the *Rubaiyat,* a volume that Melville would later acquire (Sealts #392) and commented on some of Vedder's early and recent paintings. In the light of Hazlitt's remarks about the ideal, this assessment would have interested Melville, who continued to enjoy Vedder's art and, in the last months of his life, dedicated *Timoleon* to the painter.

TO GRAPPLE FROM ART'S DEEP

Over Melville's working career, the habit of thinking of the art analogy became engrained in his writing procedures so that, with great ease, he slips into the pictorial mode of description, analogy, and analysis. In chapter 80 of *Moby-Dick,* for instance, he gives an account of a biological theory proposed by Lorenz Oken: "It is a German conceit, that the vertebrae are absolutely undeveloped skulls." Then he has Ishmael recall that "the Germans were not the first" to demonstrate the idea, and adds that "A foreign friend once pointed it out to me, in the skeleton of a foe he had slain, and with the vertebrae of which he was inlaying, in a sort of basso-relievo, the peaked prow of his canoe" (349). The artistic act of inlaying in basso-relievo, a delicate art, mixes with the rather shocking revelation of the materials of his cannibal art, and we recall that Queequeg, another artistic cannibal, is in the habit of carving Yojo, his little god image, and spends much time embellishing the lid of his coffin with the signs of a lost art. In the poem entitled "Venice" in *Timoleon,* Melville finds, as a "kindred art" to the construction of that beautiful city, the work that "a worm can do" as the "little craftsman of the Coral Sea" works to build

his marvelous gallery
And long arcade,
Erections freaked with many a fringe
Of marble garlandry. (*Collected Poems* 229)

Nature as artist, even the worm as artist, competes with the best work of man and surpasses it. "Disinterment of the Hermes" seems to be a reproof to those who go about "raking arid sands / For gold more barren," but lines deleted from the poem indicate a vital but repressed plan: "The Hermes, risen, renews its span / In resurrection never proved in man" (239; Stein 126). Poems left unpublished demonstrate his continued consideration of the picturable in the sister arts. A brief piece, "In the Hall of Marbles," which he carefully assures the reader in an epigraph is made up of "Lines recalled from a destroyed poem," reflects upon the way in which, in contrast to the "Attic years," our own "arts but serve the clay," and concludes that, in the words of the sibyls, "Man fell from Eden, fall from Athens too" (388–89). "The Medallion" (387–88) meditates upon the work of miniature art forms that fix in one static image "The ground-expression, wherein close / All smiles at last" and contrasts it to the poetic art "Whose verse the years and fate imbue / With reveries where no glosings reign." "The Old Shipmaster and His Crazy Barn" casts the architectural art in a new light. No doubt the barn was as trim and in plumb as any shipmaster might have required, but Nature, the great artist, has intervened to render it "Bewrinkled in shingle and lichened in board." It takes on some of the appearance, at least to a shipman, of a ship whose "gaunt timber shrieks / Like ribs of a craft off Cape Horn" (379). Though neighbors, as utilitarian in outlook as the man in "Rip Van Winkle's Lilac," advise pulling the wreck down, the shipmaster knows that "a Spirit inhabits, a fellowly one," and, feeling "touchy as tinder / Yea, quick to take wing," he will not get rid of the mirror image of his own ruin and imminent death.

In his study of Melville's poetry, William H. Shurr suggests that the poem "In the Pauper's Turnip-Field" was probably inspired by Jean Francois Millet's painting *The Man with the Hoe* (190) and finds the connection in the shape of the hoe, or mattock, that the man in the painting, and in the poem, leans against. Melville knew Millet's work from the volume he owned about the Barbizon painters (Sealts #362). Shurr finds the poem's theme in mortality, "the imminence of death," but the poem, contrasting the "preachment" of the nearby crow with the "homily of my hoe," seems to be more about the living condition of pauperdom and brutalizing labor, certainly the subject of the Millet painting.

The visual arts receive some historical criticism in the ekphrasis of "Puzzlement as to a Figure Left Solitary on a Unique Fragment of Greek Basso-Relievo."

Perhaps this is a piece that he promised John Hoadley he would try to purchase from a shipman (*Correspondence* 453). The terms of the poem are enticing. The relief sculpture, broken from a larger work, may show Artemis looking toward someone else whose identity may only be conjectured. But the puzzlement is that it may not even be Artemis, the virgin huntress and Apollo's sister, for the face carved there "breathes too much of Eve's sweet way." Melville thus connects, in his paradoxical manner, the pagan and the Christian, as he had in portraying Clarel's Ruth as a discordant combination of Eve and a nereid. Then, the piece might be like a fragment of a Keatsian Greek urn, which uninterruptedly shows its lovers, but, here, only "*somebody* meets her sight," a somebody who can never be ascertained. This leads the poet to speculate, as a viewer might do while imposing a coherent narrativity upon this incoherent fragment of a tale untold:

> Why, could one but piece out the stone—
> Complete restore its primal state,
> Some handsome fellow would be shown,
> Some lover she would fascinate
> By that arch look—(408)

But the depicted lady would have to be someone other than Artemis, who "high, austere, / Chill as her morn," could never look so at a potential lover; and the viewer, reluctant to destroy his own tale, is forced to conclude "Nay—can it be? / Again methinks 'tis Artemis" and interrogates the vanished artist, "Rogue of a Greek! and is it she?"[8] The poet, finding her look arch, is scarcely less arch himself in proposing that the sculptor brings the human into a portrayal of the godly in making "austere Artemis a coquette," and so is likely of a later date than the classical Greek age, from a time, perhaps, when "faith's decay begot thine art." In the sense that Palestine had become Niebuhrized by the time of Melville's "pilgrimage and poem," it seems that Greek religious idealizations are Niebuhrized into the "impudence of sweet persiflage."

A brief poem with the long title "Suggested by the Ruins of a Mountain-Temple in Arcadia, One Built by the Architect of the Parthenon" catches up a number of Melville's themes of art and life:

> Like stranded ice when freshets die
> These shattered marbles tumbled lie:
>> They trouble me.

> What solace?—Old in inexhaustion,
> Interred alive from storms of fortune,
> The quarries be! (407)

William Bysshe Stein finds "gloomy implications" in the poem, for the ruined temple "discourages belief in the romantic notion of imperishable artistic beauty ... nothing of human creation survives temporal contingency" and so "Melville despairingly acknowledges the futility of the awe" (121–22). However, there is a cancelled final verse that opens up the laconic speech of the poem—"But, tell, shall time's consummate year / As fair a temple yield, thy peer, / Replacing thee?"—and rather explicitly offers the solace requested in the second verse. It seems likely that Melville cut out the finale because he found his second stanza answering its own question. The solace lies in the fact that the quarries from which come the marble of the ruined temple are inexhaustible and, buried alive, could still provide the replacement temple that he contemplates, at least briefly, in what he must have concluded was an ill-considered sop to a weakened poetic convention. Melville is terse about his provisionally hopeful feelings because, as he wrote about James Thomson's poetry, "As to his pessimism, altho' neither pessimist nor optimist [sic] myself, nevertheless I relish it in the verse if for nothing else than as a counterpoise to the exorbitant hopefulness, juvenile and shallow, that makes such a bluster in these days." A guarded optimism about a rejuvenation of Attic spirit and artistry might seem in order in 1885 if America were to offer the world a new Athens, but it could not be the subject of bluster.

There is room for the sublime in Melville's picturesque. "In the Desert" is a marvelous ekphrasis of light:

> Never Pharaoh's Night,
> Whereof the Hebrew wizards croon,
> Did so the Theban flamens try
> As me this veritable Noon.

In the clarity of noon, light and atmosphere predominate: "Like blank ocean in blue calm / Undulates the ethereal frame." The poem ends in apostrophe:

> Holy, holy, holy Light!
> Immaterial incandescence,
> Of God the effluence of the essence,
> Shekinah intolerably bright. (240)

In his copy of Bartlett's *Forty Days in the Desert,* Melville had marked passages about "the dead heat of noon," when "the hot film trembled over the far-stretched and apparently boundless sands." In the early mornings, before sunrise, "there is a glorious radiance through the vast open concave of the sky," but by noon one felt the "terrible and triumphant power of the sun upon this wide region of sterility and death" (Cowen 1:163–64). As Barbara Novak put it, "Light is, of course, more than any other component, the alchemistic medium by which the landscape artist turns matter into spirit" (41), and a number of Melville's contemporaries, including Sanford R. Gifford, were attempting to make light a central element in their paintings. In *The Empire of the Eye,* her study of American landscape art, Angela Miller speaks of the paintings of Gifford and John Frederick Kensett in which "Resonant, light-suffused atmosphere melded topographic divisions into a vividly seamless whole" (243). This feature of painting, now labeled "luminism," is characterized by Ila Weiss as "the mystery of marginal visibility," where air is "a space-filling medium, a plastic material nearly transparent, holding light, and physically continuous with the substance of tangible nature" (18). Part of its tangibility in Melville's poem rests in the strength of its heat. It is "one flowing oriflamme" and the "fiery standard" of God. Napoleon's troops are "bayonetted by this sun," this "immaterial incandescence" and "effluence of the essence," powerful terms for what William Bysshe Stein calls "a note of almost mystical tension" (136). Without alluding to any specific artwork or painter, Melville's "luminist" poem catches up the intense endeavors of a whole school of painting.[9]

"The Great Pyramid" discovers the sublime in the architectural, as the poet doubts the merely human in its construction:

> Your masonry—and is it man's?
> More like some Cosmic artisan's.
> Your courses as in strata rise,
> Beget you do a blind surmise
>   Like Grampians.

Mountainous, the pyramid cleaves "the blue / As lording it," and in its powerful stance "All elements unmoved you stem" and dares "Time's future infinite" as it wears "Eld's diadem" (241). Seeing the pyramids in 1857, Melville had recorded his sense of immensity in "Precipice on precipice, cliff on cliff. Nothing in Nature gives such an idea of vastness" and was "oppressed by the massiveness & mystery" as they "still loom before me—something vast, indefinite, incomprehensible, and awful" (*Journals* 75–76). In the conclusion of the poem, he comes at last to the builders who, incomprehensibly, have moved into the terrain of art commanded only by inhuman powers:

> Craftsmen, in dateless quarries dim,
> Stones formless into form did trim,
> Usurped on Nature's self with Art,
> And bade this dumb I AM to start,
>   Imposing him.

The paradox that not even Nature, with its almost infinite art-creating resources, can match "in vastness" this man-made artwork is a powerful comment on Melville's concept of art. In the poem "Art," he had considered the "unlike things" that "must meet and mate" in artistic creation—flame and wind, patience and energy, humility and pride, instinct and study, love and hate, audacity and reverence. The contradictions, almost unendurable, merge in a spiritual, agonistic act:

> These must mate,
> And fuse with Jacob's mystic heart,
> To wrestle with the angel—Art. (231)

Notes

1. But cautionary advice continues. Giovannini finds fault with some discussions of the relationship between the sister arts and generalizes that often "the area of analyzable affinity is relatively small" (193). Merriman expresses his "misgivings" about "the parallel of the arts" but finds some "faint affirmation" when he discusses "rhetorical devices," and adds that the "kinds and amount of information offered to the reader are controlled by the author's selection of what is rather confusingly called point-of-view in regard to literature." Such a treatment seems to Merriman "a real possibility" (312).

2. In addition to Witemeyer, excellent discussions of the art analogy as applied to specific authors and works can be found in Viola Hopkins Winner, who uses such devices as "framing" to express what Henry James is attempting in his descriptions of paintings; in Wendy Steiner, whose discussions of Keats and Hawthorne show clearly how each author fits ekphrastic description within the framework of narrative; in Marianna Torgovnick, whose "vocabulary that suggests several methodologies" provides a useful "continuum" that "begins with *decorative* uses of the visual arts and continues through *biographical, ideological,* and *interpretive* uses" (13). Two studies of Eliot and the visual arts build on Witemeyer's work: Hilary Frasier, "Titian's *Il Bravo* and George Eliot's Tito: A Painted Record," *Nineteenth Century Literature* 50 (Sept. 1995): 210–17; and Abigail S. Rischin, "Beside the Reclining Statue: Ekphrasis, Narrative, and Desire in *Middlemarch*," *PMLA* 111 (Oct. 1996): 1121–32.

3. A census of the prints that Melville had available for study reveals the large dimensions of his knowledge, for in addition to the expected artists, Raphael, Titian, Tintoretto, Rembrandt, Rubens, Dürer, and many others, there are engravings of works by lesser-known artists, including Claude Joseph Vernet, Spagnoletto, Nicholas Lancret, John Van Huysum, J. B. Oudry, Paul Potter, Sebastian Bourdon, and Nicholas Berghem, among others.

1. THE SISTER ARTS

1. For a good analysis of the fortunes of "iconic" and other terms, see Lund chap. 1. In *Museum of Words* James Heffernan surveys the topic in its broadest aspects and sets useful parameters for considering the limits of ekphrasis. See also Aisenberg for a specifically gendered reading of pictorialism. Kurman and Alpers discuss the use of the technique in two specific literary genres.

2. See my "Wrestling with the Angel" for fuller discussions of the art analogy in some of the poems in *Timoleon*. Shurr and Stein offer extremely helpful readings of Melville's poetry.

3. Melville read Haydon's *Encyclopedia Britannica* article on painting and his autobiography with journals, a book that gives an appealing account of the artist's life and work, likes and dislikes in the art world, and encounters with artists, poets, and friends in the early years of the nineteenth century (Sealts #262, #263).

4. See Steiner chap. 3 for an excellent, full discussion of Keats's use of pictorialism in "The Eve of St. Agnes" and comments on several other Keats poems. In her view, the eighteenth-century argument (Lessing and others) against *ut pictura poesis* did not succeed in "eliminating paintings from romantic symbolism, the dichotomizing of the spatial from the temporal arts and of mimesis from expressivity" (56). Jack presents a convincing account of Keats's sources in the sister arts and his use of the art analogy in his poems.

5. Melville's probable knowledge of Browning's poetry is discussed in Hershel Parker's supplementary notes to *Clarel,* where attention is called to the publication of "My Last Duchess" under the title of "The Duke's Interview with the Envoy" in *The Literary World* on September 8, 1849. Baker observes that Melville may have used some characteristics of Browning himself in the depiction of Derwent and may have had occasion to use *The Return of the Druses* as well (14–15). Parker prints an interesting marginal note from the copy of Vasari that Melville owned. Melville writes "Attain the highest result— / A quality of Grasp," and Parker associates these remarks with the lines from "Andrea del Sarto" which assert that "a man's reach should exceed his grasp" (647). The injunction to "Get in as much as you can" applies well to the packed paragraphs of Melville's prose and to the condensed, solid lines in much of *Clarel.*

6. Richard J. Zlogar discusses Irving's use of Dutch genre painting, which "serves as a reference of central importance and lends its characteristic mode of composition to the tale" (62). See also Ringe.

7. For a good account of James's use of a number of pictorial devices, see Winner. She discusses "framing," where "through visual imagery or description it is circumscribed and set apart from the rest of the narrative" (70). As a part of framing, "an art object itself sometimes provides the center of James's living pictures" (71–72). Tintner treats the use of Holbein, Pinturicchio, and Daumier in James's fiction, as well as other fascinating topics, and speaks engagingly of James's use of "a variety of devices to call the reader's attention to a well-known painting or, occasionally, a piece of sculpture" (x) and, in the essays, calls our attention to these devices.

8. It is possible that Melville read Charles Dickens's *Pictures from Italy* (1846), a brief, quick sketch of travels. The chapter on Venice, "An Italian Dream," may not have held much in the way of art talk; but letters to John Forster spoke of "thinking over again those silent speaking faces of Titian and Tintoretto," and his observation that "it is something past all writing of or speaking of."

2. THE ARTS OBSERVED

1. Accounting for this American craze for the Cenci portrait, Barbara Novak speaks of Guido's paintings as offering "a suitable blend of bathos and sentiment quite in keeping with some of the more lurid nineteenth-century American examples" (207). Spencer Hall's essay on the Cenci painting concentrates on its use in Hawthorne's *The Marble Faun*. In considering the effect of the picture upon novelists, Louise K. Barnett asserts that buyers of the prints after the portrait "were attracted not by art but by the titillating Cenci history which the portrait mediated" (170). Melville, like his contemporaries, liked pictures that told stories, as mythological paintings did, or were associated with narratives. It is possible that his desire to see the Cenci portrait was stimulated by a book that he seems to have acquired during the art tour, Valery's *Historical, Literary, and Artistical Travels in Italy* (Sealts #533). Valery described the painting as "the pathetic head of La Cenci, dressed with elegance and coquetry ... supposed to be the work of Guido's early youth," quoted Beatrice's supposed speech to the executioner on the scaffold, and provided a translation, to the effect that "you loosen my soul for immortality." She was "the true type of an Italian maiden, and the head attributed to Guido has wonderfully expressed this ardent, simple, and tender character" (Valery 568–69).

2. See Gollin and Idol for an account of Hawthorne's attitude as being American: "Like his countrymen who came to Italy in increasing numbers at mid-century, Hawthorne brought high expectations of particular works of art, which were often fulfilled but sometimes thwarted" (87). James Jackson Jarves put it another way by condemning "American tourists" who pass through a Venetian church "without once noticing the paintings on the ceilings, turned away in disgust from Tintoretto, hurried into the church, paused a moment before some flashy modern trick of art, and in five minutes had made the tour of a building which contains enough, if properly studied, to have occupied them for as many months" (3).

3. Hawthorne liked to say that his love of Dutch art was probably proof of "a taste still very defective" (*Notebooks* 317). But the influence of the Dutch masters was strong in American art, and painters like William Sidney Mount had these precursors firmly in mind as they painted genre pictures of the commonplace in American life. As Barbara Novak points out, "Dutch art did not have the intellectual credentials that would have rendered it acceptable to official criticism," quoting Jarves: "'Those whose aesthetics are in sympathy with its mental mediocrity will not desert it for anything I can say'" (Novak 232).

4. Sophia Hawthorne was especially interested in the art of Flaxman, "the modern ancient," and knew his illustrations for Homer, Hesiod, Aeschylus, and Dante. At the Old Manse, she and Hawthorne possessed some of Flaxman's prints (Gollin and Idol 25, 30). There seems to have been a general American interest in the Englishman's work; the illustrated Dante and Homer, in Bohn editions, were widely advertised.

5. See Gretchko, "New-York Gallery of Fine Arts." *The Literary World* published accounts of exhibitions at the New-York Gallery and the showings of the Art-Union.

6. John F. McDermott's offers an excellent account of Charles Deas's brief career, his mental illness, beginning around 1849, and his early death. Pictures of a *Wounded Pawnee, Sioux Ball-Playing*, and *Western Scenery* were among those offered for distribution by the Art-Union in 1848 (McDermott, "Deas" 310) and might have been seen by Melville.

7. See Soria 22, 122–55, 184–85, 188. The volume illustrates the varied forms of Vedder's artworks and suggests some of the themes that might have interested Melville. Soria's biography of Vedder gives valuable information about his continued contacts with America in the

years after he had settled in Italy. Vedder did not know of Melville's dedication until some time after Melville's death, but he did correspond with Elizabeth Melville about the volume.

8. See Clark 84. Clark offers a useful account of trends in American art during the second half of the nineteenth century.

9. See *The National Academy of Design Exhibition Record, 1861–1900*, 340–42, 969–70.

10. I am indebted to Robert C. Kaufmann, reference librarian at the Thomas J. Watson Library, Metropolitan Museum of Art, New York City, for the information about Mrs. Allan Melville.

11. Wallace's record of the Reese collection is provided with excellent reproductions of some of the buildings shown in Melville's prints. See Short and Marovitz in Sten, *Savage Eye,* and Boudreau for discussions of Melville's knowledge of architecture and use of it in his writings.

12. In *Melville and Turner,* Robert Wallace has given an excellent account of Melville's reading, and probable reading, of art materials for the early years, up to 1851. Christopher Sten extends our knowledge of Melville's reading in his "Overview" to his edited volume, *Savage Eye.* See also my "Melville's Reading in the Visual Arts" in ibid.

13. For an interesting account of Goethe's many encounters with the sister arts, see Robson-Scott.

14. For James's use of Lambinet in *The Ambassadors,* see Winner 74–78. Tintner discusses the uses made of Pinturicchio and Daumier.

15. In other letters, Melville comments on the visual arts. An 1869 letter to Elias Dexter, who framed a mezzotint of *The Healing of the Blind* (possibly after Nicolas Poussin's painting) for him, gave Melville the opportunity to say, "I am glad, by the way, that my chance opinion of the picture receives the confirmation of such a judge as yourself.—Let me thank you for the little print after Murillo" (*Correspondence* 409). Writing to John C. Hoadley in 1877, he spoke of a ship "from Girgente" whose mate "has in his possession some stones from those magnificent Grecian ruins, and I am going to try to get a fragment, however small, which I will divide with you" (*Correspondence* 453).

16. The careful unraveling by Berthold in his essay on Dürer and by Wallace in his study of the engravings in the Ambrose group demonstrates how much can be learned from close study of the visual sources of Melville's literary works. During the last long period of his study and writing (1857–91), Melville turned more and more to his books and magazines to give him the direct experience of the sister arts, and his familiarity with the subjects of his studies led him often to use these sources with little regard for the reader's knowledge of them. Hence, the simplest-sounding poem, line, or allusion often requires a careful search through what the author may have been reading or recalling as he wrote.

17. The March 1846 issue of *The Eclectic* had Sartain's engraving of *Caius Marius on the Ruins of Carthage,* after a painting by John Martin. In 1847, a Sartain engraving of *The Cave of Despair,* after Charles Eastlake's painting, was featured. Among the "Shakespeare Gallery" engravings were pictures of Miranda, Mistress Page, Viola, and a number of other Shakespearean heroines. In addition to "The Ship *Essex,* stove in by a whale," Duncan's big collection of stories featured illustrations of the *Burning of the Kent, Explosion of the Steam Boat Helen McGregor, Loss of the Ship Hercules,* and some less calamitous scenes, including *The Eddystone Light House* and the *Frigate Constitution, Commonly called "Old Ironsides."*

3. REDBURN

1. Wallace suggests that the picture "corresponds quite closely" to one of the engravings in Melville's collection, a scene after Claude Joseph Vernet's *Figures on a Shore in a Storm* (*Melville and Turner* 9), but the toasted brown waves suggest a quieter scene than a storm. For the second picture, Wallace suggests another engraving that Melville owned, *A Storm* by Willem Van de Velde (9–10), but it seems odd that Melville would use a Dutch picture to make a point about a picture that he insists and establishes is French by his reference to Froissart. The canvas that Redburn describes appears to feature a calm scene rather than a storm, and Melville seems to be working from paintings he has seen rather than from engravings, as his emphasis on color shows.

2. Commenting unfavorably on Goupil's assuming some of the functions of the American Art-Union by setting up an "International Art-Union," *The Literary World* (141 [Oct. 13, 1849]: 317–18) did find some good things to say about the French firm, notably that it had brought pictures, "some of them of high merit," to New York, including Paul Delaroche's *Napoleon Crossing the Alps*. One page of *The Literary World* (116 [Apr. 21, 1849]: 366) contained a Goupil advertisement for statuettes of "Powers's Greek Slave" in bronze, porcelain, and plaster. Colman, as well as Williams & Stevens, advertised their wares on the same page. The February 1849 issue of *Knickerbocker's Magazine* reminded readers in its editorial section that Goupil offered opportunities to see examples of recent European art.

3. See Wallace, "Melville after Turner" for a careful analysis of Ruskinian theory and its influence on Melville's work. The comment on detail is on page 290. The Ruskin quotation, from the third volume of *Modern Painters* (1856), came much later than Melville's *Redburn*, but the use of painterly detail was a staple of art discussion.

4. When *Modern Painters*, "by a graduate of Oxford," appeared in America in 1847 under the imprint of Wiley and Putnam, the lengthy review in *North American Review* in January 1848 (vol. 66:114–16) took sharp issue with Ruskin's uncomplimentary remarks about Salvator and Dutch art and enunciated some principles about landscape painting that American artists and writers continued to cling to. Melville might have agreed more with William Hazlitt, who reviewed Lady Morgan's biography of Salvator (1824) at length, and concluded that the paintings "have a boldness of conception, a unity of design, and felicity of execution, which, if it does not fill the mind with the highest sense of beauty and grandeur, assigns them a place by themselves, which invidious comparison cannot approach or divide with any competitor." There is no definite evidence that Melville read *Modern Painters* as early as 1847 or was influenced very much by it in the composition of *Redburn* or *Moby-Dick*. Wallace finds much evidence of Ruskinian thought, some gained, no doubt, secondhand, behind Melville's writings of this period. But I am not sure that Melville's formal aesthetics progressed very far beyond an old-school appreciation of Salvator Rosa. In a poem like "At the Hostelry," written in the 1870s, perhaps, he is still puzzling out the possibilities of a term like "picturesque." His imaginative and creative appropriation of *ut pictura poesis* for his fiction and poetry is a different matter; it soars while his rationalization of it is busy limping.

5. Peter Bellis argues that the older Redburn, as narrator, "maintains a steadily ironic distance from the boy's linguistic inexperience" (86). Bryan Short usefully refers to the subtitles given to Redburn as "a source of identity in between the maturity implied by the narrative art and the lost paternal or childhood origins responsible for Wellingborough's disabled sense of

self" (69). The "older" Redburn intrudes as narrator in such passages as the account of the Moorish arch that he sees and seems to remember having seen before. His "perplexity in this matter was cleared away" by seeing a print of the scene that he recalls having seen before (206).

6. "The Rime of the Ancient Mariner" 4.278–79; Keats, "Lamia" 1.45–47. Henry F. Pommer cites the Miltonic passage for its apparent influence on *The Confidence-Man* (82). His examples of Miltonic influence on *Redburn* do not cite the Aladdin's Palace scene.

7. A description of the temple of Cholula appears in Prescott's "Appendix, Part I." The history gives a vivid account of the storming of the temple in Book 5, chapter 2. A passage in Book 1, chapter 4 exhibits Prescott's pictorial sense, which Melville may have been able to draw upon: "In casting an eye over a Mexican manuscript, or map, as it is called, one is struck with the grotesque caricatures it exhibits of the human figure; monstrous, overgrown heads, on puny misshapen bodies, which are themselves hard and angular in their outlines, and without the least skill in composition. On closer inspection, however, it is obvious that it is not so much a rude attempt to delineate nature, as a conventional symbol, to express the idea in the most clear and forcible manner." Prescott's language, like Melville's, is suggestive rather than specific in its descriptions of an art form strange to European or American eyes. In *Moby-Dick,* Melville will have Ishmael react in similar ways to "primitive" art.

8. For Melville's use of theurgic magic in *The Confidence-Man,* see P. L. Hirsch's "Melville's Ambivalence toward the Writer's 'Wizardry.'" For the connection with Bulwer-Lytton, see my note on sources for goetic and theurgic magic. Melville's interest in Pompeii and its art continued to his last years. In "'House of the Tragic Poet,'" Robert A. Sandberg reprints a pencil draft of the short prose piece that Melville composed, apparently as part of an unfinished book, about the "Burgundy Club." The sketch begins with an allusion to the name of the "disinterred" house, calling it "a hypothetical name bestowed by the antiquarians, and probably, because of the gravely dramatic character of certain frescoes on the walls within" (4). Unfortunately, Melville does not describe the frescoes. In "'The Adjustment of Screens,'" Sandberg gives an interesting account of the place of this sketch in Melville's uncompleted book and relates it to "At the Hostelry," the poem about a symposium of artists (433–36).

9. Bryan Short's references to "Harry Bolton's unspoken secret, his unrevealed inner self" (71) and to "Harry's peculiarities" (78) offer promising hints about Harry's character and his behavior in the episode in Aladdin's Palace. Toward the end of the novel, Redburn observes that Harry is "not unlike the soft, silken, quadruped-creole, that, pursued by wild Bushmen, bounds through Caffrarian woods" (253). To be a creole is to be native to, and nourished by, a particular region—and, in Harry's case, an exotic region. The Caffrarian woods, with variants of *kafir* and *kafara,* are the woods of infidelism and skepticism. This, too, offers to Redburn's visual imagination a vivid picture reinforced by references to "the girlish youth," to Harry's being "put down for a very equivocal character," and to "his effeminacy of appearance."

4. *MOBY-DICK*

1. Melville's 1849–50 journal comments on what he viewed of the arts, and Horsford's edition, with extensive notes, is indispensable. See also Wallace's long account of Melville's art tour in England and on the Continent (*Melville and Turner* 249–306). See Sealts as well as my "Melville's Reading in the Visual Arts" 40–45.

2. In "The Glassy-Eyed Hermit" Gretchko suggests that Melville's addition of the hermit and crucifix to the landscape is derived from Hieronymus Bosch's painting *The Temptation of St. Anthony*, which shows a hermit occupying a hollow tree. Other elements in the painting correspond to the description Melville gives (14–15). Richard S. Moore analyzes the passage as an attack on "the pastoral vision upon which it is based" and adds that the picture's "effects depend upon a deadening of the sensibility rather than heightened awareness" (66–67).

3. John Bryant's *Melville and Repose* gives an excellent account of backgrounds and discusses some of Melville's works using the picturesque. As Bryant indicates, Hussey provides a clear treatment of the subject. See also Hipple and Manwaring.

4. There would have been little in artworks from colonial New England to support Ishmael's characterization of the Spouter-Inn painting. It may be that Melville was thinking of such later paintings as *Saul and the Witch of Endor,* a subject treated by Benjamin West and Washington Allston, or of West's *Death on the Pale Horse.*

5. The elements in this portrayal of the inn have some things in common with the Dutch paintings that Melville admired. The bar resembling a right whale's head links Ishmael's thinking to the Dutch genre. He will later view such a head in homely terms, seeing an "inelegant resemblance to a gigantic galliot-toed shoe" where "that old woman of the nursery tale, with the swarming brood, might very comfortably be lodged" (*Moby-Dick* 333).

6. For pictures of an idol resembling Yojo and the kinds of tattooing that Melville must have had in mind for Queequeg, see Jaffé (41–48). Bryan Wolf argues that Ishmael, with all his ability to explain and interpret, is surrounded by "a world that repeatedly asserts its otherness to him" (164). "What Ishmael recognizes in Queequeg," Wolf continues, "is a system of language different from his own" (171). This is true as well of Queequeg's carvings on the coffin lid. Unable to decode the communication, Ishmael sees it only as artwork. John F. Birk argues that the voyage of the *Pequod* "is nothing less than a modern-day journey of the Egyptian god-peopled 'cosmic ship'" and that, as an Osiris figure, Queequeg reenacts the legend of that god. A chest "set off with all the ornaments of art" is made as a coffin by his enemies to hold the body of Osiris. The play of the chapter on "Queequeg in His Coffin" would then be a playful misrepresentation of the catastrophe of the murder and dismemberment of Osiris (291). Like Osiris, Queequeg is brightly garbed, though his colorful clothing is the tattooing on his body.

7. Melville's fondness for topographical prints is displayed in Robert Wallace's two accounts of the prints surviving from the Melville collection. "The Reese Collection" is especially rich in showing churches, other buildings, and landscapes.

8. See Wallace's *Melville and Turner* 7–8, 453–62 for the relationship of this painting to Turner's *Waves Breaking on a Lee Shore.*

9. Ibid. 456–57. It seems unlikely, however, that Melville saw the Turner painting. Manfred Putz rightfully characterizes the chapel painting by speaking of "a tone of irony which occasionally borders on satire and parody. What eventually emerges from the ironies is that the joke is rather on the viewer than on the picture (162).

10. A copy of *The Martyrdom of Saint Sebastian,* after the painting by Guido Reni, was acquired by the Boston Athenaeum in 1838 (Harding 72). The long article in the *North American Review* contains other matters that would have interested Melville. It mentions a painting of the Bay of Naples as well as Domenichino's *Jacob Wrestling with the Angel* and canvases by Claude and Salvator Rosa. Among the copies cited in the piece are de Brackelaer's of the Rubens painting *Descent from the Cross.* The author quotes from Sir Joshua Reynolds on this work as well as on the companion painting of *Simeon Bearing Christ in his Arms.* Ahab, who stands

before his officers "with a crucifixion in his face," is being represented as such paintings would present him. The expression on Christ's countenance as he was taken from the cross was a challenge for painters and sculptors of many pietas. Vasari, required reading for Melville, described the pieta of Michelangelo by saying, "There is besides a most exquisite expression in the countenance, and the limbs are affixed to the trunk in a manner that is truly perfect."

11. See *Piazza Tales* 403–04, 742–43. Melville's concealed allusion seems to be based on Byron's description but may have been bolstered by engravings of the statue.

12. See Short, "Like Bed of Asparagus" 106. The language of antique architecture is predominant in the writings of Austen Layard and other writers. Reviewers of Egyptological studies used architectural terms. See *North American Review* 41 (Oct. 1823): 233–42 for an article on Saint-Martin's book on the Zodiac of Denderah, with comments on Vivant Denon's study of the same subject.

13. Stuart M. Frank reproduces many iconographic representations of the whale that Melville mentions. It seems fairly unlikely that Melville could have seen some of the artworks that Ishmael catalogs in these chapters. Mansfield and Vincent 748–50 offer some sources for Melville's knowledge.

14. Moore suggests that Melville had the engravings of Giovanni Battista Piranesi in mind as the source of his references to the "finest Italian line engravings" (148–50). He certainly knew Piranesi's work, and at least one Piranesi engraving still exists from the large Melvillean collections. See Furrow. The Piranesi engravings are used prominently in *Clarel*.

15. See *Piazza Tales* 401. Melville seeks familiar analogies for facial expressions of busts and statues by alluding to "a countenance more like that of a bacchanal or the debauchee of a carnival" to describe a Socrates, who also bears "the broad and rubicund phiz of an Irish comedian." A Julius Caesar might be "a good representation of the President of the New York and Erie Railroad," and a Seneca has a face "like that of a disappointed pawnbroker, pinched and grieved." The "delicate features" of a Nero "are only those of a genteelly dissipated youth, a fast and pleasant young man such as those we see in our own day." A sense of narrativity infuses Melville's prose as he tries to find the suitable terms for the abstractions of sculpture.

16. As Berthold points out, the publication of articles in *The Illustrated Magazine of Art* on Dutch painters was in 1853–54, and *The Works of Eminent Masters,* a selection of the articles with illustrations, appeared in 1854 (227–29). All of this came too late to affect the composition of *Moby-Dick,* but Melville's acquisition of *The Works* in 1871 and, even later, of books that featured the Dutch painters attests to his long and continuing interest in the genre. As Wallace notes, Melville's collection of prints includes works of Metzu, Mieris, Cuyp, and Ostade (Wallace, "Melville's Prints and Engravings" 80–83).

17. On April 24, 1857, Melville visited Holland, where he saw an "old galliot" and pictures by Rembrandt, Teniers, Potter, and Breughel. He "Passed through Haarlem" but apparently did not stop to see the great organ (*Journals* 127). Vincent points out that the source of Melville's "cranial details come from Scoresby," including the comparison to the shoemaker's last (*Trying-Out* 255).

18. A copy of *Judith with the Head of Holofernes,* after the painting by Christofano Allori (1577–1621), was acquired by the Boston Athenaeum in 1838 (Harding 71, Plate 3). Melville was especially acquainted with the work of Veronese. At Versailles, on December 6, 1849, he saw "Titan overthrown by thunderbolts &c." (*Journals* 34, 345), likely a painting by Veronese. Samuel Rogers, whose collection Melville viewed, had at least one Veronese painting. The references in *Moby-Dick* to "Great Jove himself being made incarnate in a snow-white bull" (189) and to

the first view of the white whale, which contrasts him with "the white bull Jupiter swimming away with ravished Europa clinging to his graceful horns" (548), may be at least partially indebted to the Veronese *Rape of Europa*, though Gretchko (*Loomings* 35–37) perceptively suggests Titian's *The Rape of Europa* as a source.

19. Lorenz Oken's inaugural lecture at the University of Jena in 1807 outlined his theory "that the head is none other than a vertebral column, and that it consists of four vertebrae, which I have respectively named Auditory, Maxillary or Lingual, Ocular and Nasal vertebra" (*Elements of Physiophilosophy* xii). When Goethe claimed precedence for this discovery, a long drawn-out feud erupted between the two men. For a good account of the event, see the biography of Goethe by G. H. Lewes. Melville was familiar with *Elements of Physiophilosophy*; he quoted from the book in a presentation note to John C. Hoadley. See my "Lorenz Oken and *Moby-Dick*."

20. During his tour of the gallery at Dulwich, Melville saw "Titians." As Horsford points out, the gallery contained a Europa that "was attributed to Titian." The St. John that Melville reported seeing at Dulwich is identified by Horsford as possibly, Guido Reni's *St. John in the Wilderness* (*Journals* 20, 298–99).

21. Novak, *American Painting in the Nineteenth Century* 46–47. A similar whiteness can be found in West's *Saul and the Witch of Endor* and in Allston's painting of the same subject (50–51).

22. A convenient reprint of *The Magus* was issued by University Books in 1967. The volume is divided into two books, the first dealing with a variety of subjects under the rubric of the occult philosophy. Book 2 contains magnetism, cabalistical and celestial magic, and an account of the lives and writings of "ancient and modern magi, cabalists, and philosophers." Its subjects include the numerology that is treated by Sachs in her study of *Moby-Dick* as well as the astrology that Melville uses in *Mardi*, according to Maxine Moore's study of the author. Like other such books, *The Magus* is amply provided with plates illustrating cabalistical, geomantic, and zodiacal signs and symbols.

23. See *Clarel* 1.6.10. Bezanson's note to this line (723) identifies the organ as the kind of instrument providing music for Banvard's showing of the panorama. See Carothers and Marsh, who discuss *Moby-Dick* as a verbal panorama. McDermott's *The Lost Panoramas of the Mississippi* offers an informative account of Banvard's life and work as well as a fascinating study of this outdated and evanescent art form. See also McDermott, "Newsreel—Old Style," *Antiques* 44 (July 1932): 10–13. Collamer M. Abbott offers a good account of the panoramas that Melville might have seen in Boston and New York.

24. McDermott, *Lost Panoramas* 136. Lewis's interesting account is published in *Motion Picture in 1848: Henry Lewis' Journal of a Canoe Voyage from the Falls of St. Anthony to St. Louis*, ed. Bertha L. Heilbron (St. Paul: Minnesota Historical Society, 1936). Abbott's "Melville and the Panoramas" offers many suggestive details of panoramic art that Melville might have seen and discusses "the hyperbolic panoramic technique as an important element in Melville's style" (14).

25. See the excellent illustrated article by Elton W. Hall for views of whaling scenes by Russell. The whaling panorama "was a painting 8½ feet high and approximately 1,300 feet long" (26). The article gives a good account of the many whaling prints designed by Russell.

26. In addition to Denon, there were other possible sources open to Melville. Edward Everett's article "The Zodiac of Denderah," appearing in the *North American Review* in October 1823, presented much relevant information. Henry Wheaton's "Egyptian Antiquities," in the *North American Review* in October 1829, a review of Denon, offered valuable information about the temple.

27. Gretchko's "Melville's Hindu Sources" is indispensable for tracing out the complexities of Melville's borrowings and fabrications for this passage. He carefully disentangles the extent of Melville's debt to William Ward and Thomas Maurice and shows how the two sources were joined in Melville's composition. An illustration of the Matse Avatar that Melville might have seen is reproduced in Frank, along with an illustration of the cavern-pagoda (6–7); see also Dorothee Finkelstein's comments on the illustration and its associations (156–57).

5. PIERRE

1. Melville knew Bulwer-Lytton's *The Last Days of Pompeii, Zanoni,* and *The Pilgrims of the Rhine.* For relationships between the novel and *Zanoni,* see the "Historical Note" (*Pierre* 370–71). Simms's *Beauchampe* (1842), a novel closely based upon the "Kentucky Tragedy," is a particularly tantalizing source, dealing with murder and with suicide and attempted suicide in prison. One contemporary reviewer of *Pierre* thought that Melville "has dressed up and exhibited in Berkshire, where he is living, some of the ancient and most repulsive inventions of George Walker" (*Pierre* 380). Walker's sensational novels included *Haunted Castle* (1792), *The Three Spaniards* (1800), and *The Midnight Bell* (1824).

2. *Pierre* was a "long brain-muddling soul-bewildering ambiguity," and "a torrent rhapsody uttered in defiance of taste and sense," a "compendium of Carlyle's faults" with "incoherent ravings, and unearthly visions" (*Pierre* 380–84).

3. See Nathalia Wright, "*Pierre:* Melville's Inferno"; Charles Watson, "Melville and the Theme of Timonism"; James Duban, "The Spenserian Maze of Melville's *Pierre*"; and Paul A. Smith, "Melville's Vision of Flux and Fixity in *Pierre.*"

4. Dennis Berthold gives an admirable account of Dutch genre painting and the prints Melville owned (218–45). Books purchased in later years continued to demonstrate the pleasure Melville gained from the works of Dutch artists; see Gower's *The Figure Painters of Holland* (1880; Sealts #233) and Cundall's *The Landscape and Pastoral Painters of Holland* (1891; Sealts #169). Melville's interest in Flaxman's pictures drawn from Dante is documented by Schless, who reproduces the Flaxman drawing of the lovers (68–69). Flaxman's Homeric illustrations appeared in the Pope translations of the *Iliad* and the *Odyssey,* published in many editions during the nineteenth century

5. Among many other pieces, *The Literary World* included a review of Tuckerman's *Artist Life* (Oct. 30, 1847, 297–99), notices of a Thomas Cole exhibition (Apr. 8, 1848, 186–87), a note on "third-rate copies" of old masters (Apr. 27, 1848, 228), a sonnet on Murillo's *Flight into Egypt* (June 17, 1848, 389), a sonnet on *The Greek Slave* (Aug. 5, 1848, 530), a review of Lanzi's *History of Painting* (Feb. 10, 1849, 124), a notice of Lodge's translation of Winckelmann (Mar. 17, 1849, 251), and a story about the opening of a new gallery at the Art-Union (Sept. 22, 1849, 253–54). In addition to these and many other stories, notices, poems, and reviews, the magazine frequently carried advertisements for books about art. A typical full-page advertisement for July 8, 1848, listed among its thirty-one items for sale Haydon's *Lectures on Painting and Design,* Hazlitt's *Criticisms on Art,* Lanzi's *History of Painting in Italy,* Pilkington's *General Dictionary of Painters,* Goethe's *Theory of Colors,* and Sir Joshua Reynolds's *Literary Works* (457).

6. Smith's middle name is given sometimes as "Rubens" (in *The Dictionary of American Biography*) and as "Ruben" (in Lynes). He was said to have an "assertive personality" that made him unpopular, but was a good teacher. His topographical water colors of Boston and environs are attractive. From his father he learned the art of mezzotint, and his work in that me-

dium was that "of an able draftsman." The portrait of Allan Melvill is now in New York's Metropolitan Museum.

7. Murray calls attention to the resemblance between this description and Ames's portrait. Ames also painted a portrait of Melville's mother, a famous one of Governor Clinton, and portraits of Solomon Allen, Leonard Gansevoort, Charles Genet, and General William Irvine. His miniatures are well known. Melville may not have known Ames but was probably well enough acquainted with his work as a painter.

8. The quotation is taken from Henry F. Cary's translation of Dante (1814), which Melville purchased in 1848 in the Bohn edition of 1847. The Flaxman illustrations play an important role in this passage. See Nathalia Wright, "Melville's Inferno"; and Hillway 203.

9. Twitchell (1820–1904) is a more obscure artist than either Smith or Ames. Neither *The Dictionary of American Biography* nor *The National Cyclopedia of Biography* contains a sketch, and he is not to be found in the standard histories of American art. He lived near Troy, New York, and was associated with artistic circles in Albany. Two of his portraits are in the New-York Historical Society (see Catalogue of American Portraits, New-York Historical Society, New York City). One of these is a copy that he made of a portrait of James Fenimore Cooper painted by his teacher, Charles Loring Elliott.

10. See *The Literary World* 106 (Feb. 10, 1849): 127–30; 107 (Feb. 17, 1849): 153–54, which reprint, from the *London Examiner,* a long portion of a review of Layard. In the July 7, 1849, issue (127:9–10) is a review of *The Monuments of Nineveh.*

11. See Finkelstein (148–49) for information on Fraser (1783–1856), who wrote colorful romantic novels of Eastern adventures and accounts of travels and explorations, including *Narrative of a Journey into Khorasan, 1821-22* (1825), *Travels and Adventures in the Persian Provinces* (1826), and *Travels in Koordistan, Mesopotamia . . .* (1840).

12. Murray cites Tschudi's *Travels in Peru* and a review of the book appearing in *The Literary World* (Feb. 27, 1847, 80–83; Murray 466–67). Tschudi and the magazine excerpt deal with the veil and skirt as "useful auxiliaries in the numerous intrigues" of the Limean women. Melville used the terms effectively in "Benito Cereno" in his description of the figurehead of the Spanish ship, a sculpture gruesomely completed by the skeleton of Aranda, masked for most of the story by a "manto" of canvas.

13. Among the prints in the Reese collection are views of Woburn Abbey, Llanthony Abbey, Ostenhanger House, Croyland Abbey, and Barfriston Church (Wallace 40–42).

14. Horsford's extensive notes for the journal offer many details (*Journals* 262, 271, 275, 281, 289, 300, 333, 337, 339, 348–49).

15. Murray conjectures that the original of Melville's church may be the First Associate Presbyterian Church (1803–24), which continued as the South Baptist Church (1824–48), and finally was converted into business and office space in 1848 (484).

16. See Bamberg's edition of *The Confession of Jeroboam O. Beauchamp* for an account of literary treatments of the case. Ridgely's study of Simms (86–88) is useful, as are the essays by Jillson and Gates, and Yaggy calls attention to the connection with Simms's novels.

17. Hillway finds in the Enceladus passage an intimation that "man partakes, therefore, of the divine substance of the god and the evil substance of the Titans." He "thus reveals his semi-divinity by seeking truth and independence of action but finds himself tightly bound by his earthly limitations" (209–10).

18. Fuseli's name and works were better known in America than those of many of his contemporaries. Dunlap recommended his writings to anyone who wished to study art. In

"The Fall of the House of Usher," Poe evokes Fuseli's nightmarish pictures in his attempt to describe the paintings of Roderick Usher. In addition to the *Lectures,* Fuseli wrote and translated much. Lavater's *Aphorisms* and Winckelmann's *History of Ancient Art* were among his translations, and his edition of Pilkington's *Dictionary of Painters* was much-used.

19. The firm of Goupil was praised by *The Literary World* for seeming "desirous to identify themselves, in some measure, with American art" (Apr. 22, 1848, 228). The issue for September 30 contains a full-page advertisement for a lithograph of W. S. Mount's *The Power of Music* and paintings by contemporary French and German artists (700). The issue of April 21, 1849, has Goupil's advertisement for statuette reproductions of Hiram Powers's *The Greek Slave*. On October 13, 1849, the magazine printed a story about Goupil's plan to establish an "International Art-Union," debated the propriety of such a move, and disapproved of it (317–18).

20. Melville's poem "The Marchioness of Brinvilliers" is an ekphrastic description of a picture of the marchioness by Charles Le Brun. The story of the marchioness features another poisoner, another execution, and another ambiguous portrait. Cohen, ed., *Selected Poems* 238–39, and Shurr 244–46 tell the story, discuss sources, and analyze the poem.

6. CLAREL

1. Horace Vernet (1789–1863) traveled in Palestine in 1840 and produced a number of paintings of biblical scenes. He apparently "took the view that as all the characters of the Bible had looked like Arabs, it was legitimate to paint Judah as a bedouin sheikh, Tamar as a rather forthcoming and leggy houri" (Shepherd 100). Wilkie went to the Holy Land and was drowned on the return voyage to England in 1841. Among the engravings in Melville's collection is one after Turner's *Peace—Burial of Wilkie*. We have no record of what pictures of Wilkie Melville might have seen, but his interest in the painter continued for many years. At some time after 1881, he acquired John William Mollett's *Sir David Wilkie* (1881), which offered a brief account of the painter's life and career and reproduced engravings of a number of Wilkie's works.

2. In his biography of Hawthorne, Edwin Haviland Miller describes the Concord Manse with its bust of Apollo and quotes a Channing poem (210, 222). The description of the house in the Berkshires includes pictures by Leonardo da Vinci and Salvator Rosa and a bust of Antinous as well as the Apollo bust (305–06).

3. Melville's knowledge of Boccaccio is supported by the conjecture that he either owned a volume or borrowed one from Evert Duyckinck. Sealts quotes from an entry in Duyckinck's diary on October 1, 1856, that Melville "cited a good story from the Decameron the Enchantment of the husband in the tree" (#71a). The date coincides with Melville's setting off for Europe and the Holy Land on October 11. In Italy, on March 28, 1857, he would record a visit "to Fiesole. Boccaccio's villa" (*Journals* 116). Duyckinck may have owned any of several nineteenth-century editions: the Bohn edition of *The Decameron or Ten Day's Entertainment of Boccaccio* (1849), translated by W. K. Kelly and, alas, not illustrated; an edition published in London and New York (1845, 1851) and "embellished with twenty-one engravings on steel by G. Standfast"; or *The Decameron, with Coloured Aquatint Plates* by J. Findlay (London 1822). Melville may also have had access to *Stories of Boccaccio* "with eleven original etchings by Leopold Flameng" (London 187?). See F. S. Stych, *Boccaccio in English* (Westport, CT: Greenwood Press, 1995) 14–15. Melville was always keen for knowledge about the Italian writer. In reading *Table Talk* (Sealts #266a), he marked Hazlitt's remark in the essay "On Reading Old

Books" that "The only writer among the Italians I can pretend any knowledge of, is Boccaccio, and of him I cannot express half my admiration. His story of the Hawk I could read and think of from day to day, just as I would look at a picture of Titian's!" In a back flyleaf of the Hazlitt volume, Melville carefully noted "Story of the Hawk (Boccaccio)" with the volume and page number (Cowen 1:651, 653).

4. Bezanson correctly identifies the temple of Sunium as one dedicated to the worship of Poseidon (*Clarel* 747); however, that attribution did not occur till 1898, when an inscription was discovered that made it clear. All during the nineteenth century, the fane was identified as a temple of Minerva. In addition to Wordsworth, see, for instance, Henry M. Baird's *Modern Greece: A Narrative of a Residence and Travels in That Country* (New York: Harper and Brothers, 1856) 292. Both Baird and Wordsworth provide engravings of the ruins of the temple.

5. In *The Anatomy of Melancholy,* Robert Burton recites the details of man's iniquity: "The greatest enemy to man is man himself." Melville acquired a copy of Burton in 1848 and also a volume entitled *Melancholy; as it Proceeds from Disposition and Habit, the Passion of Love, and the Influence of Religion* (Sealts #102, #103).

6. Sharon Furrow quotes an interesting passage from De Quincey's *Confessions of an English Opium Eater* in which De Quincey and Coleridge discuss Piranesi's prints, alluding to the "mighty engines and machinery, wheels, cables, catapults, etc., expressive of enormous power put forth, or resistance overcome" (249). It seems that Melville did own a Piranesi print that shows a Roman arch rather than the labyrinths of his poetic ekphrasis.

7. THE VISUAL IMAGINATION

1. Daniel Göske suggests that a painting of *St. Michael and the Dragon,* a subject treated by Raphael and Guido Reni, is the source of Melville's description. In Göske's view, Melville reverses the iconography of the picture, which would usually portray the saint with his foot upon the prostrate demon. He sees a similar device in Hawthorne's later treatment of the theme in *The Marble Faun* (212–13, 219). He is, perhaps, straining too hard to find a plausible source. The masked figures in Melville's ekphrasis hardly seem to match any picturable concept of demon and angel, even the one proposed by Hawthorne some seven years after "Benito Cereno." A "satyr" and a recumbent figure would seem to argue the "mythological" source that Melville quite properly attaches to it rather than a bit of religious allegory.

2. Duban's suggestion that Melville could have read about diptychs in Sir Charles Eastlake's *Materials for a History of Oil Painting,* a book withdrawn from the Boston Athenaeum during a visit to the family in that city, is excellent further proof of Melville's absorption in the literature of the sister arts. In *Melville and Turner,* Wallace makes an equally convincing case for Melville's probable study of Eastlake's various publications (156–71).

3. Marovitz makes very good use of the engravings that Melville studied in William M. Thomson's *The Land and the Book; or, Biblical Illustrations . . . of the Holy Land.* Melville seems to have been acquainted with Thomson's 1859 book from the date of its publication (Sealts #523). There are excellent prints of scenes in Jerusalem and at the Mar Saba monastery, and Marovitz supplements these with photographs he has taken.

4. Gretchko links the landscape of the "Tartarus" sketch with "a sublime painting by Thomas Cole," *The Notch of the White Mountains* ("White Mountains" 127–38). As he points out, Melville would have been very aware of the quality of Cole's artistry and almost surely had seen numerous examples of his work.

5. The Civil War was covered in great detail in all sorts of pictorial modes. Photographs rendered scenes and portraits. Engravings printed in the magazines such as *Harper's Illustrated Weekly* offered a running account of persons, engagements, and weapons. As Hennig Cohen points out in his edition of *Battle-Pieces*, the battlefield art of Alfred and William Waud probably influenced the poetry of Melville's volume (25–28).

6. Vincent's rendering of the prose passage in *Collected Poems* needs to be compared with the manuscript of the text (30–31) and genetic text (236) in Ryan's dissertation on *Weeds and Wildings*. John Bryant's "Toning Down the Green" provides an excellent and suggestive reading of "Rip van Winkle's Lilac" as a central element in Melville's idea of the picturesque.

7. See, for example, "Art: The Academy Exhibition," *Appleton's Journal* 11 (Apr. 25, 1874): 540; "The National Academy of Design," *Frank Leslie's* 26 (Oct. 1888): 385–94; "Fine Arts: Forty-Second Exhibition of the National Academy of Design," *The Nation* 4 (May 2, 1867): 359; "Literature and Art," *Galaxy* 7 (Jan. 1869): 138-9; "Art," *Atlantic Monthly* 31 (Apr. 1873): 503–05, a review of the last volume of G. Henry Lodge's translation of Winckelmann's *History of Ancient Art;* "The New York Art Season," *Atlantic* 48 (Aug. 1881): 193–202.

8. Stein finds that "Melville's astonishment at the unusual execution hints at his dissatisfaction with the stylized abstractions of Artemis, their neutralization of her role as the patron of the life-giving powers of nature" and believes that "he is probably thinking of the stereotyped association that he once incorporated in 'The Tartarus of Maids,' her fatal punishment of the hunter Actaeon who glimpsed her in the nude" (131). But in this fragment of basso-relievo, her nudity would be somewhat in question since she has "a quiver thrown / Behind the shoulder" and is bent over to adjust "her buskin light," so that the Actaeon element, famous in paintings, doesn't seem quite relevant.

9. It is hardly possible to know if Melville kept up his interest in the paintings of Sanford R. Gifford or read critiques of his work, but Gifford was often praised for producing paintings in which, as Angela Miller puts it, "Resonant, light-suffused atmosphere melded topographic divisions into a virtually seamless whole" (243). This distinctive "luminism" or, as Miller puts it, "atmospheric luminism" (244), was a characteristic of Gifford's work throughout his career and is a part of the late paintings he produced after a journey to the Middle East and Palestine. In her study of Gifford's paintings, Weiss devotes her first chapter to observations on luminism and points out that "Since air, in light, is the heart of Gifford's aesthetic, I have preferred to distinguish his personal style as 'aerial-luminism'" (19).

Bibliography

Abbott, Collamer M. "Melville and the Panoramas." *Melville Society Extracts* 101 (June 1995): 1–14.

Aisenberg, Katy. *Ravishing Images: Ekphrasis in the Poetry and Prose of William Wordsworth, W. H. Auden, and Philip Larkin*. New York: P. Lang, 1995.

Alberts, Robert C. *Benjamin West*. Boston: Houghton Mifflin, 1978.

Allston, Washington. *Lectures on Art and Poems and Monaldi*. Ed. Nathalia Wright. Gainesville, FL: Scholars' Facsimiles and Reprints, 1967.

Alpers, Svetlana. "*Ekphrasis* and Aesthetic Attitudes in Vasari's *Lives*." *Journal of the Warburg and Courtauld Institutes* 23 (1960): 190–215

Arvin, Newton. *Herman Melville*. New York: William Sloane, 1950.

Baker, S. C. "Two Notes on Browning Echoes in *Clarel*." *Melville Society Extracts* 44 (Nov. 1980): 14–15.

Bamberg, Robert D., ed. *The Confession of Jeroboam O. Beauchamp*. Philadelphia: U of Pennsylvania P, 1966.

Barnett, Louise K. "American Novelists and the 'Portrait of Beatrice Cenci.'" *New England Quarterly* 53 (June 1980): 168–83.

Barrell, John. *The Political Theory of Painting from Reynolds to Hazlitt*. New Haven: Yale UP, 1986.

Bellis, Peter J. *No Mysteries Out of Ourselves: Identity and Textual Form in the Novels of Herman Melville*. Philadelphia: U of Pennsylvania P, 1990.

Bender, John B. *Spenser and Literary Pictorialism*. Princeton: Princeton UP, 1972.

Berthoff, Warner. *The Example of Melville*. Princeton: Princeton UP, 1962.

Berthold, Dennis. "Dürer 'At the Hostelry': Melville's Misogynist Iconography." *Melville Society Extracts* 95 (Dec. 1993): 1–8.

———. "Melville and Dutch Genre Painting." In Sten, ed., *Savage Eye* 218–45.

Birk, John F. "Unsealing the Sphinx: The *Pequod*'s Egyptian Pantheon." *American Transcendental Quarterly* 5 (Dec. 1991): 283–99.

Boudreau, Gordon V. "Of Pale Ushers and Gothic Piles: Melville's Architectural Symbology." *ESQ* 18.2 (1972): 67–82.

Brodhead, Richard H. *Hawthorne, Melville and the Novel*. Chicago: U of Chicago P, 1977.

———, ed. *New Essays on* Moby-Dick. London: Cambridge UP, 1986.

Brodtkorb, Paul, Jr. *Ishmael's White World: A Phenomenological Reading of* Moby-Dick. New Haven: Yale UP, 1965.

Bryant, John. *Melville and Repose: The Rhetoric of Humor in the American Renaissance*. New York: Oxford UP, 1993.

———. "Toning Down the Green: Melville's Picturesque." In Sten, ed., *Savage Eye* 145–61.

Bulwer-Lytton, Edward. *The Last Days of Pompeii*. London: J. M. Dent, 1906.

Burke, Bernard. *The General Armory of England, Scotland, Ireland and Wales, Comprising a Registry of Armorial Bearings from the Earliest to the Present Time*. London: Harrison, 1884.

Callow, James T. *Kindred Spirits: Knickerbocker Writers and American Artists, 1807–1855*. Chapel Hill: U of North Carolina P, 1967.

Carothers, Robert L., and John L. Marsh. "The Whale and the Panorama." *Nineteenth Century Fiction* 26 (Dec. 1971): 319–28.

Chase, Richard, ed. *Selected Tales and Poems by Herman Melville*. New York: Holt, Rinehart and Winston, 1950.

Clark, Eliot. *History of the National Academy of Design, 1825–1953*. New York: Columbia UP, 1954.

Coffler, Gail. "Classical Iconography in the Aesthetics of Billy Budd, Sailor." In Sten, ed., *Savage Eye* 257–76.

———. "Melville, Dana, Allston: Analogues in Lectures on Art." *Melville Society Extracts* 44 (Nov. 1980): 1–6.

———. *Melville's Classical Allusions*. Westport, CT: Greenwood, 1985.

Cohen, Hennig, ed. "Melville and the Art Collection of Richard Lathers." *Melville Society Extracts* 99 (Dec. 1994): 1–25.

———, ed. *Selected Poems of Herman Melville*. Carbondale: U of Southern Illinois P, 1968.

Cowen, Wilson Walker. *Melville's Marginalia*. 2 vols. New York: Garland, 1987.

Davis, Clark. *After the Whale: Melville in the Wake of* Moby-Dick. Tuscaloosa: U of Alabama P, 1995.

Davis, Merrell R. *Melville's* Mardi: *A Chartless Voyage*. New Haven: Yale UP, 1960.

Dillingham, William B. *An Artist in the Rigging*. Athens: U of Georgia P, 1972.

———. "'Neither Believer nor Infidel': Themes of Melville's Poetry." *Personalist* 46 (1965): 501–16.

Dryden, Edgar A. *Melville's Thematics of Form: The Great Art of Telling the Truth*. Baltimore: Johns Hopkins UP, 1968.

Duban, James. *Melville's Major Fiction: Politics, Theology, and Imagination*. DeKalb: Northern Illinois UP, 1983.

———. "The Spenserian Maze of Melville's *Pierre*." *ESQ* 23.4(1977): 217–25.

———. "Transatlantic Counterparts: The Diptych and Social Inquiry in Melville's 'Poor Man's Pudding and Rich Man's Crumbs.'" *New England Quarterly* 66 (1993): 274–86.

Finkelstein, Dorothee Metlitsky. *Melville's Orienda*. New Haven: Yale UP, 1961.

Flexner, James Thomas. *That Wilder Image: The Painting of America's Native School from Thomas Cole to Winslow Homer*. New York: Bonanza, 1962.

Fogle, Richard Harter. "Melville and the Civil War." *Tulane Studies in English* 9 (1959): 61–89.

Forsyth, Joseph. *Remarks on Antiquities, Arts, and Letters During an Excursion in Italy, in the Years 1802 and 1803*. Boston: Wells and Lilly, 1818.

Frank, Stuart M. *Herman Melville's Picture Gallery*. Fairhaven MA: Edward F. Lefkowicz, 1986.

Furrow, Sharon. "The Terrible Made Visible: Melville, Salvator Rosa, and Piranesi." *ESQ* 19 (1973): 237–53.

Fuseli, Henry. *Lectures on Painting*. New York: Garland, 1979.

Gates, W. B. "William Gilmore Simms and the Kentucky Tragedy." *American Literature* 32 (May 1960): 158–66.

Georgoudaki, Ekaterina. "Djékis Abbot of Thessaloniki and the Greek Merchant in Herman Melville's *Clarel*." *Melville Society Extracts* 64 (Nov. 1985): 1–6.

Gilman, William F. *Melville's Early Life and* Redburn. New York: New York UP, 1951.

Giovannini, G. "Method in the Study of Literature in its Relation to the Other Fine Arts." *Journal of Aesthetics and Art Criticism* 8 (1950): 185–95.

Goethe, Johann Wolfgang von. *The Auto-Biography of Goethe*. 2 vols. Trans. John Oxenford. London: Henry G. Bohn, 1848.

Gollin, Rita K., and John L. Idol, Jr. *Prophetic Pictures: Nathaniel Hawthorne's Knowledge and Use of the Visual Arts*. Westport, CT: Greenwood, 1991.

Göske, Daniel. "Dark Satyrs, White Enthusiasts: Hawthorne's and Melville's Variations on 'St. Michael and the Dragon.'" *Princeton University Library Chronicle* 54 (1993): 207–24.

Gretchko, John M. J. "The Glassy-Eyed Hermit." *Melville Society Extracts* 48 (Nov. 1981): 14–15.

———. "Melville at the New-York Gallery of the Fine Arts." *Melville Society Extracts* 82 (Sept. 1990): 7–8.

———. *Melvillean Ambiguities*. Cleveland: Falk and Bright, 1990.

———. *Melvillean Loomings: Essays on* Moby-Dick. Cleveland: Falk and Bright, 1992.

———. "The White Mountains, Thomas Cole, and 'Tartarus': The Sublime, the Subliminal, and the Sublimated." In Sten, ed., *Savage Eye* 127–38.

Hagstrum, Jean H. *The Sister Arts: The Tradition of Literary Pictorialism and English Poetry from Dryden to Gray*. Chicago: U of Chicago P, 1958.

Hall, Elton W. "Panoramic Views of Whaling by Benjamin Russell." In *Art and Commerce: American Prints of the Nineteenth Century, Proceedings of a Conference Held in Boston, May 8–10, 1975*. Charlottesville: UP of Virginia, 1978.

Hall, Spencer. "Beatrice Cenci: Symbol and Vision in *The Marble Faun*." *Nineteenth Century Fiction* 25 (June 1970): 85–95.

A Handbook for Travellers in Central Italy. Part II. Rome and Its Environs. 4th ed. London: John Murray, 1856.

Harding, Jonathan P. *The Boston Athenaeum Collection: Pre–Twentieth Century American and European Painting and Sculpture*. Boston: The Boston Museum, 1984.

Hawthorne, Nathaniel. *The French and Italian Notebooks*. Ed. Thomas Woodson. Columbus: Ohio State UP, 1963.

———. *The Marble Faun*. Columbus: Ohio State UP, 1968.

Heffernan, James A. W. *Museum of Words: The Poetics of Ekphrasis from Homer to Ashbery*. Chicago: U of Chicago P, 1993.

Heffernan, Thomas F. "Melville and Wordsworth." *American Literature* 49 (Nov. 1977): 338–51.

Heine, Heinrich. *The Poems of Heine*. Trans. E. A. Bowring. London: Bohn, 1861.

Hillway, Tyrus. "Pierre, the Fool of Virtue." *American Literature* 21 (1949–50): 201–11.

Hipple, Walter J., Jr. *The Beautiful, the Sublime, and the Picturesque in Eighteenth-Century British Aesthetic Theory*. Carbondale: Southern Illinois UP, 1957.

Hirsch, P. L. "Melville's Ambivalence Toward the Writer's 'Wizardry': Allusions to Theurgic Magic in *The Confidence-Man*." *ESQ* 31 (1985): 100–115.

Howe, Winifred E. *A History of the Metropolitan Museum of Art*. 1913. New York: Arno, 1974.

Hussey, Christopher. *The Picturesque: Studies in a Point of View*. New York: Putnam's, 1927.

Jack, Ian. *Keats and the Mirror of Art*. Oxford: Oxford UP, 1967.

Jaffe, David. *The Stormy Petrel and the Whale*. Baltimore: David Jaffe, 1976.

James, Henry. *Literary Criticism: French Writers, Other European Writers, the Prefaces to the New York Edition*. New York: Library of America, 1984.

Jarves, James Jackson. *The Art-Idea*. New York: Hurd and Houghton, 1864.

Jillson, Willard Rouse. "The Beauchamp-Sharp Tragedy in American Literature." *The Register* (Kentucky State Historical Society) 36 (1938): 54.

Jones, William Powell. *Thomas Gray, Scholar: The True Tragedy of an Eighteenth-Century Gentleman*. Cambridge: Harvard UP, 1937.

Kenny, Vincent. *Herman Melville's* Clarel: *A Spiritual Autobiography*. Hamden, CT: Archon, 1973.

Krieger, Murray. *Ekphrasis: The Illusion of the Natural Sign*. Baltimore: Johns Hopkins UP, 1992.

Kring, Walter D. "Introduction." *The Endless, Winding Way in Melville: New Charts by Kring and Carey*. Ed. Donald Yannella and Hershel Parker. Glassboro, NJ: The Melville Society, 1981. 1–9.

Kroeber, Karl, and William Walling, ed. *Images of Romanticism: Verbal and Visual Affinities*. New Haven: Yale UP, 1978.

Kurman, George. "Ekphrasis in Epic Poetry." *Comparative Literature* 26 (1974): 1–13.

Landow, George P. "Ruskin's Version of 'Ut Pictura Poesis.'" *Journal of Aesthetics and Art Criticism* 26 (Summer 1968): 521–28.

Lanzi, Luigi. *The History of Painting in Italy*. 3 vols. Trans. Thomas Roscoe. London: Henry G. Bohn, 1847.

Lewes, George Henry. *The Life of Goethe*. New York: Ungar, 1965.

Lund, Hans. *Text as Picture, Studies in the Literary Transformation of Pictures*. Lewiston, NY: Edwin Mellen, 1992.

McDermott, John F. "Charles Deas: Painter of the Frontier." *Art Quarterly* 13 (1950): 293–311.

———. *The Lost Panoramas of the Mississippi*. Chicago: U of Chicago P, 1958.

Mansfield, Luther S., and Howard P. Vincent, eds. *Moby-Dick*. By Herman Melville. New York: Hendricks House, 1952.

Manwaring, Elizabeth Wheeler. *Italian Landscape in Eighteenth Century England*. New York: Oxford UP, 1925.

Markels, Julian. *Melville and the Politics of Identity, from* King Lear *to* Moby-Dick. Urbana: U of Illinois P, 1993.

Marovitz, Sanford E. "Melville's Temples." In Sten, ed., *Savage Eye* 77–103.

Martineau, Harriet. *Eastern Life, Present and Past*. Philadelphia: Lea and Blanchard, 1848.

Mason, Ronald. *The Spirit Above the Dust: A Study of Herman Melville*. Mamaroneck, NY: Paul P. Appel, 1972.

Maugham, W. Somerset. *The Gentleman in the Parlour*. New York: Doubleday, Doran, 1930.

Melville, Herman. *The Battle-Pieces of Herman Melville*. Ed. Hennig Cohen. New York: Thomas Yoseloff, 1963.

———. *Clarel*. Ed. Walter Bezanson. Evanston and Chicago: Northwestern UP and the Newberry Library, 1991.

———. *Correspondence*. Ed. Lynn Horth. Evanston and Chicago: Northwestern UP and the Newberry Library, 1993.

———. *The Collected Poems of Herman Melville*. Ed. Howard P. Vincent. Chicago: Hendricks House, 1947.

———. *Journals*. Ed. Howard C. Horsford. Evanston and Chicago: Northwestern UP and the Newberry Library, 1989.

———. *Mardi*. Ed. Harrison Hayford, Hershel Parker, and G. Thomas Tanselle. Evanston and Chicago: Northwestern UP and the Newberry Library, 1970.

———. *Moby-Dick*. Ed. Harrison Hayford, Hershel Parker, and G. Thomas Tanselle. Evanston and Chicago: Northwestern UP and the Newberry Library, 1988.

———. *Pierre, or the Ambiguities*. Ed. Harrison Hayford, Hershel Parker, and G. Thomas Tanselle. Evanston and Chicago: Northwestern UP and the Newberry Library, 1984.

———. *The Piazza Tales and Other Prose Pieces*. Ed. Harrison Hayford, Alma MacDougall, and G. Thomas Tanselle. Evanston and Chicago: Northwestern UP and the Newberry Library, 1987.

———. *Redburn, His First Voyage*. Ed. Harrison Hayford, Hershel Parker, and G. Thomas Tanselle. Evanston and Chicago: Northwestern UP and the Newberry Library, 1969.

———. *Typee: A Peep at Polynesian Life*. Ed. Harrison Hayford, Hershel Parker, and G. Thomas Tanselle. Evanston and Chicago: Northwestern UP and the Newberry Library, 1968.

———. *White-Jacket, or the World in a Man-of-War*. Ed. Harrison Hayford, Hershel Parker, and G. Thomas Tanselle. Evanston and Chicago: Northwestern UP and the Newberry Library, 1970.

Merriman, James D. "The Parallel of the Arts: Some Misgivings and a Faint Affirmation." Parts 1 and 2. *Journal of Aesthetics and Art Criticism* 31 (Winter 1972): 153–64; 31 (Spring 1973): 309–21.

Miller, Angela. *The Empire of the Eye: Landscape Representation and American Cultural Politics, 1825–1875.* Ithaca: Cornell UP, 1993.

Miller, Edwin Haviland. *Salem Is My Dwelling Place: A Life of Nathaniel Hawthorne.* Iowa City: U of Iowa P, 1991.

Mizener, Arthur. *The Sense of Life in the Modern Novel.* Boston: Houghton Mifflin, 1964.

Moore, Maxine. *That Lonely Game: Melville,* Mardi, *and the Almanac.* Columbia: U of Missouri P, 1975.

Moore, Richard S. *That Cunning Alphabet: Melville's Aesthetics of Nature.* Amsterdam: Rodopi, 1982.

Morgan, H. Wayne. *New Muses: Art in American Culture, 1865–1920.* Norman: U of Oklahoma P, 1978.

Moses, Carol. *Melville's Use of Spenser.* New York: Peter Lang, 1989.

Murray, Henry A., ed. *Pierre; or, the Ambiguities.* By Herman Melville. New York: Hendricks House, 1949.

The National Academy of Design Exhibition Record, 1861–1900. Comp. and ed. Maria Naylor. 2 vols. New York: Kennedy Galleries, 1973.

Nevius, Blake. *Cooper's Landscapes: An Essay on the Picturesque Vision.* Berkeley: U of California P, 1976.

Novak, Barbara. *American Painting and the Nineteenth Century: Realism, Idealism, and the American Experience.* New York: Praeger, 1969.

———. *Nature and Culture: American Landscape and Painting.* New York: Oxford UP, 1980.

Oken, Lorenz. *Elements of Physiophilosophy.* London: Ray Society, 1847.

Perkins, Robert F., and William J. Gavin III. *The Boston Athenaeum Art Exhibition Index, 1827–1874.* Boston: The Library of the Boston Athenaeum, 1980.

Plaidy, Jean. *A Triptych of Poisoners.* London: Robert Hale, 1970.

Pommer, Henry F. *Milton and Melville.* New York: Cooper Square, 1970.

Putz, Manfred. "The Narrator as Audience: Ishmael as Reader and Critic in *Moby-Dick.*" *Studies in the Novel* 19 (Summer 1987): 160–74.

Richards, Bernard. "Ut Pictura Poesis." *Essays in Criticism* 21 (1971): 318–25.

Ridgely, J. V. *William Gilmore Simms.* New York: Twayne, 1962.

Ringe, Donald A. *The Pictorial Mode: Space and Time in the Art of Bryant, Irving, and Cooper.* Lexington: U of Kentucky P, 1971.

Robillard, Douglas. "Melville's *Clarel* and the Parallel of Poetry and Painting." *North Dakota Quarterly* 51 (1983): 107–20.

———. "Melville's Reading in the Visual Arts." In Sten, ed., *Savage Eye* 40–54.

———. "A Possible Source for Melville's Goetic and Theurgic Magic." *Melville Society Extracts* 49 (Feb. 1982): 5–6.

———. "The Visual Arts in Melville's *Redburn.*" *Essays in Arts and Sciences* 12 (Mar. 1983): 43–60.

———. "Wrestling with the Angel: Melville's Use of the Visual Arts in *Timoleon.*" In Sten, ed., *Savage Eye* 246–56.

Robson-Scott, W. D. *The Younger Goethe and the Visual Arts.* Cambridge: Cambridge UP, 1981.

Ruskin, John. *Modern Painters.* 5 vols. New York: Wiley and Putnam, 1865.

Ryan, Robert C. "*Weeds and Wildings Chiefly: With a Rose or Two,* by Herman Melville: Reading Text and Genetic Text, Edited from the Manuscripts, with Introduction and Notes." Ph.D. diss. Northwestern University, 1967.

Sachs, Viola. *The Game of Creation.* Paris: Editions de la Maison des sciences de l'homme, 1982.

Samson, John. *White Lies: Melville's Narratives of Facts.* Ithaca: Cornell UP, 1989.

Sandberg, Robert A. "'House of the Tragic Poet': Melville's Draft of a Preface to His Unfinished Burgundy Club Book." *Melville Society Extracts* 79 (Nov. 1989): 1–7.

———. "'The Adjustment of Screens': Putative Narrators, Authors, and Editors in Melville's Unfinished Burgundy Club Book." *Texas Studies in Literature and Language* 31 (Fall 1989): 426–50.

Schless, Howard H. "Flaxman, Dante, and Melville's *Pierre.*" *Bulletin of the New York Public Library* 64 (Feb. 1960): 65–82.

Scott, Grant F. *The Sculpted Word: Keats, Ekphrasis, and the Visual Arts.* Hanover, NH: UP of New England, 1994.

Sealts, Merton M., Jr. *Melville's Reading.* Columbia: U of South Carolina P, 1988.

Shepherd, Naomi. *The Zealous Intruders: The Western Rediscovery of Palestine.* London: Collins, 1987.

Short, Bryan C. "Form as Vision in Melville's *Clarel.*" *American Literature* 50 (1979): 553–69.

———. "'Like Bed of Asparagus': Melville and Architecture." In Sten, ed., *Savage Eye* 104–16.

Shurr, William H. *The Mystery of Iniquity: Melville as Poet, 1857–1891.* Lexington: U of Kentucky P, 1972.

Smart, Alastair. "Pictorial Imagery in the Novels of Thomas Hardy." *Review of English Studies* 12 (1961): 262–80.

Smith, Paul A. "Melville's Vision of Flux and Fixity in *Pierre.*" *ESQ* 32.2 (1986): 110–21.

Soria, Regina. *Perceptions and Evocations: The Art of Elihu Vedder.* Washington DC: Smithsonian Institution, 1979.

Spitzer, Leo. *Essays on English and American Literature.* 1962. New York: Gordian Press, 1984.

Staël, Madame de. *Corinne: or Italy.* Trans. Isabel Hill. Boston: Estes and Lauriat, n.d.

———. *Germany.* Notes and appendices by O. W. Wright. 2 vols. New York: Derby and Jackson, 1859.

Star, Morris. "Melville's Use of the Visual Arts." Ph.D. diss. Northwestern University, 1964.

Stavis, Barrie. *John Brown: The Sword and the Word.* New York: A. S. Barnes, 1970.

Stein, William B. *The Poetry of Melville's Late Years: Time, History, Myth, and Religion.* Albany: SUNY P, 1970.

Steiner, Wendy. *Pictures of Romance: Form Against Content in Painting and Literature.* Chicago: U of Chicago P, 1988.

Sten, Christopher, ed. *Savage Eye: Melville and the Visual Arts.* Kent, OH: Kent State UP, 1991.

———. *The Weaver-God, He Weaves: Melville and the Poetics of the Novel.* Kent, OH: Kent State UP, 1996.

Stevens, Wallace. *Letters of Wallace Stevens.* Selected and edited by Holly Stevens. New York: Knopf, 1972.

Thorp, Willard. "Redburn's Prosy Old Guidebook." *PMLA* 53 (Dec. 1938): 1145–56.

Tintner, Adeline R. *Henry James and the Lust of the Eye*. Baton Rouge: Louisiana State UP, 1993.

Torgovnick, Marianna. *The Visual Arts, Pictorialism, and the Novel*. Princeton: Princeton UP, 1985.

Valery, Antoine Claude Pasquin. *Historical, Literary, and Artistical Travels in Italy, a Complete and Methodical Guide for Travellers and Artists*. Paris: Baudry, 1852.

Vincent, Howard P. *The Trying-Out of* Moby-Dick. Boston: Houghton Mifflin, 1949.

Wallace, Horace Binney. *Art and Scenery in Europe, with Other Papers*. New York, 1857.

Wallace, Robert K. *Melville and Turner: Spheres of Love and Fright*. Athens: U of Georgia P, 1992.

———. "Melville after Turner: 'The Piazza,' The Crayon, and Ruskin." *Nineteenth-Century Contexts* 19.3 (1996): 285–303.

———. "Melville's Prints: The Ambrose Group." *Harvard Library Bulletin* 6 (Spring 1995): 13–50.

———. "Melville's Prints: The Reese Collection." *Harvard Library Bulletin* 4 (Fall 1993): 5–42.

———. "Melville's Prints and Engravings at the Berkshire Athenaeum." *Essays in Arts and Sciences* 15 (June 1986): 59–90.

Warren, Robert Penn, ed. *Selected Poems of Herman Melville*. New York: Random House, 1970.

Watson, Charles N., Jr. "Melville and the Theme of Timonism: From *Pierre* to *The Confidence-Man*." *American Literature* 44 (1972–73): 398–413.

Weiss, Ila. *Poetic Landscape: The Art and Experience of Sanford R. Gifford*. Newark: U of Delaware P, 1987.

Wenke, John. *Melville's Muse: Literary Creation and the Forms of Philosophical Fiction*. Kent, OH: Kent State UP, 1995.

Whelpley, J. D. "Lessing's Laocoon." *American Review* 13 (Dec. 1851): 17–26.

Wellek, Rene. "The Parallelism between Literature and the Arts." *English Institute Annual 1941* (New York: Columbia UP, 1942). 29–63.

Whitburn, Diane, and Merrill Whitburn. "Melville's Vasari." *Melville Society Extracts* 75 (Nov. 1988): 9.

Winner, Viola Hopkins. *Henry James and the Visual Arts*. Charlottesville: UP of Virginia, 1970.

Witemeyer, Hugh. *George Eliot and the Visual Arts*. New Haven: Yale UP, 1979.

Wolf, Bryan. "When Is a Painting Most Like a Whale?: Ishmael, *Moby-Dick,* and the Sublime." In Brodhead, ed., *New Essays on Moby-Dick* 141–79.

Wordsworth, Christopher. *Greece: Pictorial, Descriptive, and Historical*. London: William S. Orr, 1839.

The Works of Eminent Masters, in Painting, Sculpture, Architecture, and Decorative Art. 2 vols. London: John Cassell, 1854.

Wright, Nathalia. *American Novelists in Italy. The Discoverers: Allston to James*. Philadelphia: U of Pennsylvania P, 1965.

———. "*Pierre:* Herman Melville's *Inferno*." *American Literature* 32 (May 1960): 167–81.

Wright, Thomas. *Early Travels in Palestine*. London: Bohn, 1848.

Zlogar, Richard J. "'Accessories that Covertly Explain': Irving's Use of Dutch Genre Painting in 'Rip Van Winkle.'" *American Literature* 54 (Mar. 1982): 44–62.

Yaggy, Elinor. "*Pierre:* Key to the Middle Enigma." Ph.D. diss. University of Washington, 1946.

Zoellner, Robert. *The Salt-Sea Mastodon: A Reading of* Moby-Dick. Berkeley: U of California P, 1973.

Index

Ahab (of *Moby-Dick*), 117; compared to Pierre, 120; portrait of, 80–84

Allston, Washington, 28, 92; influence on Melville, 16–17

Ambrose group, of Melville's engravings, 21

America: art of, 26–30, 104, 119; landscapes of, 126–27

American Scenery (Willis), 125

Ames, Ezra, 103-104, 185n.7

Architecture: in *Clarel*, 145–52; influence on Melville, 32-33, 83; Melville's engravings of, 111–12; in *Pierre*, 100; in "The Bell-Tower," 161

Art, 86, 110; dealers in, 50, 119, 179n.2, 186n.19; descriptions as introduction to themes, 58–59; invented, for ekphrasis, 71, 131, 155; and life, 68–69; Melville's collection of, 20–21, 25, 28, 32–33, 175n.3, 178n.11, 181n.7, 184n.4; Melville's themes of, 96–97, 171–72; and nature, 86, 170, 174; and the picturesque, 166–68; practical uses for, 92–95, 141; prints *vs.* originals, 35; and tourists, 12–13, 20, 22, 34, 42–44, 177n.2. *See also* Engravings

"Art," 170

Art allusions: in *Clarel*, 152–54, 156–57; in *Moby-Dick*, 97–98; and pictorialism, 48–49, 62–64, 66, 67; in *Pierre*, 100

Art analogy, 105, 175n.2; Melville's comfort with, 48, 158, 169–70; in *Moby-Dick*, 83, 92; in *The Piazza Tales*, 159; in *Pierre*, 101, 109; in *Redburn*, 69

Art criticism: by Hazlitt, 37–38; by Ishmael, 84-85; in magazines, 38–40; parody of, 102–3

Art education, 185n.18; Melville's, 33–40, 50, 70, 76, 105, 176n.3, 180n.1

Art knowledge: Melville's, 88–91, 95–97, 103, 119, 168, 178n.12, 178n.16; Melville's range of, 20–33

Art-Union, 39, 102–3

Arvin, Newton, 69; on *Pierre*, 99–100, 113

"At the Hostelry," 7, 166, 179n.4; influences on, 24, 45

Banvard, John, 95–96, 183n.23

Barrett, Francis, 94, 183n.22

"Bartleby, the Scrivener," 5, 159–60

Bartlett, William Henry, 42, 59–60, 173; as source for *Clarel*, 123, 125, 145–46, 147–48

Battle-Pieces and Aspects of the War, 163–64, 188n.5. *See also specific poem titles*

MELVILLE AND THE VISUAL ARTS

was composed in 10/13 Minion

on Power Macintosh 7100/80 using PageMaker 6.0

at The Kent State University Press;

printed by sheet-fed offset

on 50# Turin Book Natural

notch case bound over binder's boards

in ICG cloth

and wrapped with dust jackets printed in two colors

on 100# enamel stock finished with film lamination

by Braum-Brumfield, Inc.

designed by Diana Gordy

and published by

THE KENT STATE UNIVERSITY PRESS

Kent, Ohio, 44242